PUTIN'S RUSSIA

Anna Politkovskaya

PUTIN'S RUSSIA

Translated from the Russian by
Arch Tait

THE HARVILL PRESS
LONDON

Published by The Harvill Press 2004

15

This book has been selected to receive financial assistance from
English PEN's Writers in Translation programme, in association with
Bloomberg : www.englishpen.org/writersintranslation

This book has been inscribed in the List of the UNESCO Collection of
Representative Works by the Clearing House for Literary Translation
(www.unesco.org/culture/lit)

First published in Great Britain in 2004 by
The Harvill Press
Random House, 20 Vauxhall Bridge Road,
London SW1V 2SA

Random House Australia (Pty) Limited
20 Alfred Street, Milsons Point, Sydney,
New South Wales 2061, Australia

Random house New Zealand Limited
18 Poland Road, Glenfield,
Auckland 10, New Zealand

Random House South Africa (Pty) Limited
Endulini, 5A Jubilee Road, Parktown 2193, South Africa

The Random House Group Limited Reg. No. 954009
www.randomhouse.co.uk/harvill

A CIP catalogue record for this book is available from the British Library

Papers used by Random House are natural, recyclable products made from
wood grown in sustainable forests; the manufacturing processes conform
to the environmental regulations of the country of origin

Typeset by SX Composing DTP, Rayleigh, Essex
Printed in the UK by CPI Bookmarque, Croydon, CR0 4TD

CONTENTS

INTRODUCTION

This book is about Vladimir Putin but not as he is normally viewed in the West. Not through rose-tinted spectacles.

Why is it difficult to sustain the rosy point of view when you are faced with reality in Russia? Because Putin, a product of the country's murkiest intelligence service, has failed to transcend his origins and stop behaving like a lieutenant-colonel in the Soviet KGB. He is still busy sorting out his freedom-loving fellow countrymen; he persists in crushing liberty just as he did earlier in his career.

This book is also about the fact that not everyone in Russia is prepared to put up with Putin's behaviour. We no longer want to be slaves, even if that is what best suits the West. We demand our right to be free.

This book is not an analysis of Putin's politics. I am not a political analyst. I am just one human being among many, a face in the crowd in Moscow, Chechnya, St Petersburg and elsewhere. These are my emotional reactions, jotted down in the margins of life as it is lived in Russia today. It is too soon to stand back, as you must if you want to analyse anything dispassionately. I live in the present, noting down what I see.

MY COUNTRY'S ARMY,
AND ITS MOTHERS

The Army in Russia is a closed system no different from a prison. Nobody gets into the Army or into prison unless the authorities want them there. Once you are in, you live the life of a slave.

Armies everywhere try to keep what they do quiet, and perhaps this is why we talk about generals as if they were members of an international tribe whose personality profile is the same all over the planet, irrespective of which particular President or state they are serving.

There are, however, some peculiarities specific to the Army in Russia, or rather to relations between the Army and the civilian population. The civilian authorities have no control over what the Army gets up to. A private belongs to the lowest caste in the hierarchy. He is nobody. He is nothing. Behind the concrete walls of military barracks, an officer can do anything he wants to a soldier. Similarly, a senior officer can do anything he fancies to a junior colleague.

You are probably thinking that things surely cannot be that bad.

Well, they aren't always. Sometimes they are better, but only because a particular humane individual has called his subordinates to order. That is the only time there is a ray of hope.

"But what about the country's leaders?" you may wonder. "The

President is the Army's ex-officio Commander-in-Chief and hence personally responsible for what goes on, isn't he?"

Unfortunately, when they make it to the Kremlin, our leaders make no attempt to rein in the Army's lawlessness but are more likely to give senior officers ever greater power. Depending on whether or not a leader indulges the Army, it either supports him or undermines him. The only attempts to humanise the Army were made under Yeltsin as part of a programme of promoting democratic freedoms. They didn't last long. In Russia, holding on to power is more important than saving soldiers' lives, and under a barrage of indignation from General Headquarters Yeltsin ran up the white flag and surrendered to the generals.

Putin hasn't even made any attempts. He is an officer himself. End of story. When he first appeared on Russia's political radar screen as a possible head of state rather than as an unpopular Director of the universally detested Federal Security Bureau (FSB), he began making pronouncements to the effect that the Army, which had been diminished under Yeltsin, was henceforth to be reborn, and that all it lacked for its renaissance was a second Chechen war. Everything that has happened in the northern Caucasus since then can be traced back to this premise. When the Second Chechen War began, the Army was given free rein, and in the presidential elections of 2000 it voted as one for Putin. The Army has found the present war highly profitable, a source of accelerated promotion, more and more medals, and the rapid forging of careers. Generals on active service lay the foundation for careers in politics and are catapulted straight into the political élite. For Putin rebirth of the Army is a done deed after its humiliations under Yeltsin and defeat in the First Chechen War.

How exactly Putin has helped the Army we shall see in the stories that follow. You can decide for yourself whether you would like to live in a country where your taxes sustain such an institution. How you would feel when your sons turned 18 and were conscripted as "human resources". How satisfied you would be with an Army from which soldiers deserted in droves every week, sometimes whole squads or entire companies at a time. What would you think of an Army in which, in a single year, 2002, a battalion, more than 500 men, had been killed not fighting a war but from beatings? In which the officers stole everything from the 10-rouble notes sent to privates by their parents to entire tank columns? Where officers are united in hatred of soldiers' parents because every so often, when the circumstances are just too disgraceful, outraged mothers protest at the murder of their sons and demand retribution.

No. U-729343. Forgotten on the Battlefield

It is November 18, 2002. Nina Levurda, retired after 25 years as a schoolteacher, is a heavy, slow-moving woman, old and tired and with a string of serious ailments. She has been waiting for hours, as she has many times over the past year, in the unwelcoming waiting room of the Krasnaya Presnya Intermunicipal Court in Moscow.

Nina has nowhere else to turn. She is a mother without a son: even worse, without the truth about her son. Lieutenant Pavel Levurda was born in 1975. To the Army he is No. U-729343. He was killed in Chechnya at the start of the Second Chechen War, the war that, according to Putin, saw the Army reborn. How it was reborn we shall see from the tale of the last months of No. U-729343. It is not the fact that he was killed but the circumstances of his death and the events that followed it which have compelled Nina to do the rounds of legal institutions for the past eleven months. She has had just one aim: to get a precise legal answer from the State as to why her son was left behind on the battlefield. And, coincidentally, to ask why, since his death, she has been treated so abominably by the Ministry of Defence.

As a child, Pavel Levurda dreamed of a career in the Army. Not a common state of affairs nowadays. Boys from poor families do apply for places at the military academies, but their aim is to get degrees and then get discharged. The endless self-congratulatory reports from the President's office about increasing competition for admission to military institutes are entirely true. But this has less to do with any increase in the Army's prestige than with the abject poverty of those seeking an education. The same situation explains the catastrophic shortage of junior officers in military units. When junior officers graduate from military college, they simply fail to appear at the garrisons to which they have been posted. They suddenly become "seriously ill" and send in certificates testifying to all manner of unexpected disabilities. This is not difficult to arrange in a country as corrupt as Russia.

Pavel was different. He really wanted to be an officer. His parents tried to talk him out of it because they knew what a hard life it was. Petr Levurda, his father, was himself an officer, and the family had spent their lives being shifted around remote garrisons.

Quite apart from that, in the early 1990s everything was falling apart in the wake of the Soviet Empire. A school-leaver would have had to have been mad, everyone agreed, to choose to go to a military academy that couldn't even feed its students.

Pavel insisted on his dream career and went away to study at the Far East College for Officers of the Armed Forces. In 1996 he was commissioned as an officer and sent to serve near St Petersburg. Then, in 1998, he was thrown into the frying pan: 58 Army.

Fifty-eight Army has a bad reputation in Russia. It is synonymous with the degeneration of the armed forces. Of course this began before Putin. He does, however, bear a heavy responsibility, in the first place for the fact that the total anarchy among officers goes unchecked, and in the second for effectively placing officers above the law. To all intents and purposes, they are not prosecuted no matter what crimes they commit.

Fifty-eight Army was, in addition, the Army of General Vladimir Shamanov. A Hero of Russia who fought in both Chechen wars, he became notorious for his exceptional brutality towards the civilian population. General Shamanov is retired now. He resigned and became Governor of Ulyanovsk Province, benefiting from his role in the Second Chechen War when he was never off the television screen. Each day he would inform the country that "all Chechens are bandits" who thoroughly deserved to be eliminated. In this he enjoyed Putin's full support.

The staff headquarters of 58 Army is in Vladikavkaz, the capital of the Republic of North Ossetia-Alaniya which borders Chechnya and Ingushetia. Its troops fought in the First Chechen War and they are still fighting there now. The officers' corps of 58 Army, following the example of their general, were also renowned for their exceptional brutality towards both the people of Chechnya and their own soldiers and junior officers. Rostov-on-Don is the location of the General Headquarters of the North Caucasus Military District, to which 58 Army is subordinate. The greater part of the archive of the Rostov Committee of Soldiers' Mothers consists of files relating to desertion by privates as the result of beatings by officers of 58 Army, which is also well known for the blatant theft of supplies from their warehouses and for wholesale treason. They sell weapons stolen from their own stores to field commanders of the Chechen resistance. That is, they aid the enemy.

I personally know many junior officers who have gone to extra-ordinary lengths to avoid serving in 58 Army. Levurda, however, decided otherwise. He didn't break ranks, he wrote letters which made heavy reading, he came home on leave, and his parents saw their son becoming more and more morose. No matter how often they urged him to resign, however, he would reply, "What must be done must be done." Pavel Levurda clearly was someone the authorities would have been justified in describing as a young

Russian with a special sense of duty towards his Motherland and a profound patriotism. In fact, he was hoping for a genuine, rather than a Putinesque, rebirth of the Russian Army.

In 2000, Pavel Levurda had another opportunity to refuse to go to war in the northern Caucasus. Few would have blamed him. Many junior officers found ways to obtain instant exemption. But, as Pavel explained to his parents, he felt he couldn't desert his soldiers.

On January 13, 2000 Pavel went off to war, first reporting to 15 Motorised Infantry Guards Regiment of the 2 (Taman) Guards Division (Army Unit 73881), in Moscow Province. On January 14 Nina heard her son's voice on the telephone for the last time. He had signed a special contract to go to Chechnya, and . . .

It was clear enough what that dreadful "and" portended.

"I cried. I did my best to change his mind," Nina remembers. "But Pavel said there was no going back. I asked my cousin who lives in Moscow to go straight to the Taman Division, to try to talk him out of it. When she got to the unit she found she had missed him by just a few hours. He had already flown out to Mozdok." This small town in North Ossetia is on the border with Chechnya. When the war began, it was the main base of the Unified Command of Forces and Troops mobilised for Putin's "anti-terrorist operation".

And so, on January 18, 2000. No. U-729343 found himself in Chechnya.

"At present I am on the south-western outskirts of Grozny . . ." wrote Pavel in his first and only letter to his parents from the war. It is dated January 24, 2000.

The city is blockaded from all directions, and there is serious fighting going on there. The gunfire does not stop for a minute. The city is burning, the sky is completely black. Sometimes a mortar shell falls nearby, or a fighter plane launches a missile right by your ear. The artillery never lets up. The losses in the battalion have been appalling. All the officers in my company have been put out of action. The officer who commanded this unit before me was blown up by one of our own booby traps. When I went to see my company commander he carelessly grabbed his rifle, sending a round into the ground a few centimetres away from me. It was sheer luck I wasn't hit. Everyone laughed. They said, "Pasha, there have been five commanding officers of the unit before you, and you almost didn't last five minutes!" The men here are all right but not strong-willed. The officers are on contract, and the soldiers, with a few exceptions, though very young, are holding out. We all sleep together in a tent, on the ground. There is an ocean of lice. We're given shit to eat. No change there. What lies ahead we don't know. Either we'll attack who knows where, or we'll just sit around until we turn into idiots, or they'll pull us out and pack us off back to Moscow. Or God knows what. I am not ill, but I feel so low. That's all for now. Love, kisses. Pasha

This might not seem a good letter for reassuring one's parents. In war you lose the ability to be reassuring and forget what might shock someone far away when you have been shocked a hundred times more yourself.

It later became clear that Pavel's letter really was intended to reassure his parents. When he wrote it, he wasn't in fact lying in a tent wondering what lay ahead. From at least January 21, he was actively involved in the "serious fighting", having first taken command of a mortar unit and, shortly afterwards, of an entire company. The other officers were indeed "out of action" and there was no-one else to take command.

Neither was he "on the outskirts" of Grozny.

On February 19, assisting the battalion's intelligence groups to break out of an encirclement and "covering the retreat of his comrades" (according to the citation nominating him for the Order of Valour) from the village of Ushkaloy, Itum-Kalin District, Lieutenant Levurda was severely wounded and died of "massive haemorrhaging following multiple bullet wounds".

So he died in Ushkaloy. In the winter of 2000 the fighting was at its fiercest there – a desperate partisan war in highland forests, on narrow paths. But where was Pavel's body?

No coffin containing Nina Levurda's son's remains came home to the family to be buried. His remains, she discovered, had been lost by the very State he had tried with such desperate loyalty to serve.

Having taken on the roles of military prosecutor and investigating officer, Nina found out that on February 19, the official date of her son's death, the "comrades" whose retreat he was covering did indeed get away. They simply abandoned Pavel, along with six other soldiers who had saved them, by breaking through the encirclement, at the scene of heavy fighting. Most of those left behind were wounded but still alive. They shouted for help, begged not to be abandoned, as the inhabitants of the remote mountain village later testified. The villagers bandaged some of the wounded themselves, but could do no more. There is no hospital in Ushkaloy, no doctor, not even a nurse.

Pavel Levurda was left behind on the battlefield and then forgotten. It was forgotten that his body was lying there. It was forgotten that he had a family that would be waiting for his return. The survivors simply stopped thinking about those who had died so that they might live.

What happened to Pavel Levurda after his death is typical of our Army. This disgraceful episode encapsulates its thinking. For the Army, a human being is nothing. No-one keeps track of the troops. There is no feeling of responsibility towards the families.

They only remembered about Pavel Levurda on February 24,

when, according to information provided by General Headquarters in Chechnya, Ushkaloy was completely cleared of Chechen fighters and "came under the control" of Federal forces. (This explanation was in fact concocted later to prove that "there was no objective possibility" of recovering Pavel's body.)

On February 24, in fact, the Army collected from Ushkaloy the bodies of only six of the seven soldiers who had broken through the encirclement. They couldn't find Pavel Levurda, so they forgot about him again.

Back home, Pavel's mother was hysterical. The only communication she had had was that official letter of February 7. The Ministry of Defence's "hotline" wasn't much help. Talking to the duty officers there was like talking to a computer about the grief that was relentlessly grinding her down. "Lieutenant Pavel Petrovich Levurda is not on the list of those dead or missing." Such was the invariable reply.

Nina listened to the "fully informative" hotline for several months. Unbelievably, even after she had located Pavel's remains by her own efforts, even when she had been officially notified of his death, the commanding officers had not got round to updating the information on their database.

But to return to our story . . . On May 20, three months after the fighting in Ushkaloy, local police discovered "a burial site containing the body of a man showing signs of violent death". However, it was only on July 6, after another one and a half months of Nina's daily telephone calls to the hotline and the local Army commissariat, that the police filled in the relevant form, "Orientation/Task No. 464", in response to a missing-person inquiry.

On July 19 the form finally reached the CID in Bryansk, where Pavel's family were living. Nina, rushing round every conceivable office, had lodged a missing-person inquiry at the police station there. So it was that on August 2, Detective Constable Abramochkin, an ordinary policeman, came round to see Pavel's parents.

The only person at home was another Nina, Pavel's 14-year-old niece. DC Abramochkin asked her some questions about Pavel, discovered what belongings he had had with him, and was greatly surprised to find he was talking to the family of a soldier. Having been assigned this routine investigation, it was DC Abramochkin and not an official from the Ministry of Defence who informed the mother of a hero that her son had officially been classified as missing without trace, and that from February 20 his entitlement to all forms of provision and allowances had been cancelled. The Itum-Kalin police asked Abramochkin to go round to the parents in Bryansk to find out "the postal address of the permanent deployment of Army Unit 73881 in which Levurda, P. P. had been serving" so they could contact its commanding officer in order to establish the circumstances relating to the death of a person who, from his mother's description, appeared to resemble one of their officers!

The quote is from the official correspondence. It tells us a lot both about the realities of the Army and about the nature of the war Putin is waging in the Caucasus. In this Army the right hand has no idea what the left hand is doing, so it is easier to post a letter to parents far away than to telephone through to General Headquarters in Hankala (the military base near Grozny).

DC Abramochkin, seeing the state the family was in, strongly advised Nina Levurda to go to Rostov-on-Don as soon as she could. He had heard that the remains of the unknown soldier from Ushkaloy had been taken to the main military mortuary there for identification by Colonel Vladimir Shcherbakov, Director of 124 Military Forensic Medical Laboratory, a man well known and respected in Russia. It should be noted that Shcherbakov does this work not at the behest of commanding officers, generals or General Headquarters, but because his heart tells him it is the right thing to do.

Abramochkin also advised Nina Levurda not to expect too

much, because, as we say, "anything can happen in Russia," where mix-ups involving dead bodies are only too common. The Bryansk Committee of Soldiers' Mothers was in the meantime helping with the Levurda saga, and it was only through their good offices and the efforts of DC Abramochkin that the élite 15 Guards Regiment and the even more élite Taman Guards Division finally twigged that the seventh body, left behind by his "comrades", just might be that of Pavel Levurda.

"We arrived in Rostov on August 20," Nina tells me. "I went straight to the laboratory. There is no security on the entrance. I walked in and went into the first inspection room I came to. I saw the inspector had a head separated from its body on a stand on his examination table. More precisely, it was a skull. I knew immediately that it was Pavel's head, even though there were other skulls next to it."

Is there any way of assessing or compensating the distress caused to this mother?

Of course there isn't. In any case who can argue against forensic inspectors needing to have skulls on their tables?

And yet . . . What an artless lot we are becoming, thoughtless, crass and, because of it, amoral.

Nina was given sedatives after the encounter with her son's skull, which she had indeed correctly recognised. At this precise moment a representative of Pavel's unit came rushing in to see her. DC Abramochkin, having learned the unit's address from the bereaved parents, had sent a telegram, and the commanding officer had sent a representative to Rostov to take care of the formalities.

The representative showed Nina a notice. She looked at it and fainted. In the notice Guards Lieutenant-Colonel A. Dragunov, acting commanding officer of Army Unit 73881, and Guards Lieutenant-Colonel A. Pochatenko, chief of staff of the same unit, requested that "Citizens Levurda" be informed that "their son, while on a military mission, true to his military oath, manifesting steadfastness and courage, has died in battle". The unit was trying to cover the tracks of its wretched "forgetfulness".

When Nina had recovered, she read the notice more carefully. There was no indication of when her son had died.

"Well, what about the date?" Nina asked the representative.

"Just write it in yourself, whatever you like," he replied.

"What do you mean, write it in?" Nina shouted. "The day Pasha was born is his date of birth. Surely I have a right to know the date of his death!"

The representative shrugged, as if to say, "Don't ask me," and handed her a further extract from an order to the operational forces to "remove Lieutenant Levurda from the list of members of the Regiment". This too bore no date and indicated no reason but did have various stamps and signatures at the bottom. Again, with the artless gaze of a child, the representative asked Nina to fill in the blanks herself and hand it in, when she got home, to the local Army Commissariat so that Pavel could be removed from the register.

Nina said nothing. What is the point of talking to a person who has no heart, no brain and no soul?

"But surely that's easiest, isn't it? Rather than me having to go all the way to Bryansk?" the representative continued uncertainly.

Of course it was easier. There is no denying that being artless, being crass, can make life easier. Take our Minister of Defence, Sergey Ivanov, a crony of the President since Putin worked for the FSB in St Petersburg. Every week Ivanov appears on television to deliver the President's war bulletins. With the inflections of Goebbels on Second World War newsreels, he tell us that nobody will make us "kneel down before terrorists", that he intends to pursue the war in Chechnya to some supposed "victorious conclusion". We never hear a word from Minister Ivanov about the fate of the soldiers and officers who enable him and the President not to seem to be kneeling down before terrorists. This political line is wholly neo-Soviet: human beings do not have independent existences, they are cogs in the machine whose function is to implement unquestioningly whatever political escapades those in power dream up. Cogs have no rights. Not even to dignity in death.

It is so much more bother not to be crass. For me that would mean being able to see beyond the "General Line of the Party and Government" to the details of how it is implemented. In the present instance, these details are that, on August 31, 2000, No. U-729343 was finally buried in the city of Ivanovo, to which Pavel's parents had moved in order to escape the dark associations of Bryansk. The forensic inspectors in Rostov returned Pavel's head to Nina. Unfortunately, that seemed to be all the remains they had.

Many people in Russia have heard of Nina Levurda because, having committed what remained of her son to the earth, on the ninth day after the funeral she set off to the headquarters of 15 Regiment in Moscow Province. When she started out from Ivanovo, her intention was only to look Pavel's commanding officers in the eye and to read in them, when confronted by their officer's mother, at least some remorse for all the things they had "forgotten" to do.

"Of course, I didn't expect them to apologise," Nina says, "but I did think I might at least see some sympathy in their faces."

When she arrived at the Taman Division, however, nobody wanted to see this mother. The commanding officer was simply unavailable. Nina sat for three days waiting to meet him, without food, tea, sleep or anyone paying attention to her. Senior officers scurried to and fro like cockroaches, pretending not to notice she was there. It was then that Nina Levurda vowed to sue the State, to bring an action against the Ministry of Defence and Minister Ivanov for the moral suffering they had caused her. Not in connection with her son's death: he did after all die in the performance of his duty. But in respect of what happened subsequently. Translated from convoluted legal jargon into plain speech, she wanted to know who was responsible.

What happened next? First, the Order of Valour awarded posthumously to Nina's son was presented to the family in the Army Commissariat in Ivanovo. Second, the Army took its revenge. The Ministry of Defence and the Taman Division went on the warpath against this mother who had dared to express her outrage at their behaviour.

This is how they went about it. In just under a year there were eight court hearings, the first on December 26, 2001, the last on November 18, 2002, none of which came to any conclusions whatsoever. The court did not even get round to considering the substance of Nina's writ, because in their impunity the representatives of the Ministry of Defence ignored the hearings completely. And they were right to do so. The case of "Nina Levurda against the State" first came before Judge Tyulenev (Krasnaya Presnya Intermunicipal Court, Moscow). He decided that a mother "has no right to information" about the body of her own son, and the Ministry of Defence was accordingly under no obligation to supply her with such information. Nina went to the Moscow City Court, where, in view of the manifest absurdity of the previous verdict, the case was referred back to the Krasnaya Presnya Court for a new hearing. The State machine's technique against the bereaved mother was a systematic boycott of the court sessions by Minister Ivanov's official representatives and by Land Forces Command, of which the Taman Division and 15 Regiment are part. They simply failed to appear, brazenly and systematically. So Nina Levurda had to keep going back to Moscow from Ivanovo, only to find herself confronted with an empty dock, her journey wasted. A simple woman dependent on her State pension, which aims only to keep you from starving, and with a husband who had taken to the bottle after Pavel's funeral as a way to escape from their suffering.

In the end, Judge Bolonina of the Krasnaya Presnya District Court, to whom the case had been referred from the Moscow City Court, became exasperated. At the fifth hearing missed by the defendants, she fined the Ministry of Defence 8,000 roubles. Paid for by the taxpayer, of course. It is a pity this fine was not paid by Minister Ivanov to Nina Levurda. There is no provision for anything of that sort. Russian legislation protects the interests not of the weak but of the all-powerful authorities.

On November 18, 2002, after the imposition of the fine, representatives from the Ministry finally turned up in the courtroom, but they were strange representatives. They knew nothing about the case and declined to identify themselves, complaining that chaos at the Ministry of Defence was the cause of all the problems. The upshot was that the court was again adjourned, this time to December 2.

Nina was in tears as she stood in the grim corridor of the court building.

"Why are they doing this?" she asked. "You would think they had done nothing wrong."

How enviable to be Sergey Ivanov, head of our Ministry of Defence, which is so pitiless towards our people! Life is straightforward for him. He doesn't have to bother himself with details, with mothers whose sons have died in that "war on international terrorism" about which he waxes so lyrical. He does not have to hear their voices or feel their pain. He knows nothing of the lives he has destroyed, nothing of the thousands of mothers and fathers abandoned by the system after their children have given their lives for it.

"Putin can't do everything!" the President's Russian admirers protest.

Indeed he can't. As President it is his job to think about methods, about approach. He is the person who shapes them. In Russia, people imitate the man at the top.

Well, we have described his approach to the Army. He is entirely to blame for the brutality and extremism instilled in both the Army and the State. Brutality is a serious infection that can easily become a pandemic. First perpetrated against people living in Chechnya, now it is used against "our people", as the patriotically inclined like to describe Russian citizens. Including those Russians who fought patriotically against those who experienced it first.

"Well, he made his choice and followed his destiny," says Nina, wiping the tears from her face. Judge Bolonina stalks past in her robes, inscrutable. "But for heaven's sake, these are human beings!"

Are they? I sometimes wonder whether Putin really is human, not just an icy, metallic effigy. If he is human, it doesn't show.

Fifty-Four Soldiers, or Emigrating Home to Mum

People emigrate from Russia when staying any longer becomes life-threatening or provokes a massive onslaught by the State on their integrity and dignity. On September 8, 2002 this was precisely the situation in the Russian Army. Fifty-four soldiers gave up and tried to emigrate.

The training ground of No. 20 Guards Motorised Infantry Division is situated on the outskirts of the village of Prudboy in Volgograd Province. The men of No. 2 Section of Army Unit 20004 had been taken from their permanent base in the town of Kamyshin, also in Volgograd Province, to the training ground in Prudboy.

This seemed unexceptional: they were to receive training. Their instructors would be their father-figure commanding officers. On September 8, however, their father-figures, Lieutenant-Colonel Kolesnikov, Major Shiryaev, Major Artemiev, Lieutenant Kadiev, Lieutenant Korostylev, Lieutenant Kobets and Sub-Lieutenant

Pekov, decided to conduct an inquiry that was outside their remit. When the soldiers had assembled on the parade ground, they were told there was to be an investigation to find out who had stolen a Fighting Reconnaissance and Landing Vehicle (FRLV) from the training ground during the night.

The soldiers later insisted that nobody had in fact stolen the FRLV. It was right there in its usual place in the divisional vehicle park. The officers were just feeling bored. They had been drinking for days, were probably feeling ill as a result and decided to divert themselves with a bit of bullying. It was not by any means the first time this sort of thing had occurred at the Kamyshin training ground, which has a bad reputation.

After the announcement a first batch of soldiers was led into the officers' tent: Sergeants Kutuzov and Krutov, Privates Generalov, Gursky and Gritsenko. The others were ordered to wait outside. Soon they heard the cries and groans of their fellow soldiers. The offices were beating them up. The first batch were thrown out of the tent. They told their comrades that the officers had beaten them on their buttocks and backs with the hafts of entrenching tools, and kicked them in the belly and ribs. This description was unnecessary. The signs of the beatings were clearly visible on the soldiers' bodies.

The officers announced they would now take a break. The lieutenant-colonel, two majors, three lieutenants and one sub-lieutenant would be having dinner, and they informed the remaining soldiers that anybody failing to voluntarily confess to having stolen the FRLV would be beaten in exactly the same way as those now sprawled on the grass outside their tent.

Their announcement made, the officers departed to take soup.

And the soldiers? They walked out. They mutinied, choosing not to wait like sheep for the slaughter. They left behind those who were on sentry duty, since deserting your post is a criminal offence involving a court martial and being sent to a disciplinary battalion, and also Kutuzov, Krutov, Generalov and Gritsenko, who were incapable of walking.

Forming up in a column, the soldiers marched out of the training ground towards Volgograd to get help.

It is a fair distance from Prudboy to Volgograd, almost 180 kilometres. The 54 soldiers marched the entire distance in an orderly manner, making no attempt to hide, on the verge of a busy highway along which officers of No. 20 Division were travelling to and fro. Not one vehicle stopped. No-one thought to ask where the soldiers were going without an officer, which is against Army regulations.

The soldiers marched until it grew dark. They lay down to sleep in the strip of woodland beside the highway. No-one came looking for them, despite the fact that when the lieutenant-colonel, two majors, three lieutenants and one sub-lieutenant emerged from the dining room after finishing their meal they discovered a marked thinning of the numbers of No. 2 Section. They had almost no-one left to command.

The officers went to bed, having no idea where the soldiers were for whom, by law, they were personally responsible, but knowing very well that in Russia no officer is ever punished for something that has happened to a private.

Early on the morning of September 9, the 54 soldiers set off again along the highway. And again Army officers drove insouciantly by.

This detachment of soldiers blessed with self-respect was on the march for one and a half days, and nobody from No. 20 Division missed them. On the evening of September 9 they marched quite openly into Volgograd. They were observed by the police, but again nobody took any interest in them.

The soldiers marched to the city centre.

"It was about 6.00 in the evening, and we were preparing to go home when the telephone rang suddenly. 'Are you still open? May we come to see you?'" Tatyana Zozulenko, Director of the

Volgograd Province Mothers' Rights organisation, is telling me this. "I said, 'Come right in.' Of course, there was no way I was expecting what happened next. Four young privates came into our small room and said there were 54 of them. I asked where the others were, and the boys led me down to the little basement of our own building. The rest were all standing there. I have worked in this organisation for eleven years but had never seen anything quite like that before. The first thing I worried about was where we were going to put them all. It was already evening. We asked them whether they had eaten. 'No,' they replied, 'not since yesterday.' Our members ran off to buy as much bread and milk as they could. The boys fell on the food like hungry dogs, but that was something we are used to. Soldiers are very badly fed in their units, they are chronically undernourished. When they had eaten, I asked, 'What do you want the result of your action to be?' They replied, 'We want officers who beat up soldiers to be punished.' We decided to put them up for the night in Mothers' Rights, all of them in together on the floor, to give us time to sleep on it. First thing in the morning we would go to the garrison prosecutor's office. I locked the door and went home. I live nearby and thought I could come round quickly if I was needed. At 11.00 that evening I phoned them, but nobody answered. I thought they must just be tired, probably asleep or afraid of answering the phone. I was awakened at 2.00 in the morning by our lawyer Sergey Semushin. He said someone who hadn't identified themselves had called to ask him to 'secure his premises'. I was round there within minutes. There were small military vehicles outside with officers in them. They did not introduce themselves. The soldiers had disappeared. I asked the officers where they were and got no reply."

The Mothers' Rights workers also discovered that their computer system with information about crimes committed in No. 20 Division had been broken into and stripped. They found a note under the carpet from a soldier saying they didn't know where they were being taken; they were being beaten and needed help.

There is a little more to add. The officers at the training ground "missed" their soldiers only after being telephoned by their superiors. This was late in the evening of September 9, after Tatyana Zozulenko had contacted journalists in Volgograd and information about the AWOL soldiers had first gone out on the airwaves. The regional staff headquarters naturally demanded an explanation from the officers. During the night, vehicles had been driven up to Mothers' Rights, and all 54 soldiers had been removed to the guardhouse in the military commandant's office. They were then returned to their unit under the supervision of the very officers whose bullying had made the soldiers leave the training ground in the first place. Tatyana Zozulenko asked Volgograd garrison prosecutor Chernov, whose duty it is to ensure that the law is upheld in the garrison's units, why he had done that, and he replied without flinching, "Because these are *our* soldiers."

That is the key phrase in the saga of the 54. "Our soldiers" means "our slaves". Everything remains exactly as it always was in the Russian Army. A perverse understanding of the "honour of an officer" has constantly to be protected, and always takes precedence over the life and dignity of any private. The march from the Kamyshin training ground resulted, firstly, from the abhorrent Russian Army tradition that a soldier is an officer's slave. An officer is always right and can treat a soldier exactly as he pleases. Secondly, however, it resulted from the sad fact that civilian control of Army procedures, about which much was said in the Yeltsin years and a draft law was even written, is now dead and buried. President Putin shares the Army's traditional view of its officers' rights and considers civilian monitoring of the armed forces completely inappropriate.

Underlying this story is the fact that No. 20 Division – the Rokhlin Division, so called after its commander, Lev Rokhlin, a hero of the First Chechen War, today a Deputy of the State Duma

– and particularly Unit 20004, have long been notorious in Volgograd, and indeed throughout Russia.

"For an entire year we sent information to the military prosecutor's office, primarily to Mr Chernov, the garrison prosecutor, but also to everyone higher up the hierarchy, right up to the chief military prosecutor's office in Moscow, about the crimes committed by the officers of Unit 20004," Tatyana Zozulenko says. "In terms of the number of complaints we receive from soldiers, Unit 20004 is in first place. The officers beat their soldiers, extorting their 'active service payments' from those who have returned from Chechnya [No. 20 Division fought in both the First and Second Chechen Wars, and fights there to this day]. We have shouted about this from the rooftops, but nothing has happened. The prosecutor's office has decided to hush everything up. The episode at the Kamyshin training ground is a wholly predictable result of Army officers' lack of accountability."[1]

A Few Shorter Stories

Russia has a military budget, of course, and there is plenty of discussion about it. A military lobby fights for new investment and orders are paid for out of the State coffers. This is standard international practice. One important detail that does distinguish us from other countries is that we are a major arms manufacturer and deal in arms throughout the world. It was Russia that gave the world the Kalashnikov assault rifle. For many Russians this is a source of pride.

I don't, however, want to dwell on statistics. What I wonder is whether people are happy under the order President Putin has established. I consider that to be the main criterion for judging the actions of the leader of a state. Seeking an answer, I go to the Committee of Soldiers' Mothers and ask the women there: "Were your sons happy to join the Army? Did it make real men of them?" I learn a great deal from their replies.

The detail matters more than the big picture. So, at least, it seems to me.

Misha Nikolaev lived in Moscow Province. His family saw him off to the Army in July 2001. He was posted to the border guards, to a frontier post ten hours' flying time from Moscow, at the village of Goryachy Plyazh on Anuchina Island in the Lesser Kurils. These are the islands that have so vexed Russian and Japanese politicians since the end of the Second World War.

While they argue, someone has to police the border. Misha was one of those doing that job. He lasted just six months at this outpost of the Russian Far East and died on December 22, 2001. By the autumn he had already been writing alarming letters home, having discovered festering sores on his body. He asked his family to send medicine: Vishnevsky's Balm, sulfanilamide, "in fact any medicines for treating suppuration, metapyrin, antiseptic, bandages and as much sticking plaster as possible. There is nothing here." His parents sent off the parcels without complaining, aware that our Army is underfunded and thinking things could not be all that bad, since Misha was still working as a cook in the Army's kitchens. If he was seriously ill, his parents supposed, he wouldn't be allowed anywhere near food preparation.

Misha did, however, continue to cook meals for the troops even when his skin was covered with suppurating sores. The pathologist who conducted his autopsy reported that the unfortunate soldier's tissues literally split open under the scalpel. At the beginning of the twenty-first century, a Russian soldier rotted alive under the eyes of his officers, receiving no medical attention at all. What killed Misha was the complete irresponsibility of his superiors.

Dmitry Kiselev was posted to serve in the Moscow Province village of Istra. In Russia such a posting is regarded as a stroke of luck. He was close to Moscow; his parents, being Muscovites, could visit their son and battle their way through to his commanding officer if he needed help. This was not the Kuril Islands. That did not, however, save Dmitry from his officers' depravity.

Lieutenant-Colonel Alexander Boronenkov, Private Kiselev's commanding officer, had a lucrative sideline. Nothing too unusual about that in today's Russian Army. People get up to all sorts of tricks as their wages don't amount to much. This particular lieutenant-colonel, however, traded in soldiers. Istra is a dacha settlement of second homes, and Boronenkov sold his soldiers to the owners of nearby plots of land as cheap labour. The soldiers worked only for food; their pay went straight to their commanding officer. This money-making scheme is by no means unique. Indeed it is widespread: soldiers are "sold" as unpaid labourers – that is, as slaves – to wealthy people for the duration of their military service. The officers use this unpaid labour as a means of bartering with people they think of as "useful". If an officer needs his car repaired and has no money, he herds a few soldiers along to the car-repair centre. They work there unpaid for as long as the centre requires, and in return the officer gets his car mended.

In late June 2002 it was the turn of the newly conscripted Dmitry Kiselev to be sold into slavery. Private Kiselev was sent to build a house for a certain Mr Karabutov, a member of the Mir Horticultural Association in Istra District. Initially he was building a house, but then he and seven other conscripts were required to dig a deep trench the length of the plot. On July 2 at 7.00 in the evening the sides of the trench collapsed, burying three boys, including Dmitry, who suffocated under the earth. His parents tried to have Lieutenant-Colonel Boronenkov brought to trial, but he wriggled out of it. He knew a lot of "useful" people. Dmitry was the Kiselevs' only son.[2]

On August 28, 2002, Army Unit 42839 was deployed in Chechnya not far from the village of Kalinovskaya, a place where there had been no fighting for a long time. The "Grandads" were drinking themselves silly. Grandads – ordinary soldiers about to be demobbed into the reserve – are the most terrifying, murderous force in our Army. In the evening it seemed to the Grandads that they were running short of vodka, so they told the first soldier who came along, Yury Diachenko, to go into the village and "get some more from wherever you like". The soldier refused. In the first place, he was on duty guarding a section of the perimeter and had no right to leave his post. In the second place, as he explained, he had no money. The Grandads told him to steal something in the village and get them the vodka that way.

Yury, however, said firmly, "No. I won't go." They beat him brutally until 5.00 in the morning, and between beatings subjected him to cruel and disgusting humiliations. They dipped a floor cloth in the latrine and rubbed the filth in Yury's face. They forced him to clean the floor, and when he bent over took it in turns to ram the handle of the mop in his anus. To conclude their "training sessions", as they called it, the Grandads dragged Yury into the canteen and forced him to eat a 3-litre can of *kasha* (porridge), beating him if he tried to stop.

Where were the officers? That night they too were drinking themselves senseless and were physically incapable of being in charge of anything. At around 6 a.m. on August 29, 2002, Yury Diachenko was found in the provisions depot. He had hanged himself.

Siberia is not Chechnya. It is a long way removed from the war there, but even this makes no difference. Valerii Putintsev, a lad born in Tyumen Province, was posted to the Krasnoyarsk Region to serve in the district town of Uzhur, in the élite units of the strategic missile forces. His mother, Svetlana Putintseva, was delighted. As they were dealing with the most up-to-date and dangerous weaponry on the planet, officers in the missile units were held to be the most educated in the Army, not to get drunk, not to beat up conscripts and to maintain discipline. Soon however, she too began to receive distressing letters from her son, in which he wrote that the officers were no better than "jackals":

Hello, Mum! I don't want this letter to be seen by anyone other than you. In particular, please keep what I am writing from Gran. We both know the score there, and I'm sure you won't let her undermine what health she has left. I worry about her a lot. I can't accept that I have to work as a slave to benefit people I despise. More than anything in the world I want to work for the good of my own people, to better my family. It's only since being here that I have understood how important you all are . . .

Valerii was never to return to work for the good of his own people. The officers in the Uzhur barracks were completely out of control. The lieutenants robbed the soldiers of everything they had, degrading any who, like Valerii, tried to defend their dignity. In the half-year he spent in his unit, four soldiers were carried out in coffins, all of them privates, all of them beaten to death.

The officers' first game was to confiscate Valerii's uniform (our soldiers have no clothing apart from their uniforms). They told him that now he had to ransom it. They assumed he would write home and ask for money to be sent as a matter of urgency. Valerii resisted. He knew that his mother lived very modestly with his grandmother, an old-age pensioner, his sister and her little daughter, and could ill afford to send him money. For this he was brutally and repeatedly beaten. In the end he had had enough. He turned on the officers and was sent to the guardhouse for insubordination. Pretending he was attempting to escape, they wounded him badly. Svetlana Putintseva became anxious and rang the unit's commanding officer, Lieutenant-Colonel Butov, who informed her that he knew how to beat people so as not to leave any trace. Svetlana dropped everything and flew straight to Uzhur, where she found her son at death's door. He had gunshot wounds to the pelvis, the bladder, the ureter and the femoral artery. In the hospital his mother was told to find blood for a transfusion: "Urgently! We have no blood here." Alone in a strange town she was expected to find donors. She rushed back to the Army unit to ask for help. The commanding officer refused. She rushed through the city, trying to save her son. She failed. Valerii, lacking a transfusion, died on February 27, 2002. In one of his last letters he had written to Svetlana, "I wasn't expecting much help from the officers. All they are capable of is humiliating people."

Back to Moscow Province. It is the morning of May 4, 2002. Army Unit 13815 in the village of Balashikha. Two boilerwomen working in the plant that provides heating for the unit hear cries for help from nearby. They rush out and see that a trench has been dug in the middle of the courtyard, in which a soldier has been buried up to his neck. The women dig down, cut the rope binding him hand and foot, and help him out of the pit.

At this moment Major Alexander Simakin appears in a towering rage. He shouts at the women to leave the soldier alone. He is teaching Private Chesnokov a lesson, and if they do not go back to the boilerhouse immediately he will have them sacked.

Private Chesnokov, having escaped from the pit, deserted from the unit.

The Russian Army has always been one of the most fundamental pillars of the State. To this day it is typically a prison camp behind barbed wire where the country's young citizens are incarcerated without trial. It has correspondingly prison-like rules imposed by the officers. It is a place where "beating the crap out of someone" is the basic method of training. This, incidentally, is how Putin described the way he would deal with enemies within Russia when first he ascended his Kremlin throne.

It may be that the President finds this state of affairs agreeable, with his lieutenant-colonel's epaulettes and his two daughters at home who will never have to serve in such an Army. The rest of us, however, apart from the officer caste who revel in their status as petty gangsters above the law, are deeply unhappy about it. This is especially true of those who have sons, and all the more so if their sons have reached conscription age. They have no time to wait for the Army reforms that have been promised for so long but that will invariably get stalled along the way. They fear having their sons leave home only to be posted straight to some Kamyshin training ground, or to Chechnya or to some other place from which there is no return.

OUR NEW MIDDLE AGES,
OR WAR CRIMINALS OF
ALL THE RUSSIAS

We currently have two kinds of war criminals in Russia. Their crimes relate to the Second Chechen War, which began in August 1999 just as Vladimir Putin was appointed Prime Minister. The war – a feature of his first presidential term – continues to this day.

All the prosecutions for war crimes have had one common attribute: their outcome has been determined on ideological rather than legal grounds. *"Inter armas silent leges."* In time of war the laws are silent. Those found guilty have been sentenced, not after due legal process but in accordance with whichever ideological winds were blowing from the Kremlin.

The first kind of war criminals are those who really were involved in fighting a war. On the one hand there are members of the Russian Army engaged in a so-called anti-terrorist operation in Chechnya. On the other hand are the Chechen fighters who oppose them. The former are cleared of the crimes they have committed: the latter have crimes pinned on them with scant regard for the law. The former are acquitted by the judicial system even where there is manifest proof of guilt (which is rare, since the prosecutor's office usually makes no attempt to collect evidence against them). The latter are given the severest sentences possible.

The best-known Federal case is that of Colonel Budanov,

commanding officer of 160 Tank Regiment of the Ministry of Defence of Russia. On March 26, 2000, the very day Putin was elected President, Budanov abducted, raped and murdered an 18-year-old Chechen girl, Elza Kungaeva, who lived with her parents in the village of Tangi-Chu, on the outskirts of which Budanov's regiment was temporarily deployed.

The best-known Chechen case is that of Salman Raduev. Raduev was a renowned Chechen field commander, a brigadier who had been carrying out terrorist raids since the First Chechen War, when he had commanded the so-called Army of General Dudaev. Raduev was caught in 2001, sentenced to life imprisonment and died in mysterious circumstances in Solikamsk High-security Prison. Solikamsk is an infamous "prison city" with salt mines in Perm Province in the Urals. It has been a place of exile since Tsarist times. Raduev was a symbol of those fighting for Chechen freedom from Russia. There are many court cases like his; as a rule, they are heard behind closed doors in order to conceal information from the public. The need for this is often obscure. Occasionally it is possible with great difficulty and in great secrecy to obtain the court record of criminal cases brought against Chechen fighters. The accused are found guilty without any wasting of time on the collection and considering of evidence.

Accordingly, none of the first category of those accused of war crimes, whether Federal or Chechen, gets a fair trial. After sentence is passed, Chechen fighters sent off to remote labour colonies and prisons do not survive for long. Opinion polls show that even those who support the government and the President's war effort in Chechnya believe they are "got rid of" at the behest of the authorities. Almost nobody in Russia believes the Russian judicial system is fair. Almost everybody believes the judiciary is subordinate to the executive branch of government.

The second kind of war criminal is the individual who happened to be in the wrong place at the wrong time, people run over by the juggernaut of history, people who are not fighters but who just happen to be Chechens when somebody needs to be convicted. A typical case is that of Islam Hasuhanov. Everything about it is redolent of Stalin's purges, which peaked in 1937. Witness statements are beaten out of people; torture and pyschotropic drugs are used to break the will of the accused. This is the hellish path a majority of Chechens have travelled who have found themselves in the torture chambers not only of the FSB but of all the other security agencies rampaging in Chechnya. People were tortured by the henchmen of the late Ahmat-Hadji Kadyrov who, until his assassination, was head of the pro-Moscow Chechen puppet government; they are tortured in the military commandant's posts, tortured in pits on the territory of Army units, tortured in solitary-confinement cells at police stations.

All this is coordinated and managed by the FSB. These are Putin's people, they enjoy Putin's support, and they carry out Putin's policies.

Stalin Will Always Be with Us

THE FILE

Islam Sheikh-Ahmedovich Hasuhanov was born in 1954 in Kirghizia. From 1973 he served in the Soviet Army. He graduated from the Kiev Higher Naval Political College. From 1978 he served in the Baltic Fleet, and from 1989 in the Pacific Fleet. In 1991 he graduated from the Lenin Political Military Academy, Moscow. As a submarine officer who had graduated from a military academy, Hasuhanov would have been regarded as the élite of the Russian Navy. He retired to the Reserves in 1998 with the rank of captain first class from the position of deputy commander of a large B 251 nuclear submarine. From 1998 he lived in Grozny. He was head of the Military Inspectorate in the government of Aslan Maskhadov and head of Maskhadov's operational staff. He is married to Maskhadov's niece, his second wife, and has two sons. Hasuhanov took no active part in the First or Second Chechen War and was never in hiding from the Federal authorities. Having been arrested on April 20, 2002 in the district centre of Shali by special units of the FSB as an "international terrorist" and "one of the organisers of illegal armed formations [IAFs]", he was sentenced by the Supreme Court of the Republic of North Ossetia-Alaniya to twelve years' detention in a strict-regime labour camp.

THE PREHISTORY OF THE TRIAL

What happens to a man after he is picked up by the FSB? Not the Cheka of 1937, not the Cheka of Solzhenitsyn and the Gulag, but the modern one funded by the taxpayers of today? Nobody has any hard facts, but everybody is frightened, just as they used to be.

And just as under the Soviet regime, only very rarely does anything get out. One of those rare instances is the case of Islam Hasuhanov.

According to the file of Criminal Case No. 56/17, Islam Hasuhanov was arrested on April 27, 2002 in Mayakovsky Street in Shali and charged under Article 222 of the Criminal Code of the Russian Federation with "being in possession of and bearing firearms". This would lead one to expect some evidence of the existence of the alleged weapons.

In actual fact, armed individuals wearing masks, as is usual in Chechnya, burst at dawn into the house of Hasuhanov's relatives, where he was living with his family. They dragged him off to an unknown destination without even bothering to plant any firearms on him; he had none of his own. The Federal special units operating in Chechnya in the search for "international terrorists" have long been confident that they can get away with anything. This time they were acting on a tip-off from an informer, and had no doubt they were picking up one of the leaders of an IAF whose fate was already sealed. As he would not be surviving, no pistol, no assault rifle was registered as material evidence.

The charge under Article 222 was allowed to stand anyway. The falsified date of April 27 was also left intact. Such missing weeks are a characteristic feature of our anti-terrorist operation in Chechnya. A man is arrested and goes missing. The first week of his detention is the most terrible. No organisation is responsible for him, none of the security agencies admits to knowing anything about him. His relatives search desperately, but it is as if he does not exist. This is when the intelligence services beat everything they need out of him.

Hasuhanov has barely any recollection of the period between April 20 and 27. Beatings, injections, more beatings, more injections. Nothing beyond that. The record of the court hearing ten months after that terrible week states: "For the first seven days I was held in the FSB building in Shali, where I was beaten. Dating from that time I have 14 broken ribs, one rib in my kidney."

What did they want to get out of Hasuhanov before he died from his injuries? They demanded that he should lead them to Maskhadov.[3] After that he could die. The trouble was, Hasuhanov didn't lead them to Maskhadov, and with the robust good health of a submarine officer, he didn't die either.

On April 30 it was decided to formalise the case against him. In order to do so, he was dragged off (the public prosecutor of Chechnya at the time was Alexander Nikitin) to a temporary interrogation unit in another Chechen district centre, the village of Znamenskaya. This centre was blasted from the face of the earth by a female suicide bomber on May 12, 2003. Afterwards there was general satisfaction in Chechnya, where most people felt that justice had been done at last. How many people had been tortured there and were secretly buried in the area!

When Hasuhanov arrived in Znamenskaya he looked like death. His body resembled a sack, but he was breathing. The torture continued under the supervision of Lieutenant-Colonel Anatoly Cherepnev, deputy head of the investigative section of the directorate of the FSB for Chechnya. Cherepnev was to be the main investigator in the Hasuhanov case, deciding on the level of torture and directing the process to obtain the required evidence.

From the court record:

"Why were violent means being used against you?"

"In all the interviews all they were interested in was where Maskhadov was and where the submarine was that I supposedly was intending to hijack. Those were the two questions in connection with which violent means were used against me."

Hasuhanov could not lead his questioners to Maskhadov because he had last seen him in 2000 and subsequently had only virtual contact with him using audiocassettes. When necessary, Maskhadov would record one and send it to Hasuhanov using a courier. Occasionally Hasuhanov would reply. One of the couriers had become an FSB informer. The last time before his arrest that Hasuhanov had received a cassette was in January 2002, and he had replied two days before. On the tapes Maskhadov usually asked Hasuhanov, apparently for the record, to confirm how much money he, Maskhadov, had transferred to which field commanders. We shall see why Maskhadov was asking about this.

Let us turn now to the submarine. Its story deserves to be told in some detail. Hasuhanov had been a high-ranking submarine officer before retiring. He was the only Chechen who ever became an officer of the nuclear submarine fleet, in either Soviet or post-Soviet times. Accordingly, Lieutenant-Colonel Cherepnev set about trying to incriminate him in the "planning of an IAF to hijack a nuclear submarine, gain possession of a nuclear warhead, seize Deputies of the State Duma as hostages, demand changes to the constitutional system of the Russian Federation by threatening to use a nuclear warhead and to kill hostages". This is a direct quotation from a form returned by Cherepnev to the public prosecutor's office of Chechnya with a request for permission to continue the detention of Hasuhanov. It was not refused.

Cherepnev did his utmost to incriminate Hasuhanov, but the results were unspectacular. Hasuhanov would not, and indeed could not, give in. In 1992 he had himself "built", as they say in the Navy, the very submarine Cherepnev was accusing him of planning to hijack. Hasuhanov had monitored the submarine's construction knowing that he would be serving on it. He had done this on behalf of its future crew.

Cherepnev worked hard on the story of the submarine hijacking. The FSB forged documents supposedly written by Chechen fighters on the basis of intelligence supplied by Hasuhanov. There was a "Working Plan of Chechen IAFs for carrying out an act of sabotage on the territory of the Russian Federation and hand-drawn maps of the bases of 4 Nuclear Submarine Flotilla of the Pacific Fleet" and a "Plan for conducting a terrorist act on the territory of Russia". There was naturally a helpful note added to the effect that "detailed planning of the operation was carried out on the basis of visual and reconnaissance intelligence of the region of interest to us during December 1995". It was under these words that Hasuhanov was meant to sign.

The trouble was, they could not get him to sign. The FSB set about beating him more ingeniously, although there was little that they hadn't already tried. Now, however, they were beating him for disrupting their plans.

The only things Cherepnev ever got Hasuhanov to sign (to "endorse" was the term used in the verdict), out of his mind from a combination of pain and psychotropic drugs, were blank sheets of "orders and operational instructions of Maskhadov". Cherepnev wrote in whatever he thought would go down well. Here is an example of one such falsification:

On September 2, 2000 Hasuhanov issued a combat instruction ordering all field commanders to scatter small nails, nuts, bolts and ballbearings on highways and routes of deployment of Federal forces in order to disguise mines and explosive devices. Thus, availing himself of his leading role in the IAF, by his deliberate actions Hasuhanov incited other participants of the IAF to commit terrorist acts directed at opposing the establishment of constitutional order on the territory of the Chechen Republic.

Cherepnev also demanded that Hasuhanov sign the minutes of his interrogations without reading them. Here is an example of their quality:

> Question [supposedly asked by Cherepnev]: You have been shown a photocopy of an Address to Russian Officers, No. 215 of November 25, 2000. What testimony can you give? Answer [supposedly given by Hasuhanov]: The preparation and distribution of such documents was a component part of the propaganda carried out by the operational directorate of the armed forces of the Chechen Republic of Ichkeria under my immediate leadership. The Addresses referred to were intended to counteract the Russian mass media in respect of their coverage of the progress of the anti-terrorist operation. I understood that distribution of such documents could lead to destabilisation of the situation on the territory of the Chechen Republic, but continued my activities . . .

This is typical of the Army's literary style. For a whole month Hasuhanov was tortured in Znamenskaya so that material of this calibre could be accumulated.

From the court record:

> "And when as a result of these beatings I no longer understood or reacted to anything, I was given injections

and transferred to the FSB in North Ossetia. They didn't want to admit me to the interrogation unit there because their doctor said that, as a result of the earlier beatings, I would die within 48 hours. I was then taken to a timber mill, Enterprise No. YaN 68–1."

"Were you given any medical assistance?"

"I just lay in the timber mill recovering for three months."

What timber mill is this? Mention is occasionally made of it in stories about people who have vanished without trace after "purges" in Chechnya. Some who have been there and survived call it a lumber camp, a term from Stalin's times; others call it a timber mill. Its official title is Enterprise No. YaN 68–1, and it comes under the administration of the Ministry of Justice of the Republic of North Ossetia.

What we do know about the "timber mill" is that it receives people who have been beaten half to death by officers of the law-enforcement agencies (primarily FSB agents). The enterprise closes its eyes to the fact that these people have no identification documents. These are non-persons who have vanished without trace after their encounter with the Feds.

We owe a debt of gratitude to those who work at the "timber mill" for illegally accepting the outlawed into their enterprise. They have saved many from otherwise certain death: those who were supposed to die but whom the Feds simply couldn't be bothered to shoot as they were brought from Chechnya to Ossetia, and those who were brought to the mill to die without the FSB getting its hands dirty. Nobody knows how many people have died there in the course of the Second Chechen War or who they were. They have left behind not so much as a grave mound. On the other hand we do know how many survived. Hasuhanov is one of those. A guard took pity on him, no more than that, and every time the man was on duty he would bring milk for Hasuhanov from his home.

Hasuhanov thus survived yet again, and yet again found himself facing Cherepnev. In the Chechen directorate of the FSB they have a rule that anyone who survives interrogation is put on trial. Not many do, and hence trials of "international terrorists" are few and far between. It is, nevertheless, expedient that there should be some at least. Within the overall conduct of the anti-terrorist operation it is thought desirable to sentence the occasional "terrorist". Western leaders do ask Putin questions from time to time, he demands information from the FSB and the prosecutor general's office, and they do their best to oblige. Only, of course, when someone survives.

VLADIKAVKAZ

Vladikavkaz is the capital of the Republic of North Ossetia-Alaniya, which borders on Chechnya and Ingushetia. Ossetia too is a fully paid-up member of the anti-terrorist operation. Mozdok in North Ossetia is the main military base where Federal groupings are formed up before being sent to Chechnya. It was the scene of two major suicide bombings in 2003: on June 5 a woman got on a bus transporting military pilots and blew herself up; and on August 1 a man crashed a truck loaded with a ton of explosives into a military hospital.

Vladikavkaz is the traditional setting for many fabricated court cases against "international terrorists". The local lawyers act less as counsels for the defence than as functionaries in close liaison with the court, the FSB and the prosecutor's office. Vladikavkaz is also where agents of the Chechen directorate of the FSB often have extended spells of duty, preferring to bring their victims there to interrogate them, as far away from the war as possible.

Cherepnev now went to Hasuhanov in Vladikavkaz and found him a lawyer. Since June 1, 2003 Russia has had a progressive new code of criminal procedure in conformity with the highest European standards. Among other things, it prohibits interrogating a suspect without a lawyer being present, but of course, "when necessary", everything continues as before. At all events, from April 20 until October 9, 2002, for almost six months, Hasuhanov had no legal representation at all. Not until his skull had healed over and his fractured ribs and broken hands had recovered at the timber mill could he be readied for a court appearance.

Here again, the detail is of interest. On October 8 Cherepnev summoned Hasuhanov to an interrogation and instructed him to address an application to him. Cherepnev dictated the following: "I request you to provide me with a lawyer for the preliminary investigation. Up to the present time I have had no need of the services of a lawyer, and in this connection I have no complaints against the investigative services. I request you to appoint an advocate chosen at the investigator's discretion . . ." On October 9, then, Hasuhanov had his first interrogation in the presence of Alexander Dzilikhov, a Vladikavkaz legal-aid defence lawyer. Hasuhanov suspected he was an FSB agent;[4] Dzilikhov did nothing to cause him to change his mind. He gave Hasuhanov no advice, sat passively at the interrogations and said nothing.

From the court record:

"You may say whether there is a difference between the evidence you gave before a lawyer was present and after, and if so, what that difference is."
"There is a difference. Before, I was not given the record to read at the end of an interrogation. After the appearance of a lawyer, I was."

In all, Hasuhanov had three such interrogations in the presence of a defence lawyer, on October 9, 23 and 24, 2002. More precisely, in the course of these three days Cherepnev simply copied the testimony beaten out of him in Znamenskaya on to new forms, and these became "testimony in accordance with the code of criminal procedure".

Cherepnev declared that October 25 would be the final day of the investigation. He informed Hasuhanov that he would shortly receive the text of the indictment and that he was to sign it as quickly as possible. So that he should have no illusions, Hasuhanov was taken from the solitary-confinement unit for two days, October 29–30, needless to say without a lawyer. He did not know where he was being taken. He had a hood put over his head and was led out as if to be executed. "That's it, the end," the guards said, cocking their rifles.

His execution was a hoax, designed to frighten him into signing the indictment.

Of course he signed. But he remained unbroken, and at the trial he retracted everything on which the indictment was based. The indictment was nonetheless confirmed by the new prosecutor of Chechnya, Vladimir Kravchenko, and the text migrated virtually intact into the verdict of Judge Valerii Dzhioyev.

Here are quotations from both, with my comments. It is easy to see how criminal cases are fabricated, and also how none of the counterfeiters are the least bit worried about being exposed or about the fact that these records will remain as the raw material of history (which, in accordance with Russian tradition, will surely be rewritten in the course of time).

> In April 1999 Hasuhanov . . . voluntarily entered an armed formation not permitted under Federal law. Hasuhanov made contact with Hambiev Mahomed, an aide of Maskhadov, who proposed that he provide assistance to Maskhadov using his experience to organise the work of "Military Audit", an IAF then being created.

What this is about is that, after retiring, Hasuhanov had returned home to Grozny. Unique in being a Chechen officer with an academic education, he was invited by Maskhadov to work in the

Chechen government. In 1999 this was the official republican government, financed from Moscow, and Maskhadov was the lawfully elected President of Chechnya, recognised by Moscow. The "Military Audit" that Maskhadov invited Hasuhanov to join was desperately needed. The Chechen bureaucracy was shamelessly corrupt, as indeed were the bureaucrats in Moscow, and the republican government needed a knowledgeable man capable of monitoring the flow of military funds, in particular those coming from the Russian Federal Treasury. What kind of IAF is that?

From the court record:

"Did you consider the actions of President Maskhadov to be lawful?" [the Prosecution asked].

"Yes. I had no way of knowing that Maskhadov, the government and security ministries would later be considered illegal. I knew that Maskhadov was the President. He was recognised as such by the Russian leaders, there were meetings with his ministers, financial resources were allocated, so of course I did not know that I was joining an IAF."

"Was it your job to inspect the finances and general administration of the Ministry of Internal Affairs of the Chechen Republic of Ichkeria?"

"Yes, I reported the results of the audit to Maskhadov in June 1999. I listed everything money had been spent on. I received this information from the Ministry of Internal Affairs of the Russian Federation. All the information was received through official channels. I had no reason to suppose anything was unlawful."

Hasuhanov's work before the war did indeed include the inspection of finances and administration as well as the setting up of a system to audit and monitor the financial resources allocated for maintaining the security services of Chechnya: the Ministry of

Internal Affairs, the national and presidential guards, and the Army's staff headquarters. In the summer of 1999 he established that considerable sums of money were passing through SHQ for the purchase of weaponry and uniforms but that, for example, the rocket launchers which the Ministry of Defence was ordering from the Grozny Red Hammer Factory were known to be militarily useless. This was a blatant misappropriation of funds. The same went for the purchasing of military uniforms. They were being sewn in the Chechen town of Gudremes at a price of 60 roubles per outfit, but the accompanying documentation stated that they were "Made in the Baltic States" at a correspondingly higher price.

Hasuhanov reported all this to Maskhadov, and the Director of the military audit office immediately ran into trouble with the President's security forces, who were involved in all the embezzlement. After Hasuhanov had worked in the military audit office for just a week, Maskhadov appointed him chief of staff, simply because he urgently needed honest people around him.

It was the end of July 1999. Chief of Staff Hasuhanov began work in August, a few days before the start of the Second Chechen War, in which he refused to take part.

As you read the record of the court hearings (which took place behind closed doors), you cannot help feeling the trial was a complete put-up job. Someone had decided Hasuhanov had to be sent down for a very serious offence, but no-one would say what that offence was. Was it that, back in 1999, Hasuhanov found out something which came back to haunt him in 2002–3? Was it the secret of those embezzled Federal funds? There is a suspicion that this very fraud was to a large extent the reason the Second Chechen War was started, a war to ensure that the tracks of the wrong-doers would be covered for ever. And is this the reason why the upper echelons of Russia's armed forces are still so set against peace negotiations?

Here is a further quote from the indictment:

Hasuhanov was actively involved in the work of the IAF and in 1999 was engaged in matters relating to the financing of the IAF. He devised and implemented an auditing system in respect of financial resources provided to maintain the National Guard, General Headquarters and Ministry of Internal Affairs IAFs of the self-proclaimed "Republic of Ichkeria". Having demonstrated organisational ability and efficiency in this position, Hasuhanov was appointed by Maskhadov to the post of his chief of staff in late July 1999. Actively engaged in the work of the above-named IAF, Hasuhanov was involved in formulating the basic decisions relating to opposition to the forces of the Federal government, by means which included armed opposition, in their task of restoring constitutional order to the territory of the CRI.

This would be laughable if we did not know the price exacted from Hasuhanov for this brazen falsification of history by the forces of the FSB.

From the record of the court hearing:

"Tell the court what necessity there was for you personally to be in Chechnya from the beginning of combat operations until the day of your arrest."

"I did not consider it possible to turn my back on Maskhadov because I considered him the legally elected President. I could not stop the war and did everything in my power . . . I sometimes fulfilled his requests. I was not in a fit condition to march through the forests, but what I could do I did. I saw people dying. I know what is meant by 'restoring constitutional order'. I will not conceal the fact that this entire war is genocide. However, I never called for the carrying out of acts of terrorism."

"Did you call for the killing of Federal troops?"

"In order to call for that, I would have had to have men under my command. I had no men under my command."

"Were any of the field commanders directly subordinate to you?"

"No."

I have in front of me documents marked "Official Use Only". When he was preparing the court case, Cherepnev sent out enquiries to every local FSB department in Chechnya requesting information on terrorist acts committed in their districts on "combat instructions from Chief of the Operational Headquarters of the Armed Forces of the CRI Hasuhanov". We recall the "combat instructions" Hasuhanov signed during his interrogation as blank sheets of paper, on which Cherepnev then wrote in whatever he wanted. Not surprisingly, every local department head replied that Hasuhanov was not wanted for any terrorist acts. These responses came back to Cherepnev not from Chechen fighters but from his own people.

This did not, however, halt the machinery that was to proclaim the guilt of "a leading member of the IAF", as Hasuhanov's case, after he had survived, now began to be called, despite the facts. The court paid not the slightest attention to this pile of papers "for official use", and neither did the prosecutor general's office.

THE TRIAL

The Hasuhanov case was heard behind closed doors and at great speed, from January 14 to February 25, 2003, in the Supreme Court of the Republic of North Ossetia-Alaniya, Valerii Dzhioyev presiding. The court found nothing untoward. Not in the fact that the accused had had no access to a lawyer for six months, or that the lawyer invited to act on his behalf had been chosen by those who had been beating his client, or that there was no information on the whereabouts of the accused between April 20 and 27, or that he had been tortured. The court accepted that he had been tortured but had no comment to make on the subject. Here is a quote from the verdict:

> Hasuhanov made no admission of guilt during the investigation but under physical and psychological pressure from officers of the FSB was forced to sign previously prepared records of the interrogations.
>
> "You have said that violent means were used against you," the judge told Hasuhanov. "Can you give the names of those who used violent means against you?"
>
> "I cannot give their names because I do not know them."

The court passed over this detail, the torturers having omitted to identify themselves to their victim. It even refused to commission a medical report, despite the fact that the accused had a dent in his skull. The court confined itself to asking Tebloev, the Director of the timber factory, whether Hasuhanov had stayed in his hospital section. He replied, "Yes. He was there from May 3 until September 2002 with a broken ribcage." The court took this in its stride. To quote again from the verdict:

> At the court hearing the accused, Hasuhanov, did not admit to being guilty of the crimes committed. He stated that he considered it his duty to carry out certain requests and missions for the legally elected President Maskhadov. He denied making preparations for the committing of terrorist acts or providing financial resources for field commanders. He acknowledged only that he authenticated certain orders and instructions of Maskhadov, annotating them "True copy" in his own hand.

Was that it?

Yes, that was it. The sentence was twelve years in a strict-regime labour colony without eligibility for amnesty. The prisoner's final comment was, "I wish to state that I have no intention of repudiating my beliefs. I consider what is going on in Chechnya to be a flagrant violation of people's rights. Nobody makes any attempt to catch the real criminals. While the present situation continues, there will be many more people like me in the dock."

The shroud of darkness from which we spent several Soviet decades trying to free ourselves is enveloping us again. Ever more stories are heard of the FSB using torture to fabricate cases to suit its ideological needs, implicating the courts and the prosecutor's office as its accomplices. This is now the rule rather than the exception. We can no longer pretend that it is a random occurrence.

The implication is that our Constitution is on its deathbed, in spite of all the guarantees intended to safeguard it, and the FSB is in charge of the funeral arrangements.

When I learned that Hasuhanov had been brought to the notorious Krasnaya Presnya transit prison in Moscow, a kind of distribution centre from which those already sentenced are sent off in convoys to other parts of the country, I rang the Moscow office of the International Red Cross. Those who work there are almost the only people able to visit particular prisoners. I rang them because I knew that after the torture Hasuhanov had endured he was in very poor health indeed. I asked them to visit him in Krasnaya Presnya, to provide him with medicine, to ask the prison authorities to ensure he received treatment and to get their consent to regular visits.

A week passed, during which the Moscow office considered my appeal. They rejected it, mumbling something about the situation being "very complicated".[5]

The Precedent of Colonel Budanov

On July 25, 2003, in a North Caucasus district military court in Rostov-on-Don, sentence was finally passed on a then colonel of the Russian Army, Yury Budanov, combatant in the First and Second Chechen Wars, and recipient of two Orders of Valour. He was sentenced to ten years in a strict-regime labour colony for crimes committed in Chechnya in the course of the Second Chechen War. He had abducted a Chechen girl, Elza Kungaeva, and murdered her in an exceptionally brutal manner. The court further resolved to strip Budanov of his rank and State awards.

The Budanov case began on March 26, 2000, the day Putin was elected President, and continued for more than three years of the Second Chechen War. It became a test for all of us, from the Kremlin down to the smallest villages. We all tried to make sense of these soldiers and officers who, every day, were murdering, robbing, torturing and raping in Chechnya. Were they thugs and war criminals? Or were they unflinching champions in a global war against international terrorism using all the weapons at their disposal, their noble aim justifying their means? The Budanov case became highly politicised, turning into a veritable symbol of our time. Everything that happened in those years in Russia and in the world was seen in the light of this case: September 11, 2001 in New York; the wars in Afghanistan and Iraq; the creation of an international anti-terrorist coalition; terrorist acts in Russia; the seizing of hostages in Moscow in October 2002; the endless succession of Chechen women blowing themselves up; and the Palestinisation of the Second Chechen War.

This striking, tragic case brought all our difficulties into the open. Most importantly, it demonstrated for all to see the pathological changes which the entire system of Russian justice has undergone under Putin and as a result of the war. The legal reform that the democrats had tried to implement and that Yeltsin had done all he could to promote collapsed under the pressure of the Budanov case, because for three years and more we were treated to a demonstration of the fact that we still did not have an independent judiciary. Instead we had a judicial system that did what the politicians told it to do. Moreover, we discovered that a majority of the population saw nothing out of the ordinary in this state of affairs. Today's Russian, brainwashed by propaganda, has largely reverted to Bolshevik thinking.

On July 25, 2003, the parents of Elza Kungaeva – the girl brutally strangled by the colonel – who had a better understanding than most of what was going on, did not even bother to attend the court. They were certain the man who had butchered their daughter would be acquitted.

But then a miracle occurred, both a miracle and a courageous act by Judge Vladimir Bukreev. The judge dared to find Budanov guilty and furthermore to sentence him to a far from token period of detention. Bukreev thereby set himself against the entire Russian military establishment, which had been actively rooting for Budanov. In Russia the military courts come under the jurisdiction of the country's armed forces, whose Commander-in-Chief is the President. Despite immense pressure from the Kremlin and the Ministry of Defence, Judge Bukreev decided that Budanov should receive the sentence he merited. In the process, however, the judge showed once more that today, as in the past, Russia's judicial system is in thrall to the politicians.

THE CASE

In order to dispel the myths surrounding the Budanov case let me quote from the indictment. These following excerpts, despite being written in the dry language of the prosecutor's office, testify more eloquently to the ambience of the Second Chechen War than any journalist could. They give us a feel for the situation in units deployed in the so-called "Zone of Anti-terrorist Operations", where Army anarchy rules. This ambience was the ultimate cause of the crimes committed by Yury Budanov, the former colonel of a tank regiment and commander of an élite subdivision of the Russian armed forces, a member of the Army Establishment, a graduate of the Military Academy awarded the country's highest decorations in recognition of his distinguished military service.

Indictment in respect of Colonel Yury Dmitrievich Budanov, Army Unit 13206 (160 Tank Regiment), accused . . . and of Lieutenant-Colonel Ivan Ivanovich Fedorov, Army Unit 13206, accused . . .

[Initially Budanov and Fedorov, a regimental commanding officer and his deputy, were both accused of committing crimes on March 26, 2000. Lieutenant-Colonel Fedorov was subsequently acquitted as his victim survived and publicly forgave him in the courtroom.]

The preliminary investigation has established that:

Yury Dmitrievich Budanov was appointed on August 31, 1998 to the post of commander of Army Unit 13206 (160 Tank Regiment). On January 31, 2000 Budanov was awarded the military rank of colonel. Ivan Ivanovich Fedorov was awarded the rank of lieutenant-colonel on August 12, 1997. On September 16, 1999 Fedorov was appointed to the post of chief of staff and deputy commander of Army Unit 13206 (160 Tank Regiment). On September 19, 1999, on the basis of Order of the General Headquarters of the Armed Forces of the Russian Federation No. 312/00264, Budanov and Fedorov left as part of Army Unit 13206 for duty in the North Caucasus Military District and were thereafter deployed to the Chechen Republic to engage in a counter-terrorist operation.

On March 26, 2000, Army Unit 13206 was temporarily

deployed on the outskirts of the village of Tangi . . . During dinner in the regimental officers' mess, Budanov and Fedorov imbibed spiritous liquor to celebrate the birthday of Budanov's daughter. At 19.00 hours that day Budanov and Fedorov proceeded in a drunken state, together with a group of officers of the regiment and at Fedorov's suggestion, to the intelligence company of the regiment under the command of Lieutenant R. V. Bagreev.

[It was Bagreev who subsequently forgave both Budanov and Fedorov in the courtroom for what they had done to him.]

Having inspected the state of orderliness in the tents . . . Fedorov desired to show Budanov that the intelligence company, to whose command Bagreev had been appointed on Fedorov's recommendation, could be relied upon in a combat situation. He proposed that Budanov check their readiness for action. Budanov at first declined, but Fedorov insisted. After Fedorov had repeated his suggestion several times, Budanov gave permission to test the company's combat readiness and proceeded with a group of officers to the Signals Centre. Permission having been given, Fedorov decided, without telling Budanov, to order the use of regimental armaments to open fire on Tangi. Fedorov's decision . . . was taken . . . without any actual necessity since no fire was incoming . . .

Implementing his plan in flagrant violation of the requirement of Order of the General Headquarters of the Armed Forces of the Russian Federation of February 21, 2000, No. 312/2/0091, which forbids the use of intelligence subsections without thorough preparation . . . Fedorov gave orders for firing positions to be taken up . . .

Obeying orders, Lieutenant Bagreev gave the command

to the company's personnel . . . Three combat vehicles took up combat positions. After completing targeting, some members of the crews declined to carry out Fedorov's order to open fire on a populated position. Continuing to exceed the authority of his rank, Fedorov insisted that they should open fire. Angered by the refusal of his subordinates, Fedorov began complaining to Bagreev. In a coarse manner he demanded that Bagreev should get his subordinates to open fire. Not satisfied with Bagreev's actions, Fedorov began personally to direct the activity of the company's personnel . . . the crew opened fire . . . and a house . . . was destroyed.

Having succeeded in getting the company's personnel to carry out his unlawful order, Fedorov grabbed Bagreev by his clothing and continued to address him in a vulgar manner. Bagreev offered no resistance . . . and returned to the tent of his subsection.

Budanov . . . ordered Fedorov to stop firing and report to himself. Fedorov reported that Bagreev had deliberately failed to carry out his order to open fire. Bagreev was summoned to Budanov. Budanov . . . insulted him and then punched Bagreev at least twice in the face.

At the same time, Budanov and Fedorov ordered the soldiers on guardhouse duty to tie Bagreev up and place him . . . in a pit . . . Budanov then seized Bagreev by his uniform and threw him to the ground. Fedorov booted Bagreev in the face. The soldiers on duty bound Bagreev, who was lying on the ground. Budanov, together with Fedorov, then continued to kick Bagreev . . .

After this beating, Bagreev was put in the pit, where he was left sitting with his hands and legs tied. Thirty minutes after the beating Fedorov went back to the pit, jumped in, and punched him in the face at least twice . . . This beating was stopped by officers of the regiment . . . Several minutes later Budanov came to the pit. On his orders Bagreev was pulled out. Seeing that he had succeeded in untying himself, Budanov again ordered the soldiers on duty to tie him up. When this order had been carried out Budanov and Fedorov again began beating Bagreev . . . Bagreev was again put in the pit bound hand and foot . . . Fedorov jumped down and bit him on the right eyebrow. Bagreev was left . . . until 08.00 hours on March 27, 2000, after which on Budanov's orders he was freed.

At 24.00 hours on March 26 Budanov, acting without instructions from his superiors, decided to go into Tangi personally in order to check out the possible presence at No. 7 Zarechnaya Street of members of an IAF. In order to drive to Tangi, Budanov ordered his subordinates to ready Armoured Personnel Carrier (APC) No. 391. Before departing, Budanov and the members of the crew armed themselves with standard-issue Kalashnikov-74 assault rifles. At this time Budanov informed the crew of the APC, namely Sergeants Grigoriev, Yegorov and Li-En-Shou, that their mission was to arrest a female sniper . . .

Budanov arrived at Tangi before 01.00 hours . . . On his orders the APC stopped outside No. 7 Zarechnaya Street, where the Kungaeva family lived. Budanov entered the house together with Grigoriev and Li-En-Shou. In the house were Elza Visaevna Kungaeva . . . along with her four younger brothers and sisters. Their parents were not present. Budanov asked where the parents were. Not receiving an answer, Budanov continued to exceed his authority and in contravention of Federal Law No. 3 "The Struggle against Terrorism", Article 13, ordered Li-En-Shou and Grigoriev to seize Elza Visaevna Kungaeva.

Believing themselves to be acting lawfully, Grigoriev and

Li-En-Shou seized Kungaeva, wrapped her in a blanket taken from the house, carried her from the house and placed her in the assault compartment of APC No. 391 . . . Budanov took Kungaeva back to the compound of Army Unit 13206. On Budanov's orders, Grigoriev, Yegorov and Li-En-Shou took Kungaeva, still wrapped in the blanket, to the prefabricated officers' accommodation which Budanov occupied and placed her on the floor. Budanov then ordered them to remain in the vicinity and not to let anyone through.

Remaining alone with Kungaeva, Budanov began demanding information from her as to the whereabouts of her parents and also information about the routes by which fighters passed through Tangi. When she refused to talk, Budanov, who had no right to interrogate Kungaeva, continued demanding information. Since she refused his demands, Budanov began beating Kungaeva, punching and kicking her many times on her face and different parts of her body. Kungaeva attempted to resist, pushing him away and trying to run out of the accommodation.

As Budanov was convinced that Kungaeva was a member of an IAF and that she had been involved in the deaths of his subordinates in January 2000, he decided to kill her. For this purpose Budanov seized Kungaeva's clothing, threw her down on a camp bed and, clasping the back of her neck, began to squeeze it . . . until he was sure she no longer showed signs of life . . .

Budanov's deliberate actions caused . . . asphyxia . . . Budanov called Grigoriev, Yegorov and Li-En-Shou into his quarters and ordered them to remove the body and secretly bury it away from the unit. Budanov's order was obeyed by the crew of APC No. 391. They secretly transported Kungaeva's body and buried it on one of the forest plantations, as Grigoriev reported back to Budanov on the morning of March 27, 2000.

The accused Budanov and Fedorov when questioned in respect of the present criminal charges partly admitted to being guilty of the acts of which they are accused. They changed the testimony they had given at the initial stage of the investigation.

Accused: Yury Dmitrievich Budanov

Questioned as a witness on March 27, 2000, Budanov explained that he had driven to Tangi ... discovered mines in one of the houses and detained two Chechens ... Budanov asserted that nobody had beaten Bagreev up. While carrying out a check of the combat readiness of the intelligence company ... the company had reacted incorrectly to the command "Attack". A conflict had arisen. Bagreev had insulted Fedorov ... He had then ordered the arrest of Bagreev. Budanov denied that Fedorov had given orders to fire on Tangi, or that the village had been fired on. At the end of the interrogation Budanov requested permission to write an admission of guilt regarding his having terminated the life of a female relative of citizens who were members of illegal formations in Chechnya.

Further, in an autograph admission of guilt ... Budanov gave the following information. On March 26, 2000 he had departed for the eastern outskirts of Tangi in order to take out or capture a woman sniper ... When they returned to the unit the girl was carried to his quarters ... A conflict ensued as a result of which he tore the girl's blouse and brassière. The girl continued trying to escape ... He strangled her ... He did not remove the clothing from the lower part of her body ... Budanov called the crew, ordered them to wrap the body in a blanket, drive with it to a forest plantation in the vicinity of the tank battalion and bury her.

Questioned on March 28, 2000, Budanov testified that on March 3, 2000 he had learned from operational sources that a female sniper was living in Tangi . . . he had been shown a photograph of her. This information had been made known to him by an inhabitant of Tangi who had personal scores to settle with the fighters . . . Detaining the girl, they returned to the regiment . . . He dragged her to a far corner of his quarters, threw her down on the camp bed and began to strangle her . . . The commanding officer of the APC came in with the signaller. The girl was lying in the far corner of his quarters, wearing only her pants . . . Budanov had been infuriated that she would not say where her mother was. According to information in his possession, on January 15–20, 2000 her mother had used a sniper's rifle in the Argun Ravine to kill twelve soldiers and officers.

When questioned on March 30, 2000 Budanov partly admitted his guilt . . . Budanov partially changed his testimony about Kungaeva's conduct, saying that she had told him they would get round to him in the end, and that he and those under his command would never get out of Chechnya alive. She had mouthed obscene remarks about his mother and run to the door. Her last remarks had completely infuriated Budanov . . . His pistol lay on a table next to the bed. She had tried to seize the pistol. Throwing her back on the bed, he held Kungaeva by the throat with his right hand and with his left hand held her arm to prevent her from reaching the pistol . . .

[These gradual changes to Budanov's testimony occurred because the Kremlin and the military establishment, having recovered from their shock at the unexpected audacity of the prosecutor's office in allowing itself to arrest a bemedalled serving colonel, began to pressure the officials conducting the investigation. As a result they started coaching Budanov as to what he should say in order to minimise the legal consequences and possibly even escape criminal responsibility completely.]

In the course of a further interview ... Budanov gave additional detailed testimony as to how he knew that the Kungaevs were members of an IAF. Information to this effect had been received from one of the Chechens he had encountered in January–February 2000 after the fighting in the Argun Ravine. This Chechen had passed him a photograph which showed Kungaeva holding a Dragunov sniper's rifle.

Interviewed on January 4, 2001, Budanov testified that he would plead not guilty to abducting Kungaeva. He considered that he had acted properly, given the operational information in his possession ... He had arrested her in order to pass her on to the law-enforcement agencies. He had not done so because he hoped himself to discover from the detainee where fighters were located ...

He was also aware that if the fighters learned that Kungaeva had been detained they would do their utmost to free her. It was for this reason that he decided to return to the regiment immediately. ... He did not accept that he was guilty of premeditated murder ... He was in a highly emotional state, and he was at a loss to explain how it came about that he had strangled her.

Accused: Ivan Ivanovich Fedorov

Interviewed on April 3, 2000 as a witness, Fedorov testified that on March 26, 2000 he, Arzumanyan [a comrade-in-arms] and Budanov went to inspect the intelligence company. Having completed the inspection he gave Bagreev an interim order: "Command post under attack: Take up firing positions" and indicated the location of the target. He then summoned Bagreev and asked why the combat vehicles had not taken up their firing positions. He could not remember what Bagreev replied . . . He then seized Bagreev by his clothing.

[. . . Fedorov] did not remember who gave the order to tie Bagreev's arms and legs . . . He then went up to Bagreev and struck him several times . . . On his, Fedorov's orders, Bagreev was then put in the pit. He jumped down into the pit in order to tell Bagreev exactly what he thought of him.

He, Fedorov, was pulled out of the pit by Arzumanyan. He learned only the following morning that Budanov had driven to Tangi that night . . .

On or around March 20, 2000 he saw a photograph Budanov had of a woman who, Budanov told him, was a sniper. According to Budanov this woman lived in Tangi . . . The woman appeared to be not more than 30 years old. On or around March 25, 2000 Budanov drove to Tangi and a Chechen showed him houses where fighters lived . . .

Aggrieved Party: Visa Umarovich Kungaev . . . agronomist of the Urus-Martan Soviet Farm, father of Elza Visaevna Kungaeva

Elza was the eldest child in the family . . . modest, calm, hard-working, decent and honest. She had to undertake all the housework, since his wife was ill and not allowed to work. For the same reason, Elza had the responsibility of looking after the younger children. She spent all her free time at home and did not go out. She had no boyfriends. She was awkward with members of the male sex. She had no intimate relations with them. His daughter simply was not a sniper. She was not a member of any armed formation. The suggestion was absurd.

On March 26, 2000 he went, together with his wife and children, to vote in the elections.

[Ironically, this was the day Putin was elected President.]

They busied themselves about the house. His wife got ready to go and see her brother Alexey in Urus-Martan ... He remained with the children.

They went to bed at about 21.00 hours, since there was no electricity ... At about 00.30 on March 27 he was awakened by the roar of a military vehicle ... He looked out of the window and saw strangers coming towards their house. He called his eldest daughter Elza and asked her quickly to rouse all the children, get them dressed and take them out of the house, telling her that it was being surrounded by soldiers. He, Kungaev, ran outside to find his brother, who lived some 20 metres away.

His brother was already running to see him ... On entering the house his brother saw Colonel Budanov, whom he recognised because his photograph had been published in the *Red Star* newspaper.

Budanov asked him, "Who are you?" Adlan replied that he was the brother of the owner of the house. Budanov replied rudely, "Get out of here." Adlan ran out of the house and began shouting. From what his children told him, Kungaev knew that Budanov then ordered the soldiers to take Elza. She was screaming. Wrapping her in a blanket, they took her outside. His relatives immediately came running and woke everybody to look for his daughter.

He went to the head of the village administration, the military commandant of the village and the military commandant of Urus-Martan District. At 6 a.m. they drove to Urus-Martan in order to find his daughter. On the evening of March 27, 2000 they learned that Elza had been murdered. In Kungaev's opinion Budanov abducted Elza and then raped her because she was a pretty girl.

Witness A. S. Magamaev testified that he was a neighbour of the Kungaevs. They were a poor family. They worked mainly in the fields. He had known Elza since she was born. She was a shy girl and did not associate with boys of her own age. He could say with certainty that Elza had never been a member of any armed formations.

The investigation has been unable to discover any evidence that E. V. Kungaeva was associated with or a member of any IAF.

Witness: Ivan Alexandrovich Makarshanov, former private in Army Unit 13206

On the evening of March 26, 2000 the guardhouse duty squad was called out to an emergency. On the orders of the commanding officer of the regiment, the personnel of the guardhouse duty squad bound the commanding officer of the intelligence company. Bagreev, the commanding officer of the intelligence company, was lying on the ground. Budanov and Fedorov each kicked Bagreev at least three times. Everything happened very quickly. After this Bagreev was put in a pit, the so-called *Zindan*.

After a time, when it was already dark, Makarshanov heard shouts and groans and came out of his tent. He saw that Budanov and Fedorov were in the pit where they had put Bagreev. (The tent was about 15–20 metres from the *Zindan*.) Fedorov was punching Bagreev in the face . . . Somebody shone a torch into the pit, so he saw everything clearly. Someone then pulled Fedorov out of the pit.

Until 02.00 hours on March 27 Makarshanov was in Fedorov's tent keeping the stove lit. At about 01.00 hours he heard an APC drive up to Budanov's quarters . . . He saw four persons enter Budanov's accommodation, one of whom was Budanov. One was carrying something on his shoulder, like a roll, its dimensions approximately those of a human body. He, Makarshanov, saw long hair hanging down from one end of the roll . . .

The person carrying the roll opened the doors, carried the roll inside and put it on the floor. A light was burning in the accommodation. Accordingly Makarshanov was able to see Budanov enter. The distance from the place where he was (in the tent) to Budanov's quarters was some 8–10 metres . . . The whole time after Budanov came to his quarters, he had three members of the crew of his APC standing by . . .

Other Witnesses

Witness Alexander Mikhailovich Saifullin testified that he had served with Army Unit 13206 from August 1999. From late January 2000 his duties were acting as stoker in Budanov's quarters. At approximately 05.00–05.15 hours on March 27 he entered the commander's quarters . . . Budanov was lying on the camp bed on the right and not, as usual, on the far one. The rug on the floor had been moved and was rumpled . . . and he saw that Budanov's bed was not made up. Budanov was asleep. At about 7 a.m. he entered the quarters and poured the commander a bucket of water to wash himself . . . The commander told him to tidy up in the quarters and, indicating the bed with his head, ordered him to change the blanket and all the bed linen. Saifullin set about tidying up and noticed that the blanket was damp . . . Budanov gave him an hour to clean the premises from top to bottom. When he took the bed linen from the far camp bed out of Budanov's quarters, the left corner of the sheet was wet.

Witness Valerii Vasilievich Gerasimov testified that from March 5 until April 20, 2000 he was acting commanding officer of the West Group of Troops. On the morning of March 27 he learned from the commandant of Urus-Martan that a girl had been abducted from Tangi during the night and that it was suspected that soldiers were responsible. He communicated with the commanding officers of three regiments, including Budanov of 160 Tank Regiment, and ordered that the girl should be returned within 30 minutes. With General Alexander Ivanovich Verbitsky, he himself drove first to 245 Regiment, then to 160 Regiment.

In 160 Regiment he was met personally by Budanov, who reported that everything was in order and that he had been unable to learn anything about the girl. Together with Verbitsky [Gerasimov] drove to Tangi, where at that moment some villagers were gathered. From the explanation of the father of the girl it appeared that a colonel had driven into the village during the night with soldiers in an APC, had wrapped the girl in a blanket and carried her off. They knew this colonel: he was the commanding officer of the tank regiment. At first [Gerasimov] and Verbitsky did not believe this. They returned to the regiment. Budanov was not to be found. Gerasimov ordered that Budanov should be detained.

[There is a rule in the Russian armed forces that serving personnel can be arrested only with the permission of their superior officers. For Budanov, only General Gerasimov had this status. Accordingly, we are obliged to Gerasimov for the fact that there ever was a Budanov case. The majority of commanding officers in Chechnya do not give the prosecutor's office permission to arrest those under their command who have committed war crimes and go to great lengths to protect them. Given the situation in the Anti-terrorist Operation Zone, Gerasimov's act must be regarded as very courageous. It could well have cost him his career. As the affair became a major focus of public attention, that did not occur. Gerasimov was appointed commander of 58 Army, a significant promotion.]

After his arrest Budanov was taken to Hankala [the main military base in Chechnya]. On that same evening the driver of the APC who had driven Budanov to the village admitted that on the night of March 27 they had brought a girl back and dragged her into Budanov's quarters. Some two hours later Budanov had summoned them. The girl was dead. Budanov had ordered them to take the body and bury it.

On the morning of March 28 the body was exhumed, taken to the Medical and Sanitary Battalion, medically examined, washed and returned to the parents.

When interviewed as a witness, Igor Vladimirovich Grigoriev testified that on March 27, 2000, when they returned to the unit, Budanov ordered them to carry the girl, wrapped in a blanket, into his quarters and themselves to stand guard . . . Budanov remained in his quarters with the girl. Some ten minutes after they had left the quarters, a woman's cries were heard coming from within, and Budanov's voice was also heard. Then music was heard coming from the accommodation. A woman's screams were heard for some time more coming from the same place.

Budanov was together with the girl in his quarters for between one and a half and two hours. Some two hours later Budanov called all three of them into his quarters, where the woman they had brought was lying naked on the bed. Her face was a bluish colour. The blanket they had wrapped the girl in was spread on the floor. Her clothing was lying on it in a heap. Budanov ordered them to take the woman away and bury her in secret . . . Wrapping the body in the blanket, they drove the girl away in APC No. 391 and buried the body. Grigoriev reported this back to Budanov on the morning of March 27.

Interviewed on October 17, 2000, Grigoriev elaborated that ten to twenty minutes after their leaving Budanov's quarters Budanov began shouting. What, exactly, he did not hear. There were also several screams from the girl, screams indicative of fear. When at Budanov's summons they entered his quarters, they saw the girl lying naked on the camp bed without signs of life . . . The girl had bruises to her neck, as if she had been strangled. Pointing to her, Budanov said with a strange expression on his face, "That's for you, you bitch, for Razmakhnin and the boys who died up that mountain."

The examination of Kungaeva's body revealed . . . injuries . . . on the . . . neck . . . the face . . . bruising in the right suborbital area, on the inner surface of the right thigh haemorrhaging into the . . . mouth and . . . of the left upper jaw. The corpse was unclothed . . .

The medical examination of the corpse . . . established that the injuries discovered on the neck had been caused ante-mortem . . . the cause of death was pressure on the neck from a blunt object. The bruising on Kungaeva's face and left thigh, the haemorrhaging into the . . . mouth, the injury to the right eye resulted from the action of a blunt object(s) . . . The act causing injury was a blow. The injuries referred to occurred ante-mortem . . .

Interviewed as a witness, Captain Alexey Viktorovich Simukhin, Investigator, military prosecutor's office, testified that on March 27, 2000 he received orders to bring Budanov to the landing strip of Army Unit 13206 in order for the latter to be transported to Hankala.

During the flight Budanov was very agitated, enquiring how he should behave, what he should say, and what he should do. On the morning of March 28, 2000 Simukhin travelled out as a member of the investigating team to . . . locate the body of Kungaeva . . . Simukhin wished to note that the burial site had been very carefully camouflaged, covered with turf . . . The body was in a half-sitting "foetal" position and was completely naked.

Aggrieved Party: Lieutenant Roman Vitalievich Bagreev . . . deputy chief of staff of Tank Battalion Army Unit 13206

From October 1, 1999 as a member of 160 Regiment Bagreev took part in the counter-terrorist operation. He had no scores to settle with Budanov and Fedorov.

On March 20, 2000 the intelligence company moved from . . . Komsomolskoe to . . . Tangi. It had been decided to hold a competition between the regiment's subsections to decide which company was the most orderly. The anti-aircraft section came in first. Fedorov disagreed with this result and assured everybody that the intelligence company was better . . . In order to persuade Budanov of this . . . Fedorov insisted an inspection should be carried out of the company's site.

After 18.00 hours Budanov, Fedorov, Silivanets and Arzumanyan arrived at the site. Budanov was intoxicated but entirely able to control himself. Fedorov was very drunk, his speech was slurred, and he was unsteady on his feet. Fedorov tried to persuade Budanov to check the combat readiness of the company. Budanov refused three or more times but Fedorov continued to insist. Budanov yielded to Fedorov's demands, ordering, "Firing positions. Prepare for combat."

Bagreev immediately ran towards the company's trenches. Fedorov ran behind him. The vehicles took up their firing positions. Budanov was at the Signals Centre. He knew that each vehicle always had a high-explosive fragmentation shell in its rammer tray ready for firing. There were no grounds to open fire on the village at the time, other than Fedorov's order.

After the vehicles' gun crews had taken up their positions, he gave orders to the crews to unload the fragmentation shell, load a hollow-charge shell and fire it over the houses. Such a shell, shot upwards, if encountering no obstacle, self-destructs. A fragmentation charge has no such self-destruction mechanism . . .

Vehicle No. 380 fired once over the roofs of the houses in the village. Fedorov saw this, leapt on to the second APC and ordered the gun layer to fire at Tangi. Dissatisfied with Bagreev's actions, Fedorov seized him by his clothing and abused him using obscene language. Bagreev was summoned by Budanov. When he arrived at the Signals Centre, Budanov and Fedorov were both there. They beat him up.

Inspection has established that to the south-west of the staff headquarters of Army Unit 13206 at a distance of 25 metres from the regimental command post on March 27, 2000 there was a pit above which three square-edged planks had been placed. The pit was a hollow in the ground 2.4 metres long, 1.6 metres wide and 1.3 metres deep. The walls were faced with brick, and the bottom was earthen.

[The evidence you have just read contains the first description in a Russian legal document of a so-called *Zindan*. These special torture pits were introduced on an extensive scale during the Second Chechen War. They are to be found in almost every military unit in Chechnya and are generally used for detaining arrested Chechens, as well as privates who are in disgrace. It is rare for them to be used against junior officers.]

Witness Private Dmitry Igorevich Pakhomov testified that on March 26, 2000 at about 20.00 hours Fedorov shouted at Bagreev, "I'll teach you to carry out my orders, you puppy." Bagreev was deluged with insults . . . Fedorov gave the order to tie Bagreev up and put him in the pit. There had been earlier occasions when the squad had tied up drunken contract soldiers before putting them in the pit, but for such a thing to be done to the commanding officer of the intelligence company was unbelievable.

Approximately one hour later the squad was again alerted to an emergency by Budanov. When they arrived, Bagreev was lying on the ground. Budanov and Fedorov once more started kicking him. After this, on Budanov's orders, Bagreev was again tied up and put in the pit. Fedorov then jumped down and began beating Bagreev up in the pit. Bagreev was shouting and groaning . . . Silivanets jumped down into the pit and pulled Fedorov out. At about 02.00 hours Pakhomov was in his tent when he heard rifle fire. As he later learned, this was Suslov shooting in order to bring Fedorov to his senses. He was again trying to reach Bagreev.

Budanov and Fedorov were charged. The criminal case against Grigoriev, Li-En-Shou and Yegorov was closed as the result of an amnesty.

The expert conclusion of the Standing Inter-departmental Forensic Psychological and Psychiatric Board was that Budanov was not at the time of the act with which he was charged in respect of Bagreev in a transitory pathological state of dysfunction or in a state of pathological or physiological incapacity. At the time of the murder of Kungaeva, Budanov was in a transitory, situationally induced, cumulative psycho-emotional state and was not fully aware of the nature and significance of his acts or able to use his free will to control them.

THE TRIAL

Budanov's case now moved to trial. This was the summer of 2001. The first judge was Colonel Victor Kostin of the Military Court of the North Caucasus located in Rostov-on-Don, in the same location as the North Caucasus Military District Staff Headquarters, which, as people in Russia say, is "fighting the war in Chechnya". The influence of the military on every aspect of life in Rostov-on-Don is enormous. The main military hospital, through which thousands of soldiers crippled and wounded in Chechnya have passed, is located there, and the city is home to the families of many officers posted to Chechnya. In a sense this is a front-line city, and this circumstance played a large part in how the Budanov trial developed. Pickets and demonstrations outside the courtroom, in support of Budanov, provided the trial with a running commentary, with slogans like "Russia in the Dock!" and "Free Russia's Hero!"

The first phase of the hearings lasted for more than a year, from the summer of 2001 until October 2002. The purpose of the proceedings seemed not to be to decide whether Budanov was guilty or not but to absolve him of all sins and crimes. Throughout the hearings Judge Kostin displayed manifest prejudice in favour of Budanov, turning down all representations on behalf of the Kungaevs and refusing to admit any witness who might speak against Budanov. He even refused to question Generals Gerasimov and Verbitsky, on the grounds that they had given permission to arrest the murderous colonel.

Throughout this time the prosecutor too was openly on the side of the accused, effectively acting as his defence lawyer although his duty was to act on behalf of the victims.

The situation inside the courtroom was mirrored by the situation outside it. Public opinion was generally on Budanov's side. There were meetings outside the court with red Communist flags, flowers for Budanov as he was being led into the building. The top brass at the Ministry of Defence joined in, with public pronouncements by Minister Sergey Ivanov to the effect that Budanov was "quite clearly not guilty".

The ideological basis for absolving Budanov was that, although he had committed a crime, it was a crime he had a right to commit. His treatment of Elza Kungaeva was justified on the basis that he was taking revenge on an enemy in war, because he believed the girl to be a sniper responsible for the death of officers.

The Kungaev family had major problems with lawyers from the beginning. The family was very poor, had many children, and no work, and was obliged to move to a tent in a refugee camp in the neighbouring republic of Ingushetia after their daughter's tragic death. They were afraid of reprisals from the Army for having gone to court (having been threatened on more than one occasion). As a result they found themselves without a lawyer. At this point the Memorial Civil-rights Centre based in Moscow, with a branch in Rostov-on-Don, found them lawyers and for a long time covered their fees.

The first lawyer who thus became involved in the case was Abdullah Hamzaev, an elderly Chechen who had been living in Moscow for many years and who was, moreover, a distant relative of the Kungaevs.[6] It has to be said that his efforts were not effective, rather the reverse. This was not Hamzaev's fault. It was because our society is becoming increasingly racist. It does not trust people from the Caucasus, let alone people from Chechnya. The press conferences Hamzaev called in Moscow in order to describe how difficult it was to move matters forward in the military court in Rostov-on-Don got nowhere. Journalists did not believe what he said, and accordingly no public campaign in defence of the Kungaevs resulted. That, of course, was their only hope of making any headway.

Memorial invited a young Moscow lawyer, Stanislav Markelov, to assist Hamzaev. Markelov was a member of the same Inter-republican College of Lawyers to which Budanov's lawyers belonged. The major cases Markelov had defended before and which had attracted Memorial's attention were the first in Russia to involve accusations of terrorism and political extremism: the blowing up of memorials to Emperor Nicholas II in the vicinity of Moscow, an attempt to blow up the monument to Peter the Great, and the murder by skinheads of Russian citizens of Afghan background.

Markelov was Russian, and at the time this was crucial. Memorial had made a good choice, because subsequently it was his energy, choice of tactics and ability to communicate with the press that focused a lot of attention on the trial, mainly from journalists in Moscow, both Russian and foreign. Here is what Markelov himself has to say about what he saw in the court just after taking on the case. At that time the trial was effectively taking place in camera and journalists were banned:

> "The court was in a great rush. It did not want to go into the detail of any of our requests and rejected anything that could be interpreted against Budanov ... All our petitions, for example, to call witnesses, to call in experts, to have independent examinations, were rejected. I had the impression that Judge Kostin was not even reading them ..."

"But why were there so many petitions?" I asked. "Surely you were provoking the court by deluging it with such quantities. Was that a sensible approach to take?"

"The reason was simple: the court was allowing one violation of the law after another, and it was our duty as lawyers to protest against that . . . Who were all these people we wanted to be invited into court . . . ? And why did such a furious battle develop around at least two of them . . . ? Let me remind you of the circumstances of the case: on the day before the crime was committed . . . Budanov and other officers . . . detained two Chechens . . . one of whom supposedly pointed out a house where, Budanov alleged, a family lived who supported terrorists or whose members were themselves terrorists. The names of the informers were given in the materials of the case . . . We, the defence, began trying to discover who these people were who had misled Budanov by indicating the Kungaevs' house . . . We wanted these people to come into court and explain why they had done that . . . We discovered that one 'informer' was a deaf mute. That is, he was physically incapable of hearing Budanov's question about who the female sniper . . . was. He was also physically incapable of replying . . ."

"And the other informer?"

"It was even easier to find him. It transpired that on March 26, after the meeting with Budanov, this second informer and the colonel, entirely by coincidence of course, were photographed together by correspondents of the Ministry of Defence newspaper *Red Star*. It just happened to be that day that correspondents were working in the village of Tangi-Chu, and eleven of their photographs from Tangi-Chu [were] part of the evidence . . . [This] meant that this individual could be identified from his photographs, and could then confirm to the court that on the fatal evening Budanov had gone to Tangi-Chu to capture terrorists . . .

"But here we again came up against misunderstandings and inconsistencies. We carefully studied the photographs . . . only to find they had been taken on March 25, not on March 26 . . . You will recall that it was supposedly during March 26 that the informers told Budanov about the 'female snipers' and he, thirsting to avenge his slain comrades . . . could barely contain himself . . . If, however, it turned out that the informers had told Budanov everything on March 25, then what spontaneous reactions, what feelings which completely overwhelmed the colonel and justified his behaviour, are we talking about? There were also witnesses to testify that on both March 25 and until midday on March 26, when the officers in the regiment began the binge drinking which Budanov had organised in honour of his little daughter's birthday, the colonel was calm and showed no intention of going and taking revenge on some female sniper."

"Well, let's be objective. Somebody got the dates wrong. These things happen. There's a war going on."

"No. Inconsistencies occur at every stage of the Budanov case . . . Even to a lay person, let alone a lawyer, what these inconsistencies say unambiguously is that the court absolutely *had to* call the [second] informer . . . And did Budanov go looking for a female sniper, or was he just looking for a pretty girl? . . . If so, then the idea that Budanov was a hero . . . all that ideology, is completely beside the point. It's no good the psychiatric report basing all its conclusions on his 'heroism' and 'vengeful feelings towards the sniper'. The more so since there are tell-tale references in the file to numerous earlier 'women of the colonel'. 'The Commander has brought a woman back again' is a quote from the testimony of one of the soldiers at the preliminary investigation . . ."

"What happened then?"

"The Court announced that . . . it was not a detective agency and was under no obligation to go looking for this person. Naturally, the lawyers got to work and found him themselves. He turned out to be one Ramzan Sembiev, a convict serving time in a strict-regime labour camp in Dagestan for kidnapping. What matters here, however, is not the personality of the informer or the fact that the people who were assisting Budanov committed such heinous crimes. The fact that we found Sembiev in a strict-regime labour camp meant that there should have been no difficulty at all in bringing him to the court for cross-examination. It is standard practice in Russian criminal cases for those sent to places of detention to be listed in a database to which the courts have access. To make things even easier for the judge we told him exactly where Sembiev was to be found. It was not far from Rostov-on-Don. Even then the court's response was, 'No. We do not need this man. He cannot communicate any significant information to the Court.' And as if that wasn't enough, Prosecutor Nazarov . . . delivered a speech [saying that] since the witness was a criminal he would not tell the truth, and there was therefore no sense in our 'dragging him here'. I was astonished. The prosecutor saw no distinction between the fact that, while Sembiev was a criminal in his own case, he was a witness in this one."

"What was going on?"

"The court's approach to the case was ideological. The Kremlin was applying pressure for Budanov to be absolved of his sins. Nothing was important or relevant if it could be to Budanov's disadvantage. The prosecutor's office decided not to behave in . . . accordance with its role as defined by the Constitution . . .

"During Nazarov's speech to the Court a number of other inexplicable things came out. For example, a prosecutor in Dagestan was said to have approached Sembiev in the labour camp after our application and to have asked whether he knew Budanov. Sembiev reputedly denied it and said the first time he had seen him was on television."

"Was this conversation forwarded to the court as an official document?"

"No, of course not . . ."

"Is it accurate to say that the district military court did all it could to prevent an accurate picture emerging of the crimes committed in the Budanov case? That is, did it do the exact opposite of what it was obliged to do under the Constitution and current legislation?"

"Yes, that is absolutely right. Let me cite one more instance where the court did not want the truth to come out. One of the items in . . . the case . . . was a photograph Budanov had supposedly kept for a long time which showed Elza Kungaeva with her mother, both holding rifles. Budanov claimed he had been given this photograph by Yakhyaev, the administrative head of the town of Duba-Yurt, to help him find the woman who had shot officers of Budanov's regiment during fighting in the Argun Ravine. The village of Duba-Yurt is located at the entrance to the ravine and was at the centre of fierce fighting in February 2000 in which Budanov's regiment took part. This photograph, on which the court's psychiatric consultants based their conclusions . . . was nowhere to be found in the case files. It still isn't. This means, in the first place, that the experts were lying . . . In the second place, it means that this basic piece of evidence . . . never existed. Everything in the enterprise to whitewash Budanov was premised on that photograph . . ."

"Right. But even if the photograph is missing from the case files, there is still an important witness in Yakhyaev. He could presumably have been cross-examined."

"He would have been if this court had been following the normal procedure of seeking to establish the truth and determine the guilt of each party. In Russia, however, we have a different kind of court. It is ideological, it protects the interests of war criminals and imagines that is the same as protecting the interests of the State. So here too Judge Kostin said, 'No. We do not need Yakhyaev. He will tell us nothing of importance' . . . We found Yakhyaev. He was perfectly willing to come to court but would have needed authorisation to pass through the checkpoints in Chechnya and cross the border. The court refused to give that authorisation."

"How did Judge Kostin justify his refusal also to question General Gerasimov?"

". . .The judge was not interested in hearing the general's testimony, although he could, for example, have described the colonel's state of mind in the morning immediately after committing the crime, a subject about which there was greatly conflicting evidence . . . Had Budanov had a hangover? . . . In the preliminary investigation witnesses had talked a great deal about his drunkenness . . . Was he, as the first psychiatric report claimed [there were six in all], in an altered state of mind as a result of alcoholic intoxication? Was the murder the consequence of temporary insanity? Being of unsound mind is not a condition that can pass off in a few hours . . . so Budanov must have been responsible and aware of his actions. Why then did the experts assure us that he was not aware of his actions and could not be held responsible? Was it not because they too were party to the whitewashing of Budanov?"

"Apart from that, cross-examining General Gerasimov would have helped to establish whether Budanov resisted arrest. We know that when the general came to 160 Regiment . . . to arrest Budanov, Budanov responded by summoning soldiers from the regimental intelligence company, forcing them to offer armed resistance to General Gerasimov's soldiers. The units came close to having a shoot out."

"Yes, that is exactly what happened. Budanov then pulled out a revolver. Gerasimov was afraid he was going to shoot somebody, but Budanov thought for a moment and then shot himself in the foot. This was all in the case file . . ."

"If Budanov did resist arrest, what difference would that have made?"

"A lot. In the first place, it would have been an additional offence. In the second, it would have shed important light on Budanov's personality. The court . . . added a letter . . . from General Vladimir Shamanov, now Governor of Ulyanovsk Province, to the case files. [Shamanov was an old friend of Budanov's, 160 Regiment having long fought in Chechnya under his command.] There are no new facts in Shamanov's letter, because at the time the crime was committed he was not even in Chechnya. Instead there is a great deal of ideology. He simply asserts that Budanov is 'Not guilty': he was absolutely right to detain Kungaeva as a sniper, and right to kill her when she resisted. Shamanov wrote to the court as a typical participant in the Second Chechen War, as Budanov's immediate superior, and the court happily added his letter to the case files."

"Can we say that the entire court proceedings in respect of Budanov are ideologically based if the court refused to accept specific information from direct witnesses such as General Gerasimov, Sembiev and Yakhyaev but consented to accept a patriotic text from General Shamanov, who was not in any sense a witness? Shamanov is well known as a proponent of extreme military cruelty towards the civilian population of Chechnya, and as someone who firmly believes that the Chechen people must bear collective responsibility for the actions of individual criminals."

"Yes, that's exactly right. The hearing . . . was designed to prevent a proper examination of the case and . . . to reduce everything to a 'reprisal against a Russian officer'. Quite apart from that, as I have said, the court blatantly ignored standard procedures. For example, the reading of the ten large volumes of the case files was completed in one and a half hours."

"How did the judge manage that?"

"He just leafed through them and announced that the investigation was complete. The following day the investigation resumed without any ruling to that effect . . . This will, of course, give us grounds for appeal . . ."

"Doesn't it bother you that you are a Russian defending the interests of a Chechen family? The way things have evolved here, Chechens are defended by Chechen lawyers, and Russians by Russians."

"I was invited by Memorial, which organised the defence for the Kungaev family . . . The Kungaevs found themselves without any protection at all, and the court took advantage of that. It started to hurry the case along . . . When I appeared in Rostov-on-Don, people asked me what relation I had to the Chechen diaspora. I replied, 'Look at me. None.' The second question was, 'What race are you?' I was asked this not only by Budanov supporters but by Budanov himself in the courtroom. Incidentally, he shouted constantly at me during the hearings – 'What are you getting so het up about, you tit?' for example."

"'You tit?'"

"Of course. He is a soldier. He thinks he can do as he pleases. Budanov was never reprimanded by the judge for behaving improperly in court. He could do as he pleased. I think the judge was scared of him."

"What about his own defence team, his three lawyers. Did Budanov shout at them too?"

"No, of course not. When I was really fed up with being questioned about my race, I said, 'I am a Russian, as you can see. That is precisely why I am involved in this case. I am defending the standards of Russian law.'"

Following in Budanov's footsteps, the court decided to defend customary law instead. Budanov had acted entirely in accordance with Chechen customary law: he considered the murder he committed to be retribution. The court, and Russian society, supported him in this. What the case shows is that the authorities in Russia, and the State as a whole, accept that Russian law is in abeyance in Chechnya.

PLAYING GAMES WITH PSYCHIATRIC REPORTS

One of the main features of the Budanov case was the games played with the forensic psychological and psychiatric reports.

During the three years the case ran, the colonel had the benefit of four psychiatric reports and, when the initial verdict was set aside, of a further two. The conclusions of nearly all of these were politically slanted and supported whatever the current Kremlin line happened to be.

The first two reports were compiled almost in the aftermath of the crimes, in May and August 2000 during the preliminary investigation. The first examination was carried out by the psychiatrists of the military hospital of the North Caucasus Military District and the Central North Caucasus Forensic Laboratory of the Ministry of Justice of Russia. The second report was produced by doctors of the civilian Novocherkassk Provincial Psycho-neurological Hospital.

These reports asserted that Budanov was responsible for his actions. That is, he was answerable for his crimes. This was during a period when Putin was talking a great deal about the "dictatorship of law" which needed to be established in Russia, and which meant that soldiers who committed crimes in Chechnya would be punished in exactly the same way as Chechen fighters who were members of IAFs.

Moreover, this was a time of courting the Chechens after the fierce assaults of 1999–2000 and the appointment of a new head of administration of the republic, Ahmad-Hadji Kadyrov. Kadyrov had been one of the fighters and the mufti of Djohar Dudaev, the first President of Chechnya who had been assassinated in 1996 by a smart missile targeted by Russian Federal officers. Kadyrov, having earlier declared jihad on Russia, had subsequently become a friend of the Kremlin after "fully appreciating the situation".

These two reports noted, however, that when Elza Kungaeva was strangled, Budanov was probably mentally unbalanced, and that he appeared to be exhibiting symptoms of brain damage resulting in a "personality and behavioural disorder".

The Ministry of Defence took exception to these conclusions because they had two implications. One was that since Budanov was in his right mind, he could be prosecuted to the full extent of the law. The other was that the Russian Army was employing people with brain damage which nobody bothered to assess, that such people were fighting in battles and that people with personality disorders had command of hundreds of other people and had cutting-edge weapons at their disposal.

When the trial began, it soon became clear that the psychiatrists' conclusions did not suit Judge Kostin either. There seem to have been at least two reasons for this.

The first was that Kostin is himself, as a military judge, employed by the Ministry of Defence. Russia has special military courts and military judges who try crimes committed by military personnel. These judges are totally beholden to the military establishment, entirely dependent on military leaders (from garrison commanders up to the Minister of Defence) for their living accommodation, their salaries and any prospects of promotion. So Judge Kostin's apartment and pay rise would have to come from the same headquarters to which the accused, Colonel Budanov, was subordinate.

The second reason was that by the time Budanov came to trial, political circumstances in Russia had begun to change significantly. The Kremlin had gradually stopped playing at democracy and worrying about the "dictatorship of law". In consequence, all those who had fought in Chechnya were declared heroes, irrespective of what they had done there. The President began dishing out medals and orders right, left and centre, assuring those involved in the war that the State would "never betray them". These highly charged words meant that the government intended to be lenient towards those guilty of war crimes in Chechnya, to the point of forgiving absolutely anything, and that any prosecutor's office trying to bring criminal proceedings against Federal military personnel should just pipe down.

Stories poured from the State-controlled television channels relating how honestly Budanov had fulfilled his duty, and General Shamanov was continually in evidence making patriotic speeches in praise of his comrade-in-arms. The claim that the 18-year-old Chechen girl whom the colonel had murdered was a sniper was no longer subject to doubt. Nobody now recalled that neither the investigation nor Budanov's counsel had been able to find a shred of evidence to suggest that Elza Kungaeva had had anything to do with IAFs.

The politically inspired brainwashing of the Russian population was going full tilt, preparing the ground for Budanov's acquittal.

At this very moment, the court in Rostov-on-Don was stricken by doubt as to the competence of the experts who had carried out the first two psychiatric reports, and commissioned a new one. This time it was a joint military and civilian effort, in Moscow moreover, uniting the efforts of the Central Forensic Medical laboratory of the Ministry of Defence and the Serbsky State Research Centre for Social and Forensic Psychiatry, popularly known as the Serbsky Institute.

The Serbsky's bad reputation in Russia dates from Soviet times, when dissidents – those fighting against Communism, the totalitarian lie and political unfreedom – would be certified insane. The doctors of the Serbsky Institute were invariably conscientious in carrying out the tasks they were allotted by the omnipotent KGB.

That is where Budanov was sent. When this became common knowledge, there were few doubts as to why he was being sent there. Everything possible was being done to free him of criminal responsibility, his supporters – and his opponents – said.

The official reasons for commissioning a third report were given by the court as "imprecision, contradictoriness and factual incompleteness", and because "new and more accurate data" had appeared which were important for "determining Budanov's true mental state".

It did not matter that a series of episodes described to the new commission had never happened. As these unproven facts favoured the colonel they were put before the experts, who then treated them as incontrovertible.

Not to mince matters, this was blatant falsification.

What questions did Judge Kostin address to the psychiatrists of this third commission?

Has Budanov suffered, or is he presently suffering, from any chronic mental illness?

At the time of the acts he is accused of having committed, was Budanov in a state of temporary pathological disturbance? Could he fully understand the true nature and danger to society of his acts and control them?

What psychological peculiarities of Budanov's personality could have contributed to or substantially influenced his behaviour in the situations under investigation?

Was Budanov at the time of performing the acts he is accused of in an emotional state (of stress, frustration, temporary mental aberration)?

Could Kungaeva's actions have influenced the arising in Budanov's mind of any temporary disturbance of his mental functions?

Did Kungaeva's actions provoke Budanov's behaviour?

What influence did the use of vodka have on Budanov's condition at the time of performing the actions of which he is accused?

How can Budanov's condition be assessed ... in the event of (1) his perceiving Kungaeva to be the daughter of a sniper, who was refusing to communicate the whereabouts of her mother, insulting him, attempting to escape, offering resistance? (2) attempting to gain possession of a loaded weapon? (3) his ... showing her a photograph unmasking her?

Is Budanov in need of medical treatment?

Was Budanov in a fit mental state for military service at the time of the acts of which he is accused, and is he fit for military service at the present time?

Are the conclusions of the experts given in the preliminary investigation clinically sound?"

Following is the Serbsky experts' response. Everything in their report is neatly directed towards producing the requisite image of a hero.

According to Budanov, his was a difficult birth . . . According to the testimony of his mother and sister, he was vulnerable and liable to flare up in response to a slight. He would respond coarsely or start a fight. He was particularly sensitive about unfair remarks and in such cases always tried to defend the weak, those smaller than himself, and the poor . . .

Budanov's service references show him in an exceptionally favourable light. He was disciplined, effective and tenacious. In January 1995 during the first military campaign in Chechnya, while taking part in combat operations, Budanov suffered concussion, losing consciousness for a short time. He did not seek medical attention. According to his mother and sister, after returning from the First Chechen War Budanov's personality and behaviour changed. He became more nervous and irritable . . . In his subsections Budanov created a spirit of intolerance of shortcomings and passivity. He had a highly developed sense of responsibility . . .

None of his comrades has noticed mental aberrations in Budanov. He has never been under the observation of a psychiatrist or neuropathologist.

Budanov testifies that when his regiment arrived in Chechnya . . . it was involved almost constantly in combat operations. In October and again in November 1999 Budanov suffered concussion with loss of consciousness. After this he began to suffer incessantly from headaches and dizziness with loss of vision. He became unable to tolerate sudden loud noises, became liable to flare up, lacking in restraint and irritable. He suffered mood swings, with outbursts of rage. He committed acts which he later regretted.

Budanov testifies that the most severe fighting was in the Argun Ravine from December 24, 1999 to February 14, 2000. From January 12 to 21 the regiment lost nine officers and three other ranks. Many of these were killed, Budanov testifies, by a shot to the head from a sniper. On January 17, 2000 Budanov's comrade, Captain Razmakhnin, died at the hands of a sniper. Two weeks after the fighting they succeeded in removing from the battlefield the mutilated corpse of Major Sorokotyagi, on which signs of torture were evident.

On February 8, 2000 Budanov went on leave to the Buryat Republic. His wife testifies that during this leave he was irritable and nervous. He told her that his regiment had encountered fighters of Hattab [an Arab commander] in the Argun Ravine, and that 15 field commanders of Hattab's grouping had been killed in the fighting. Because of this the fighters had declared that Budanov's regiment were "wild beasts" and proclaimed Budanov their personal enemy. They had offered a fabulous sum to have him killed.

Budanov was extremely upset by the fact that the majority of officers in his regiment had died not in open battle but at the hands of a sniper. He said he would return home only after they had "wiped out the last fighter".

On February 15, without completing his leave, Budanov returned to Chechnya. His mother and sister testify that Budanov looked in on them . . . and had changed beyond recognition. He smoked constantly, hardly spoke and "flew into a rage over nothing at all". He could not sit still. Showing photographs of those who had died and of their graves, he wept. They had not seen him in such a state before.

[According to the testimony of Captain Kuptsov, head of the medical centre of 160 Regiment, who saw Budanov every day, there were occasions when his mood might change several times within ten or fifteen minutes, from a normal, amiable frame of mind to a defensive fury. During combat these tendencies were exaggerated. In a moment of rage Budanov might hurl a wall clock to the floor or at those around him, telephones, anything that came to hand. In Kuptsov's words, Budanov's mental state had assumed "perverse forms" by October 1999 – that is, before the death of his fellow officers during the fighting in the Argun Ravine.

Budanov led attacks himself, his rifle in his hands, and took part in man-to-man combat. After the battles in the Argun Ravine he tried personally to retrieve the bodies of those who had died. After the death of officers and soldiers of the regiment on Hill 950.8 Budanov blamed himself and was in a state of constant depression. He might strike subordinates or hurl ashtrays at them. In mid-March 2000, having demanded that his tent should be tidied, he threw a grenade into the stove . . .

From mid-February 2000 the regiment was deployed in the vicinity of Tangi. Budanov was ordered to carry out intelligence and search measures, lay ambushes, carry out supplementary passport checks of the inhabitants of the village and detain suspects.

Budanov and those under his command commented that at that time the situation was very confused, and it was impossible to tell friend from foe or where the front line was. From March 22 to 24, the regiment carried out reconnaissance and search measures. They decided to inspect a number of houses in Tangi and discovered two "slaves", forcibly taken from Central Russia some ten or fifteen years earlier.

Having received information about this, on March 26, 2000 Budanov decided to check the situation in Tangi personally. Having detained two Chechens, Budanov ordered that they should be bound and put in the APC. At the regiment one presented documents in the name of Shamil Sambiev and asked to be allowed to talk to Budanov privately. After 15 or 20 minutes Budanov gave orders that they should return to Tangi, explaining that Shamil had agreed to show houses where persons associated with or assisting the fighters lived. During the journey through the village the Chechen pointed out the houses of interest to them, including a white house ... where a "female sniper" lived. In addition, Budanov had a photograph showing two or three men and three or four women with weapons in their hands.

Budanov testifies that he decided to detain this sniper without delay. On March 26 ... during lunch in the officers' mess, Budanov imbibed spiritous liquor. At 24.00 hours he decided to drive personally to ... where the Kungaev family lived. Budanov ... ordered that Kungaeva be arrested ...

He began to beat her, punching her and kicking her in the face and on various parts of the body, causing bruises to the inner surface of her right thigh and haemorrhaging in her ... mouth. Kungaeva attempted to resist ... Budanov, being certain that Kungaeva was a member of an IAF and involved in the death of those under his command, decided to kill her. He ... then summoned the crew of his APC and ordered them to take Kungaeva's body away and bury it outside the territory of the unit. This they did ...

Budanov claims he had no intention of killing Kungaeva at first, let alone of abusing her sexually. Kungaeva, however, "exploded" with curses [we recall that she did not speak Russian] directed at the armed forces of Russia, Russia itself and him personally . . . The situation became increasingly heated. Kungaeva told him the Chechens would "deal with him and his family" . . . Budanov . . . forcibly dragged her away from the door. In the course of this struggle, Kungaeva's clothing was partly torn.

According to Budanov, Kungaeva proved to be very strong. She tore his T-shirt, tore his daughter's chain with a cross from his neck, and he responded by tearing off her upper clothing. Kungaeva shouted that she "hadn't shot enough of them yet". When Kungaeva was on the second, further camp bed, she attempted to reach his pistol, which was lying on the bedside table. Budanov seized her hand, and with the other pressed her body down on to the bed, keeping his hand in the region of her throat. Kungaeva continued to threaten him. There flashed before his eyes the faces of "all the soldiers and officers who had died in the Argun Ravine".

What happened after that Budanov does not remember. When he began to recover, he saw Kungaeva lying on the bed, not moving. He called the APC crew. Budanov testifies that at this moment Kungaeva was wearing a skirt, while her vest, blouse and brassière were lying in a heap, and he was wearing his trousers. Li-En-Shou suggested burying her in the plantation. Budanov then told the members of the crew to wrap her body in the blanket and take it away . . .

After the crew left Budanov lay down and fell asleep.

[We should note that soldiers of the regiment who were guarding their commanding officer's quarters that night had said more than once during the investigation that when they entered at Budanov's summons, the colonel was wearing only his underpants. The young girl was lying on the further bed completely naked. Budanov asked the soldiers, "Anyone scared of dead bodies?", lit a cigarette and ordered them to wrap the body and bury it. He threatened that if they told anyone he would shoot them.]

At about 13.30 on March 27, according to Budanov, he met Major-General Gerasimov, acting commanding officer of the West Group.

[The actual commanding officer was Vladimir Shamanov.]

General Gerasimov complained to Budanov that he had burned down half the village and raped a 15-year-old girl. Gerasimov's remarks were insulting and included obscene language. Budanov pulled out a pistol, pointed the muzzle down and shot himself in the foot. At this point Gerasimov's bodyguard pointed their weapons at him, although after the shot Budanov himself handed Gerasimov the pistol.

At the same time the intelligence company of Budanov's regiment drove up. The intelligence company, consisting of 20 soldiers and two officers, took up positions opposite General Gerasimov's officers. A confrontation ensued, but Budanov ordered his men to lower their weapons. According to Budanov, he and Generals Gerasimov and Verbitsky then went to the staff room. Budanov subsequently wrote an admission of guilt.

When questioned ... Budanov explained the contradictions in his statements by saying that [earlier] he had been in a very bad state.

On the basis of the above, the commission has come to the conclusion that Budanov was not responsible for his actions, on the grounds of diminished responsibility . . . The acts of the victim, Kungaeva, were one of the factors causing Budanov's temporary mental breakdown . . . There is no conclusive evidence regarding Budanov's being in a state of intoxication . . .

Budanov . . . should be kept under observation and treated by a psychiatrist on an outpatient basis. Category C: Partially fit for military service.

The commission's conclusions gave the judge all the ammunition he needed under Russian law to do the bidding of his political masters and acquit the colonel.

In the first place, he could lift the burden of criminal responsibility from Budanov.

In the second place, he could send him for compulsory psychiatric treatment but as an outpatient. How long this should continue was to be determined not by the court but by the doctor treating him. The colonel could be free of all that unpleasantness a week or so after the verdict.

In the third place, the judge could safeguard Budanov's right to continue to serve in the Army, since his state of diminished responsibility had been "temporary" and situational. The military establishment insisted that the verdict be worded in this way since otherwise, as we have said, it would have appeared that their regiments in Chechnya were being commanded by individuals who were manifestly insane and who were getting away with murder.

That's the way it is in Russia. What the experts report to Russian courts, just as in Soviet times, depends not on the facts but on who is massaging them.

Let us pause to take a look at the cast of characters who provided the psychological and psychiatric grounds for exculpating Budanov:

Professor T. Pechernikova, Doctor of Medical Science (Commission Chairman), Director of the Consultancy Section of the Serbsky Institute, doctor with an international reputation, psychiatric consultant of the highest standing, with 50 years of consultancy experience;

Professor K. Kondratiev, Doctor of Medical Science, Award of Merit of the Russian Federation, Director of the First Clinical Department, with 42 years of consultancy experience;

F. Safuanov, MSc in Psychology, with 20 years of consultancy experience;

Colonel A. Gorbatko, Army Medical Service, Chief Consultant in Forensic Psychiatry of the Ministry of Defence;

Lieutenant-Colonel G. Fastovtsev, Army Medical Service;

G. Burnyasheva, Consultant Psychiatrist.

Why did the court turn to Professor Pechernikova to cobble together a politically sensitive expert report to suit the authorities?

My belief is that the choice was far from random, because in Russia things like this do not just happen. It is the way things were done in Soviet times. The spectres of Communism, its most monstrous spectres at that, are right there with us again. What follows will show that in the era of President Putin, the appalling practice of political-psychiatry-to-order has returned to become part of our everyday life, and from an unexpected direction.

On August 25, 1968 a famous demonstration took place in Red Square, Moscow. Seven people entered the square and unfurled banners reading "For Our and Your Freedom!" and "Shame on the Occupiers!" One of the seven was Natalia Gorbanevskaya, a poet, journalist and dissident who, on this occasion, was pushing a pram with her baby in it. In this manner, in a country where nobody had protested for a long time, people stepped forward who had it in them to protest against the invasion of Czechoslovakia by Soviet troops.

The demonstration of "The Seven" lasted only a few minutes before all of them were seized by the KGB agents in civilian clothing who constantly patrolled Red Square. A court subsequently sentenced two of them to terms in labour camps and sent one to a psychiatric hospital and three into exile. Gorbanevskaya was at first released since she was breast-feeding her baby.

On December 24, 1969, she was rearrested, because she had not given up her civil-rights activities.

It was then that Tamara Pechernikova made her mark on the life of our country for the first time. Pechernikova it was who, at the behest of the KGB, interrogated Gorbanevskaya in that same Serbsky Institute where, three decades later, Budanov was examined.

Pechernikova produced the medical verdict on Gorbanevskaya which the KGB required: "Schizophrenia". Which is to say that anyone displaying banners in Red Square protesting against Russian tanks in the streets of Prague must have been insane.

Another KGB diagnosis which Pechernikova rubber-stamped in 1969 was that Gorbanevskaya was a danger to society and should be subjected indefinitely to compulsory treatment in a specialised psychiatric hospital.

Natalia Gorbanevskaya, the founder and first editor of the underground *Chronicle of Current Events*, a samizdat bulletin of Soviet civil-rights activists, was to spend grim years of incarceration in the Kazan Specialised Mental Hospital. Imprisoned there from 1969 until 1972, in 1975 she emigrated with an Israeli visa. She now lives in France.

"Do you remember the name Pechernikova?" I asked Natalia Gorbanevskaya recently.

"I certainly do."

"How was your examination conducted?"

"It was biased, to say the least. They had decided in advance to diagnose me as schizophrenic . . . They had been instructed by the

KGB to send me for compulsory treatment to a specialised psychiatric hospital, and all of them, including Pechernikova, did as they were told. They knew the court would not require any justification of the diagnosis, so they did not bother giving any in their expert finding. For example, they wrote, 'Thinking illogical at times.' How did this manifest itself? Not a word. 'Gorbanevskaya presents abnormalities of thinking, emotional and critical faculties typical of schizophrenia.' What abnormalities? Not a word. And yet this phrase is absolutely crucial ... because the conclusion which followed immediately after it stated that forcible treatment was essential. During the entire month they were examining me they did not ask a single question about my poetry, although I am a poet. It was as if it did not exist. I thought they might pin megalomania on me for thinking I was a poet, but nothing of the sort happened. It's obvious now why they didn't. The symptoms of 'emotional stuntedness and frigidity' as a result of schizophrenia would make it impossible to write poetry. 'The patient willingly enters into conversation. Behaves calmly. Has a smile on her face.' Absolutely true, but what that calm was costing me! I knew that I had to keep calm and not give them any grounds for inventing symptoms, but in the end my very calmness was used as a symptom and figured in the report as: '. . . displays no anxiety regarding her future or the fate of her children'. You bet I was worried about my children, but I wasn't going to share that with KGB psychiatrists. The report goes on: 'Does not repudiate her actions. Unshakeably convinced of the rightness of her deeds. In particular, states that she acted in this way in order in the future not to feel guilty before her children.' To this day I do not repudiate my actions, and I am still convinced of the rightness of my deeds, and my children are proud of what I did. Here's some more: 'A critical awareness of the situation is absent.' The psychiatrists, including Pechernikova, considered that thinking with my own brain rather than relying on someone else meant I should be certified insane. It's worth pointing out that throughout the month I was being examined I met only with Pechernikova and Martynenko, a doctor. All the 'observations' which provided the basis for the experts' final conclusions were theirs alone. I believe they were perfectly aware of the misrepresentation and distortions, but that did not stop them from carrying out the criminal task they had been given. By now Pechernikova has a long history of carrying out criminal orders. I believe working in the Serbsky Institute irrevocably undermined both the human decency and the professional integrity of these psychiatrists . . ."

"How did this all end for you? How much time did you spend in the specialised mental hospital as a result?"

"Two years and two months. I would call it psychiatric incarceration. I spent nine and a half months in the worst hospital, the Kazan. They took me from Butyrka Prison in Moscow to Kazan in January 1971. In 1972, again by way of Butyrka, they sent me back to the Serbsky Institute for a further examination. I was another three months there. What mattered most, though, was not the length of time but the forcible treatment with neuroleptic drugs. The use of haloperidol has long been recognised as torture. Haloperidol was used in clinical practice for treating delirium and hallucinations. I had neither, unless you consider my views to have been delirious . . . The way haloperidol is administered is to give a course of treatment for a month, then to allow a break for remedial treatment, because one side-effect was Parkinsonism. Well, they injected me for nine and a half months with no remedial treatment or breaks. When they brought me back to the Serbsky Institute from Kazan and put me back on haloperidol, Pechernikova said, 'You know yourself you will have to continue to take haloperidol.' What a hypocrite!"

"Then what happened?"

"I emigrated to Paris . . . There was a lot of hilarity during my subsequent meetings with French psychiatrists when they read the account of my treatment which the Serbsky Institute had compiled. One of them told me, 'We really must go and learn from these Soviet psychiatrists: to judge from their diagnoses, we have before us a miraculous case of someone who has been cured of schizophrenia.'"

The Gorbanevskaya case was among the first of the so-called "psychiatric repressions" against dissidents in the USSR. Colonel Budanov's would-be saviour was in her heyday in the 1970s, a dire period in Russia as the Communist regime fought a war of attrition against dissidents. By then we had a perfectly respectable Constitution, and the KGB preferred to wage its war against dissidence in ways which didn't raise too much protest, in other words by diagnosing everyone they could as mentally ill and requiring compulsory treatment in specialised hospitals.

Lyudmila Alexeeva was a well-known dissident and champion of civil rights in Soviet times who was obliged to emigrate to the US as a result of political persecution. She is now the President of the International Helsinki Association. She writes in her *History of Dissidence in the USSR* that in 1971 alone, "no fewer than twenty-four out of eighty-five people found guilty of political crimes were diagnosed as mentally ill, almost one third of them". Those who could not be declared insane were found guilty of slandering the Soviet system, and here too Pechernikova was at hand.

For example, in the summer of 1978 Alexander Ginzburg was tried on a charge of slander. Tamara Pechernikova was present at that trial as a witness for the prosecution.

Ginzburg was one of the best-known Soviet dissidents, a journalist, a member of the Moscow Helsinki Group, publisher of the samizdat poetry journal *Syntax*, and the first administrator, from 1975 until 1977, of the Social Fund for Aid to Political Prisoners in the USSR and Their Families, funded by Alexander Solzhenitsyn with the royalties from *The Gulag Archipelago*.

Between 1961 and 1969 Ginzburg was three times sentenced to periods in labour camps for his activities, and in 1978 he was sentenced to eight years' detention. In 1979, under pressure from the West, he was exiled from the USSR in exchange for Soviet spies arrested in the US. He subsequently lived for many years in France, dying in Paris in 2002 from illnesses acquired in Soviet political prison camps.

This is what Arina Ginzburg, Alexander's wife and ally in the dissident struggle, told me about the atmosphere at his trial, which was held in Kaluga, a small town in central Russia:

During the trial they were dosing him up with neuroleptics, and he would simply blank out in the courtroom. They were forever giving him injections. He didn't look right. He was hardly able to walk, and he carried around a pillow slip filled with books because he had refused to have a lawyer and was defending himself. He had a long grey beard. His speech would become incoherent; he had lost his coordination. He would ask to be allowed to sit down, but they wouldn't allow it, and then he would collapse. Admittedly, they did lay off immediately after the verdict. They stopped injecting him then.

And here is a quote from the court record of that trial: "In respect of Submission No. 8 [an article in *Chronicle of Current Events* from October 12, 1976], Pechernikova, Director of the Consultancy Section of the Serbsky Institute, and Kuzmicheva, Consultant at No. 14 Psychiatric Hospital, Moscow, were cross-examined. They stated that no abuses of psychiatry exist in the USSR."

Ginzburg, of course, insisted on the opposite in court. He also wrote in samizdat about the dramatic increase in psychiatric repressions in the country and about the doings of, among others, Pechernikova.

Here are extracts from the "Submission No. 8" which Pechernikova contested:

Recently the Group for Monitoring Implementation of the Helsinki Agreement addressed a proposal to the Supreme Soviet of the USSR and the US Congress to create a joint commission to identify instances of the abuse of psychiatry. In the present document the Group reports the facts about recent psychiatric repressions known to it.

Petr Starchik, songwriter and performer, was removed on September 15 with the involvement of the police to the Stolbovaya Mental Hospital [the notorious Soviet "White Columns" psychiatric hospital, similar in function to the Serbsky Institute]. Starchik is already being injected with substantial doses of haloperidol. Entry in the admissions notes of Petr Starchik: "D.S. [Danger to Society]. Compulsory in-patient treatment in mental hospital in Kazan under Article 70 [anti-Soviet agitation and propaganda]. Discharged 1975. In recent times has been writing songs with anti-Soviet content, with gatherings of 40 to 50 persons in his apartment. Lucid during examination. Does not deny composing songs. Says, 'I have my own outlook on the world.'"

Eduard Fedotov was a clergyman in Pskov. He came to Moscow when he heard about the persecution of Orthodox Christians . . . Fedotov was arrested by the police and sent to No. 14 Mental Hospital. Currently still there. On May 7, 1976 Nadezhda Gaidar lodged a complaint with the prosecutor's office of the USSR [to which she had been directed from the reception desk of the Central Committee of the Communist Party of the Soviet Union]. She was arrested by police and taken to No. 13 Mental Hospital, where she was immediately injected with aminazine. The

Director of Section 2, L. I. Fedorova, stated, "We shall hold her here for a while to get her to stop complaining, then send her through a specialised reception centre to Kiev. They will keep her there for a short time. She will think twice next time before she goes lodging complaints."

It was in the light of such information that Dr Pechernikova testified in court that no abuses of psychiatry existed in the USSR. Her testimony led to Alexander Ginzburg being found guilty of slander and agitation against the Soviet system.

For Ginzburg the result was eight years of detention in prisons and labour camps, tuberculosis, and the loss of one lung and of a quarter of the other. Throughout his last years he was attached for 16 hours a day to an oxygen cylinder. His health had been completely undermined.

In order to understand what is going on in Russia today, we need to be aware not only of the fact that political psychiatry, with diagnoses to order, has been revived, but also of how it functions.

In the files of almost all of Pechernikova's cases, from Gorbanevskaya and Ginzburg to Budanov, we find the leitmotif of the search for social justice. Today these words are used in a completely different context, however. In the Soviet era Pechernikova regarded evidence of a search for social justice as a symptom of mental illness dangerous to society. Nowadays she considers a brutal murder to be justified by a search for social justice by the murderer. The colonel was overwhelmed by feelings of guilt over the death of his comrades at the hands of a sniper. He accordingly, understandably according to Pechernikova, killed a woman.

Is it mere chance that Pechernikova figured in the cases both of Ginzburg and of Gorbanevskaya?

The next question is whether it is mere chance that Pechernikova turned up in the Budanov case.

For the past three decades the KGB/FSB has known that Pechernikova could be relied upon. She sat it out in the shadows during the "late democratic" period of Gorbachev and under Yeltsin, but then a KGB officer with a 20-year service record became President. In the wake of Putin's rise to power, every conceivable nook and cranny in the power structure was filled by individuals with KGB service records.

Information from independent sources (unsurprisingly, there is none from official ones) suggests that more than 6,000 members of the KGB/FSB followed Putin to power and now occupy the highest offices in the land. These include the key ministries, in which they occupy the key positions: the President's office (two deputy directors, the heads of the staffing and information departments); the Security Council (deputy secretary); the government administrative apparatus; the ministries of defence, foreign affairs, justice, the nuclear industry, taxes and revenues, internal affairs, press affairs, television, radio and mass media; the State Customs and Excise Committee; the Russian Agency for National Reserves; the Committee for Financial Recovery – and so on.

Bad history, like cancer, tends to recur, and there is one radical treatment: timely therapy to destroy the deadly cells. We have not done this. We dragged ourselves out of the USSR and into the "New Russia" still infested with our Soviet bedbugs. To return to our central question: Is the resurrection of Professor Pechernikova in the Budanov case a coincidence? Well, is the return to power of the secret police in our country a coincidence?

It is not. Back in 2000, people were saying, "What if Putin did start out in the KGB in the Soviet period? He'll shape up once he is in office."

By then it was already too late. Now we find ourselves surrounded by people trusted by Putin and Putin's friends. Unfortunately they only trust their own kind. The result is that the power structures of New Russia are overrun with citizens from a particular tradition, brought up with a repressive mentality and with an understanding of how to resolve governmental problems that reflects this mentality.

Pechernikova both embodies that tradition and is a mechanism for perpetuating it. In the two decades she spent "defending the Soviet social and state system", she put in place a mechanism for controlling medical science, moulding psychiatry to fit the needs of the State security apparatus. Now, more than a decade after the fall of the visible structure of the Soviet system, she has found herself, and her very special skills, in as much demand as ever.

These are not abstractions of political theory. Pechernikova's contribution to the Budanov case had life-and-death consequences for real people just as in the 1970s and '80s.

Whether Budanov did or did not go free was a matter of fundamental importance for our times, not least for the Army, which, in Chechnya, has become an instrument of political repression. The Army was waiting for a precedent from the court in Rostov-on-Don. Could it continue to behave like Budanov?

Pechernikova, who said, "Go right ahead," provided the most important ammunition to enable Judge Kostin also to say, in law, "Go right ahead."

The signal was certainly understood that way in Chechnya, where officers picked up exactly where Budanov had left off. We could cite enough examples to fill another book.

More than a year passed. The Budanov case files would be augmented by a further three expert reports. Pechernikova's conclusions would be rejected as untenable. The Supreme Court would send back the case for a retrial, and a newly appointed military court in Rostov-on-Don would commission new reports. Prosecutor Nazarov, who had effectively defended the accused, was removed from the scene, and social justice began to peep out from behind the clouds.

And Pechernikova? Was she punished?

No chance! She was left in place.

Let us turn now to the evidence Pechernikova ignored: the underwater rocks of the Budanov case.

On the last night of her young life, the unfortunate Elza Kungaeva was not only brutally strangled but also raped. Here is a quote from the forensic report:

The burial site is a plot in the forest plantation 950 metres from the command post of the tank regiment. The body of a naked woman is discovered wrapped in a tartan blanket.

The body is lying on its left side, the legs pressed to the stomach, the arms bent at the elbows and pressed to the trunk. The perineum in the region of the external genital organs is smeared with blood, and the blanket in this place is also bloodstained.

A forensic investigation of Kungaeva's body was carried out on March 28, 2000 . . . by Captain V. Lyanenko, Director of the Medical Section, 124 Laboratory Medical Corps. On the external genital organs, on the surface skin of the perineum and on the rear surface of the upper third of the thigh are moist smears of a dark-red colour resembling blood and mucus . . . On the hymen there are bruised radial linear tears. In the buttock crease there are dried traces of a red-dark-brown colour. Two cm from the anal aperture there is a tear of the mucous membrane . . . The tear is filled with coagulated blood, which indicates it occurred ante mortem. On the side of the blanket turned towards the corpse there is a damp patch of dark-brown colour resembling that of blood . . .

Together with the body there were recovered: 1. Blouse,

woollen. Back torn (cut) vertically the full length ... 5. Knickers, worn. Removal of specimens for forensic examination not undertaken in view of the lack of suitable conditions for preserving and conserving them ...

The tears in the hymen and mucous membrane of the rectum ... resulted from the insertion of a blunt, hard object (objects) ... It is possible that such object might have been an engorged (erect) penis. It could, however, have been the haft of a small entrenching tool ...

From the very beginning of the investigation Budanov had categorically denied rape. Someone, however, had clearly violated Elza Kungaeva and, moreover, before she was murdered. Since during the last hours of Elza's life Budanov was alone with her, and since he allowed his soldiers to enter his quarters only after she was dead, one conclusion seems inescapable.

Two forensic analyses were performed during the preliminary investigation. When the court set about its whitewash of Budanov, it commissioned a third medical report for the same purpose as the new psychiatric report commissioned from the Serbsky Institute: in order to deliver the conclusions the Russian military establishment and the Kremlin wanted to hear, and so that an officer awarded two Orders of Valour should not be shown to be a rapist.

According to the third report, which contradicts everything the original medical corps examiner had seen with his own eyes, "The tears of the hymen and mucosa of the rectum occurred post mortem when the retractive capacity characteristic of living tissue had been completely lost." In other words, while someone had abused this girl, it most certainly had not been Budanov. He had an alibi. After murdering her he had gone peacefully to sleep.

To make this seem more plausible, the profuse bleeding Lyanenko had seen was interpreted as follows: "... the presence of bloodstains in the region of the external genital organs does not contradict the conclusion regarding the post-mortem origination of these injuries . . ." These "correct" experts augmented their conclusions with a side-swipe at the earlier report: "The unexplained decision by the consultant not to collect material for forensic histological analysis does not allow us to conclude more definitely at the present time . . ."

In a war zone, with nowhere to conserve histological specimens, the absence of definitive proof strengthened the colonel's alibi. Without a histological analysis, as the latest pathologists chorused, any attempt to prove rape, and that the perpetrator had been Budanov, was doomed to failure.

The needful conclusion could now be delivered: "There are no data supporting the hypothesis that the posthumous injuries were caused by an erect male sexual organ. The results of the forensic examination of the body and the material evidence give no grounds for concluding that a forcible sexual act was committed against Kungaeva."

In other words, there had been no rape.

This report "acquitting" Budanov was signed by:

I. Gedygushev, DMedSci, Award of Merit, Deputy Director of the National Centre of Forensic Medical Analysis of the Ministry of Health;

A. Isaev, CandMedSci, Director of the Department of Complex Analyses of the same centre, expert of the highest category;

O. Budyakov, CandMedSci, Award of Merit, Forensic Medicine Consultant of the Department of Complex Analyses of the same centre.

They evidently imagined that their efforts had removed a stain from the uniform of the Russian Army. From the jacket perhaps, but not from the trousers.

As the Budanov case dragged on over three years, I couldn't believe the reaction of Russia's women. We are more than half the population, and if only because of that a majority of Russians must surely despise and detest a rapist? Apparently not.

Tens of millions of Russians have growing daughters and, if only for that reason, they should understand and identify with the grief of the Kungaev family. Again, apparently not.

Interviews with Budanov's wife were shown on television. She blabbed some nonsense about her poor husband having to endure all those examinations and a trial, and about their little daughter who was tired of waiting for Daddy to come home. The country sympathised with the colonel's wife, not, it seemed, with the Kungaevs who, wait as they might, would never see their daughter again.

In 2002, when the experts accepted that Budanov had been temporarily insane at the moment of committing the murder, he was cleared of rape. No storm of indignation swept over the country. There was not a single protest demonstration, even from women's organisations. No defenders of civil rights took to the streets. Russia thought what had happened was fair enough. The report "acquitting" the colonel triggered a wave of war crimes in Chechnya, committed by soldiers who used the disastrous situation and the cruelty perpetrated by both sides as a cover. Throughout 2002, "purging" of territory continued in Chechnya on a massive scale and with extreme brutality. Villages were surrounded, men taken away, women raped. Many were killed, and even more disappeared without trace. Retaliation was elevated to become a justification for murder. Lynch law was encouraged from the Kremlin itself – an eye for an eye, a tooth for a tooth. We discovered that we were moving backwards, from stagnation under Brezhnev to the out-and-out arbitrariness of Stalin. It was terrifying to reflect that we probably had the government we deserved.

Budanov's final address to the court was scheduled for July 1, 2002, indicating that the judicial mummery of the case was about to conclude. The parents of Elza Kungaeva and their lawyers left the courtroom, unable to stomach the perverse traducing of morality and the desecration of the law. Supporters of the colonel and his military colleagues were braying outside the walls of the courtroom in the expectation that another couple of days would see them and Budanov toasting their victory in vodka.

Suddenly, something happened. Budanov's final address was abruptly cancelled. The verdict, which had been expected on July 3, was not delivered. To everyone's total surprise, a break in the hearings was announced until the beginning of October, and Budanov was taken off to Moscow again, back to the Serbsky Institute for a further, by now fourth, medical report. What was going on?

We have little reliable information as to which way the wind was blowing in the Kremlin right then so can only fall back on surmise and inference. We do know there was strong pressure on Putin from the German Bundestag, with letters and appeals addressed to him personally. Chancellor Schroeder himself had been enquiring at summit meetings as to why those trying the war criminal Budanov seemed only to be interested in getting him acquitted. Sources within the President's office say he had no answer.

You should not be surprised. In our country, with its Byzantine traditions of servility, such trivia are quite sufficient to change the course of history.[7]

The hearings started up again on October 3. The main interest centred on the conclusions of the new psychological and psychiatric report. Many were anticipating a sensation, but in the event there was only a rerun. Budanov was again found to have suffered a "temporary pathological dysfunction of his mental activity", and the verdict was hence entirely predictable: he would not bear criminal responsibility, and the court would insist on psychiatric treatment, the length of which would be decided by the doctor treating him. The underlying principle remained the same: Budanov would evade punishment.

That verdict was duly delivered on December 31, 2002. This is a special day in Russia. On December 31 there is almost nobody at work, and few people have anything serious on their minds. It is almost a religious festival, when even the remnants of civil society and Members of Parliament who are democratically inclined, and hence anti-Budanov, don't get indignant about anything because they are celebrating the New Year.

The day had been well chosen. There was no outcry about the verdict. After December 31 Russia observes two weeks of freedom from thought, when all that is shown on television is an endless succession of gala concerts, and the newspapers are not published.

The Kungaevs' lawyers naturally lodged an appeal. The lawyers wanted, of course, to get the verdict overturned, but to tell the truth they were not very optimistic. As Abdullah Hamzaev stated immediately after the verdict was announced, he was pinning most of his hopes on the European Court of Human Rights, not on the Russian judicial system, and the appeal to the Supreme Court was being made mainly because that was procedurally necessary before an appeal could be lodged in Strasbourg.

But then: a sensation! Early in March 2003 the Military College of the Supreme Court unexpectedly annulled the verdict, acknowledged all the irregularities and decreed that a retrial should take place. It was to go back to the very start of the investigation and convene in Rostov-on-Don in the same district military court, but with a different judge presiding.

On the Russian political map the Supreme Court has long been regarded as no more than a department of the President's office rather than the highest level of an independent national judicial authority. This could mean only one thing: the wind in the

Kremlin had now changed direction completely, and the President had turned his back on the slogan about a Russian officer fighting in Chechnya always being in the right. Again, as in spring 2000, Putin was trying to position himself publicly as the champion of the "Dictatorship of Law".

And the pre-election campaign for 2004 was about to begin. Putin's United Russia party, whose secretary-general, in contravention of the law, was Boris Gryzlov, the Minister of Internal Affairs, just had to win in the parliamentary elections in December 2003. The main slogans for the both these campaigns, United Russia's and Putin's, were already being worked on. The front-runner was "The Law Rules Supreme".

On April 9, 2003 the court in Rostov-on-Don reconvened. The colonel was a changed man. There was little sign of the brazen lout who almost spat at the judge and who had ceaselessly insulted the parents of the girl he had murdered. He complained he had been betrayed. He was plainly nervous. He demanded trial by jury but was refused. He then ceased to reply to questions, stuck cotton wool in his ears and sat in the dock reading. The Bench was now occupied by Colonel Vladimir Bukreev, deputy chairman of the district military court. For the first time in two years, witnesses for the aggrieved parties were called for cross-examination. This was revolution.

First to be questioned was General Gerasimov. He reported that Budanov, as the commanding officer of a tank regiment, and hence a representative of the Ministry of Defence rather than of the Ministry of Internal Affairs, had had no right to inspect the village of Tangi-Chu, or to drive into it in search of a female sniper. Searching for and arresting suspected members of IAFs was a matter for the prosecutor's office and for officers of the FSB and the police. Moreover, General Gerasimov testified that the regiment had received no orders to conduct search operations in February–March 2000. Budanov himself had "no right to be checking passports and accommodation in populated areas, and no right to be gathering intelligence there".

Then Yakhyaev, the head of the municipal administration of Duba-Yurt, was called to give evidence. This, according to Budanov, was the man who had given him the photograph of men and women carrying snipers' rifles, which had been the main reason why Budanov had gone looking for a sniper in Tangi-Chu. Yakhyaev now told the court he had given no such photograph to Budanov. This was corroborated by a certain Pankov, who had been in Chechnya as a senior FSB agent in late December 1999 and early January 2000. Pankov testified that Budanov had indeed met Yakhyaev several times in his presence, but that Yakhyaev had not given Budanov any photograph or said anything to him about a female sniper. Neither had Budanov himself made any mention to Pankov of a photograph or a sniper.

As a result, all Budanov's testimony in his own defence was discredited. On July 25, 2003 sentence was passed: ten years' detention in strict-regime labour colonies. Budanov is due for release on March 27, 2010.

Budanov undoubtedly got what he deserved, and even if that was as a result of pre-election manoeuvring and opportunistic political intrigue, one can only welcome the court's just verdict, of which there are so few in Russia. The court of the North Caucasus Military District, and its deputy chairman Colonel Vladimir Bukreev, showed great courage. It certainly cut against the grain. The majority of the Army top brass, and virtually all of the officers' corps, especially in the Caucasus, categorically rejected the verdict. Greatly incensed, they were convinced that Budanov had suffered only because he had honourably defended his Motherland. They took the ten-year sentence and the stripping of Budanov of his awards and rank as a personal insult. Let us remember that the Russian system of military courts is, to all intents and purposes, part of the military, not of the judiciary. Bukreev's rank, his accommodation and his promotion are in the gift of the Ministry of Defence and the headquarters of the North Caucasus Military District. For Judge Bukreev to find Budanov guilty was a brave act, because he was simultaneously passing sentence on himself.

WHAT ABOUT THE OTHERS?

No matter how dramatic the conflicts around the Budanov case, the story of his conviction is an exception to the rule. Political circumstances moved his crime into the limelight and brought it to the public's attention with important political consequences. This in turn forced the authorities to give permission to the court to find Budanov guilty. It all happened entirely by chance. In every other trial of a war crime in which the accused have been members of the Russian Federal forces, the charges have been frozen, and the security services have exerted themselves only to enable the criminals to escape punishment, even when truly monstrous acts have been committed.

For example, on January 12, 2002 six groups of Russian military landed in the vicinity of the Chechen highland village of Dai. They were searching for fighters, among them Field Commander Hattab, who, according to operational intelligence, had recently been wounded and was in the region.

What happened then was later to be called Budanov Case II. The members of one of the groups, ten men from a special operations unit belonging to the Central Intelligence Directorate (GRU) of General Headquarters, landed from helicopters. Seeing a minibus travelling past them on the road, they stopped it and ordered everybody to get out. They first tortured the passengers, trying to get them to reveal the whereabouts of fighters, then killed all six of them, and finished by burning the bodies.

The official information agencies promptly dubbed this brutal, lawless execution "a military clash with IAFs". There were witnesses, however, who quickly made that lie untenable. All six passengers proved to be ordinary civilians returning on a scheduled bus from the district centre of Shatoy to their homes. Among them was 40-year-old Zainap Djavathanova, the mother of seven children aged from two to seventeen years and expecting her eighth. All that remained of her was one foot in a shoe, from which her husband and older children identified her. That day she had been to Grozny to be examined by a gynaecologist.

Then there were the headmaster of the Nokhchi-Keloy village school, Said Mahomed Alskhanov, 69 years old, and Abdul-Wahab Satabaev, history teacher at the same school. They were returning from a teachers' meeting in Shatoy. The fourth body belonged to the Nokhchi-Keloy forester, Shahban Bahaev. The fifth was that of a nephew of the pregnant Zainap, accompanying her on the journey as was customary in those parts. His name was Djamalaili Musaev. The sixth body was that of the bus driver, Hamzat Tuburov, the father of five children. The entire district knew him well, because every day he drove whoever required transport from Shatoy to the various highland villages and back.

On the evening of January 12 all the murderers were arrested. The Shatoy District prosecutor's office, acting on the evidence of a chance witness, Major Vitaly Nevmerzhitsky of Military Intelligence, managed to obtain permission to do this. This was virtually unprecedented in Chechnya. The special operations troops were handed over shortly afterwards to the investigators of the military prosecutor's office, and Criminal Case No. 76002 was brought against them.

All, it would seem, according to the rules. I met Colonel Andrey Vershinin, the military prosecutor in Shatoy District, who was conducting this much-publicised case at that time, and in the spring of 2002 he was still full of optimism. He said there was more than enough proof of guilt, and that the case would most certainly come to court. It would be almost impossible to demolish it, as happens nearly every time with similar cases. Hundreds of criminal cases waiting to be brought to court are hanging round the necks of prosecutors of all levels for one simple reason: Army personnel accused of crimes are moved out of Chechnya by their commanding officers just as quickly as can be. Investigations stall, obstacles are put in the way of the prosecutor's office, its staff are intimidated, and so it is silenced.

Prosecutor Vershinin had managed to achieve what was almost impossible: he had the personnel of the GRU under arrest, while the investigation proceeded, in the guardhouse of 291 Regiment, because the military prosecutor's office had its premises within the regiment's compound. So they were under the colonel's direct, round-the-clock supervision.

Prosecutor Vershinin is not to blame for what happened next. The accused were removed from Shatoy and transferred to a prison outside Chechnya and beyond his reach. Those who actually carried out the massacre near Dai, Lieutenant Alexander Kalagandsky and Corporal Vladimir Voevodin, spent nine months in prison in Pyatigorsk and were then released because the central military prosecutor's office of Russia failed to apply to the court to extend their period of detention. The court was therefore automatically obliged to release them "on receipt of their signed undertaking not to travel outside the Shchelkovsky District of Moscow Province".

Why were these two criminals to be found in Moscow Province? Before being sent to Chechnya, both had been serving at the end of the world in Buryatia. That they had been transferred to Moscow Province meant only one thing: the Central Intelligence Directorate and General Headquarters had decided to show support for them, evidently considering that, like Budanov, they had loyally served a Motherland which had failed to appreciate the fact.

Only Captain Eduard Ulman, Special Operations, has remained in detention. It was he who, on January 12, 2002, gave the order to commit the massacre. The instigator, Major Alexey Perelevsky, remains at large.

What do you call this sort of situation? If a Chechen fighter had shot six Russian military personnel and burned their bodies, we can be quite sure he would not simply have been freed. As Abdullah Hamzaev put it, "In the 41 years I have worked for the courts, the prosecutor's office and as a lawyer, I have never before come across a criminal case where someone accused of aggravated premeditated murder was set free in return for a signed undertaking not to change his place of residence." I asked him: "If the idea of an international criminal tribunal on Chechnya, which is being discussed by the Council of Europe, ever came to be realised, would you be able to provide it with documentary evidence of cases where the Russian security services had chosen not to investigate war criminals and instead had done all they could to provide a cover-up and get them released?" Hamzaev's reply was, "As many as you like. There are hundreds of such cases."

Russia now faces the question, as the US did at the end of the Vietnam War, of how to view its soldiers and officers who everyday are murdering, looting, torturing and raping in Chechnya. Are they war criminals? Or are they unyielding combatants in the struggle against international terrorism using every means at their disposal, with the noble end of saving humankind justifying the means? Are the ideological stakes in this struggle so high that everything else should be disregarded?

A Westerner would, I hope, have a simple answer to these questions: It is for the courts to decide. As of now, Russia has no answer. Now, five years into the Second Chechen War, more than a million soldiers and officers have passed through that experience. Poisoned by a war on their own territory, they have become a serious factor affecting civilian life. They can no longer simply be left out of the social equation.

The cases of Colonel Budanov and the Dai massacre are both tragic and dramatic. The way they developed exposed our problems and where the Second Chechen War fits into our lives. They exposed our illogical thinking about the war and about Putin, and put on trial our notions of who is right and who is wrong in the northern Caucasus. Most importantly, they showed up pathological changes which have taken place in the Russian judicial system under Putin and under the impact of the war.

The legal reforms the democrats tried to pass, and which Yeltsin did everything he could to move forward, seemed to have collapsed under the pressures of the Budanov case. That their spirit lives on was vividly demonstrated by the work of Judge Bukreev and Prosecutor Vershinin. Despite the fact that there are individuals capable of taking such actions, Russia has seen clearly that we do not have an independent judiciary or prosecutor's office. Instead we still have verdicts decided by political fiat and based on the imperatives of political expediency.

TANYA, MISHA, LENA AND RINAT: WHERE ARE THEY NOW?

So, where are we now? We who lived in the USSR, where most of us had a stable job and a salary we could rely on, who had unbounded and unshakeable confidence in what tomorrow would bring. We who knew there were doctors who could cure us of all ailments and teachers who would teach us. And who also knew that we would not pay a kopek for all this. What kind of existence are we eking out now? What new roles have we been allocated?

The changes since the end of the Soviet era have been threefold. First, we underwent a personal revolution (in parallel, of course, with the social revolution) at the time of the demise of the USSR and during the reign of Boris Yeltsin. Everything vanished in an instant: Soviet ideology, cheap sausage, money and the certainty that there was a Big Daddy in the Kremlin, and even if he was a despot, at least he was responsible for us.

The second change came with the 1998 debt default. Many of us had managed to earn a bit in the years after 1991, when the market economy was effectively introduced, and there were signs that a middle class was being formed. A Russian middle class, admittedly, not like what you might find in the West, but a middle class nonetheless to support democracy and the free market. Overnight all this disappeared. By then many people were so tired of the daily struggle for survival that they could not rise to a new challenge and simply sank without trace.

The third change came under Putin, as we embarked upon a new stage of Russian capitalism with obvious neo-Soviet features. The economy in the era of our third President is a curious hybrid of the free market, ideological dogma and various odds and ends. It is a model that puts Soviet ideology at the service of big-time private capital. There are an awful lot of poor, indeed destitute, people. In addition, an old phenomenon is flourishing again: the *nomenklatura*, a ruling élite, the great bureaucratic class that existed under the Soviet system. The economic system may have changed, but members of this élite have adapted to it. The *nomenklatura* would like to live the high life like the "New Russian" business élite, only their official salaries are tiny. They have no desire to return to the old Soviet system, but neither does the new system suit them ideally. The problem is that it requires law and order, something Russian society is demanding ever more insistently, and accordingly the *nomenklatura* has to spend most of its time trying to obviate law and order to promote its own enrichment.

The result has been that Putin's new-old *nomenklatura* has taken corruption to heights undreamt of under the Communists or Yeltsin. It is now devouring small and middle-sized businesses, and with them the middle class. It is giving big and super-big business, the monopolies and quasi-State businesses, the opportunity to develop. (In Russia this means these are the *nomenklatura*'s preferred source of bribes.) This is the kind of business which in Russia produces the highest and most stable returns not only for its owners and managers but also for their patrons in the State administration. In Russia, big business without patrons, or "curators", in the State administration does not exist. All this misconduct has nothing to do with market forces. Putin is trying to gain the support of the so-called *byvshie*, the *ci-devants*, who occupied leadership positions under the Soviet regime. Their hankering after old times is so strong that the ideology under-pinning Putin-style capitalism is increasingly reminiscent of the thinking in the USSR during the height of the Period of Stagnation in the late Brezhnev years – the late 1970s and early '80s.

Tanya, Misha, Lena and Rinat are real people, not fictional characters, ordinary people who, together with the rest of the country, have been struggling to survive. They were all my friends. This is what has happened to them since 1991.

TANYA

It is early winter, 2002. The *Nord-Ost* saga has just ended. Russian society, particularly in Moscow, is in a state of shock. I appeared on television, playing a small part in these events, and as a result old friends reappeared in my life.

The late-night call was from Tanya. Actually she had always rung in the small hours, or so late at night that everyone was already asleep.

I hadn't seen Tanya, my sometime neighbour, for ten years or so. In those days she had been downtrodden, but now she was a queen. She looked triumphant and very chic, not because she was expensively dressed, which she was, but because she was self-possessed and poised. This was something new.

In the Soviet period, Tanya's life had been one long torment. Almost every evening she would come down to see me (I lived on the ground floor of an old block of flats, and she lived at the top). She would weep over how her life was completely ruined.

In those years Tanya was an engineer in a research institute and accordingly was regarded as belonging to the "Soviet scientific and technical intelligentsia", a substantial social category that no longer exists.

How did one come to belong to that stratum? At the time, a girl from a good family – Tanya was the only daughter of well-established parents – was expected to enter higher education, and if when she finished secondary school she showed no particular inclinations or aptitudes, she went to study at a technical institute, of which there were any number, and became an engineer. After graduating she was required to work for three years at the speciality the State had trained her in at its own expense. Accordingly, there was a whole army of people in the country who were deeply dissatisfied with life, young specialists who had never wanted to be engineers and who now sat out their working days in research institutes producing nothing useful whatsoever.

Tanya was a fully paid-up member of this army, with the profession of engineer of communal facilities in nuclear power stations. For days at a time and without the least enthusiasm, she would sit in her institute designing projects for drainage and water-supply systems which nobody ever built, receiving a minuscule salary in return. She was always unhappy because of a chronic shortage of money. She tried to feed and clothe her family decently, frantically ministering to her two small, perpetually sick children and her husband, a rather odd man called Andrey, a young lecturer at a prestigious technical university in Moscow.

As a result Tanya was a typical neurasthenic, endlessly tormenting herself, Andrey and the children with her bad moods, her hysteria, her depressions and her constant dissatisfaction.

To make matters worse, Tanya was from Rostov-on-Don. She had managed to move to Moscow by marrying Andrey, whom she had met on a Black Sea beach. She was regarded as little better than one of the *limitchiki*, menial "quota workers" who, in the mid-1970s, were granted temporary residence permits in Moscow in return for working in unpopular or undersupplied occupations. At that time there were no end of female "engineers" in the capital, girls from the provinces who had married Muscovites. No-one wanted to remain outside Moscow and girls from good families did their best to move there.

Tanya did not know what she wanted, but she did know very clearly what she did not want: to be an engineer and to be living in penury with the impoverished Andrey. We talked about it a lot. Tanya was angry because she saw no way out.

There were often ructions at home. In accordance with Soviet tradition, Tanya, not having a place of her own in Moscow, should have lived with Andrey in his flat, but he did not have a flat either. So they ended up sharing one large flat with Andrey's parents and his two elder brothers, each of whom also had a family and a couple of children.

All in all, it was a typical Soviet beehive, but with no option to swarm and achieve independence. Andrey, to make things worse, came from a genteel old Moscow family consisting of exceptional people. One, for example, was a famous professor who had taught the violin at the Moscow State Conservatory. He was the second husband of Andrey's grandmother, who had also been a professor of violin there. His grandmother had died long ago, but her husband was still in the beehive. Like Tanya, he had nowhere else to go.

Andrey's parents were professors of physics and mathematics. The elder brother was a professor of chemistry at Moscow University who made one discovery after another, although this had little material impact on his life.

The situation made Tanya more and more exasperated. She considered Andrey's family to be a bunch of incompetent failures despite the dozens of academic qualifications they possessed, and Andrey's family reciprocated wholeheartedly, disliking and constantly finding fault with her. Tanya, we have to remember, was from Rostov-on-Don, where even in Soviet times anyone who could trade did trade in anything they could. Illegal underground workshops flourished there. Many rich men divided their time between prison and the outside world, and no-one considered it a disgrace. The newspapers called them speculators and spivs, but the young women of Rostov were happy enough to marry them.

When we first met in the early 1980s, Tanya already thought she had made a bad mistake in marrying Andrey. Love hadn't come into it. She admitted she had simply swallowed the bait of residence in Moscow. She only came out of herself when she could produce pretty things she had picked up who knows where and was inviting you to buy them. She undoubtedly had a special gift of commercial persuasiveness. She could sell you a blouse of appalling quality at thrice the price while assuring you, "It's what people are wearing in Europe." When the fraud came to light, she would not be embarrassed in the least. This talent for speculative trade was something that Andrey's traditionalist, highly educated family despised.

Now, in 2002, Tanya invited me to her home, which turned out to be that same spacious flat in the heart of Moscow.

The flat had been magnificently refurbished. The place was crammed with the latest technology, excellent copies of famous paintings, high-quality reproduction antique furniture. Tanya was almost 50, but her skin was youthful and healthy, her clothes bright. She talked in a loud, confident voice, very openly, and although she laughed a lot her face remained unwrinkled. This could only mean she had had plastic surgery, which in turn could only mean she had made the big time.

"Has Andrey struck it rich?" I wondered to myself. Tanya strode through the rooms. Ten years ago she had preferred to whisper in this flat, to sit in the corner of one of the rooms, avoiding her in-laws.

"Well, where are the family?"

"I'll tell you, only don't faint. All this belongs to me now."

"It's yours? Congratulations! But where do they live?"

"In a minute, in a minute. Everything in good time."

A handsome young man about the age Tanya's sons must be

now, I supposed, slipped quietly into the room. The last time I'd seen her boys they'd been children, so I blurted out, "Can this really be . . . Igor?"

Igor was Tanya's and Andrey's elder son and must by then have been 24 or 25.

Tanya burst out laughing. Peals of merriment, mischievous, echoing, youthful. Not at all like Tanya.

"My name is David," the handsome, ox-eyed young man with dark curly hair murmured. He kissed Tanya's manicured hand. I remembered a time when her hands hadn't looked like that, as they had been worn by many hours of washing clothes for a large family. David drifted off into the depths of the flat. "Well, don't let me spoil things for you, girls."

Oh, dear. We really were not girls.

"All right, tell me. Reveal the secrets of your youthfulness and prosperity," I begged my old friend. "Where are your family?"

"They aren't my family any more."

"What about Andrey?"

"We split up. My sentence of hard labour came to an end."

"Have you remarried? This boy? David?"

"David is my boyfriend, short-term, just for the sake of my health, really. He's my toy boy. I'll keep him for as long as I feel like it."

"Good heavens! Who are you working for?"

"I don't work for anyone. I work for myself," Tanya answered firmly and with a metallic edge to her voice that didn't seem to go with the image of the slightly indolent, manicured lady with a young lover who was sitting opposite me.

Tanya is a happy product of the new life. In the summer of 1992, when there was nothing to eat in the majority of homes in Moscow (this was called "economic shock treatment", part of the market reforms of the then Prime Minister Yegor Gaidar), Tanya, together with her children and the rest of the professor's family, were living in the country at their old dacha.

In that terrible, hungry summer, all Muscovites, if they had a dacha, were sitting it out in their wooden shacks in the country and growing vegetables for the winter so as to have at least something to eat. The research institute where Tanya worked had closed for the summer. They had no work at all and hadn't in any case paid anybody's salaries for ages. The employees, town dwellers all, had gone off to hoe their vegetable patches or to trade in the markets which had sprung up in large numbers on the streets of starving Moscow. Tanya was busy growing vegetables of her own and looking after the children. Andrey often stayed in the city and didn't come back to sleep at the dacha because, unlike the majority of research institutes, his technological university had not closed.

One morning for some reason Tanya turned up in Moscow unexpectedly, unlocked the door of their flat, and found Andrey and a girl student in her matrimonial bed. A loud-mouthed woman from the south of Russia, Tanya bawled at Andrey so the whole apartment block could hear her.

Andrey made no excuses. He said he loved the student. The student herself said nothing, got dressed and went through to the kitchen, where she began boiling the kettle for tea as if nothing had happened.

For Tanya her rival's silence and her manifest familiarity with the layout of the flat was the last straw. She decided there and then that she hadn't been putting up with Andrey's pathetic family all her married life only to let a rival invade their space. She told Andrey not to imagine he could get away with it. He got his things together and left with the student.

That, in effect, was the day Tanya's new, completely independent life began. Andrey behaved abominably, giving her not a kopek to support herself or the children. Three years later, when Tanya had made a little money, she would in fact occasionally feed him and even buy him clothes. But not from any feeling of sympathy. Tanya fed Andrey because revenge is sweet. She gave him red caviar, a symbol of luxury in Soviet times which she could now afford. Andrey gobbled it up until it was coming out of his ears, not even blushing at the humiliation because he was so hungry. At times he even ate at the soup kitchens set up at churches, pretending for good measure to be a believer. He even learned how to cross himself.

In 1992, the summer of the free-market breakthrough, this was all still in the future. After a week, when there was nothing left to feed the children, and with her mother-in-law insisting that she must forgive Andrey and take him back, Tanya went off to trade at a nearby market.

Her mother-in-law shrieked, "The disgrace of it! The disgrace!" and took to her bed. She soon came round, however, when Tanya began buying her medicine with the disgraceful money she was making at the market. Not one of the old lady's sons, her husband or her other daughters-in-law had been able to do anything like this for her. Matters had taken on a tragi-comic aspect when it was resolved at a family council that they would never, come what may, sell off the family heirlooms, the antique furniture inherited from their forebears, the rare antiquarian music albums, the pictures by famous nineteenth-century Russian painters. Tanya's mother-in-law, lying obstinately in her bed and readying herself for death rather than disgrace, was the first to vote against the idea. In the early 1990s, other long-established families who had held on to their heirlooms through the Stalin years were selling them off on the cheap or, as people said at the time, "for a meal".

Tanya meanwhile was out at the market from 6.00 in the morning until 11.00 at night. It was not work but hard labour. It was the purest purgatory, but it had one redeeming feature: this was slavery with a price tag. Tanya stood in the market and earned real roubles which rustled in her pocket. What was more, you got your cash on the day. You stood there and you got the money, not later but right then, and that was what mattered. Tanya always came home with money. She also came home with swollen legs, barely able to put one foot in front of the other, and with enormous swollen "crab-claw" hands, incapable even of washing herself or making herself look half human. But – she was almost happy!

"You may not believe it, but I was happy not to be dependent on anyone else any more. Not on the Director of the institute who didn't pay me, not on Andrey who was giving me nothing, not on my mother-in-law with her family heirlooms and traditions. I depended solely on myself." Tanya, now rich and beautiful, told me the story of how it had all changed ten years ago. "My mother-in-law? Well, one fine day I just told her where to get off. 'Go ****** yourself!' And what do you think? For the first time she didn't preach back at me. It was a revelation. A revolution took place before my eyes. The seemingly incorruptible old Moscow intelligentsia was being broken. It was being broken by the money I was giving my mother-in-law. She stopped lecturing me because I started feeding her. Me, the one who was always in the wrong. Gradually all of them, that whole family which had looked down on me for so many years because I didn't come from the same sort of background and because, as they always said, I had inveigled Andrey into marrying me because I wanted to move to Moscow, the whole bunch learned to smile at me and even to listen attentively to what I had to tell them.

"And it was just because I was feeding them all by trading at that market. I gloried in it. I was prepared to continue doing it for just one reason: to get more and more money, more and more, and to humiliate them by rubbing their noses in it."

When Tanya returned home towards midnight she would collapse on the bed. She no longer had any time for her sons. She did not check their homework. She would collapse and then she was out like a light. Early the next morning everything started again.

Her mother-in-law began looking after Tanya's children – for the first time, it has to be said, since they had been living under the same roof. Tanya was amazed yet again.

In the market Tanya found herself working for an adroit young man who was a "shuttle", as people said then. Nikita's "shuttling" consisted of importing cheap clothes from Turkey, cheap watermelons from Uzbekistan, cheap mandarins from Georgia; in fact, anything cheap from anywhere at all. Tanya and the other women working for him sold his goods. There were no taxes, no State levies. In the market the rules were the same as inside a prison. Disagreements were resolved at knifepoint, extortion was rife, people got beaten up. The women traders were mostly in the same situation as Tanya, single women with children abandoned at home, former members of the scientific and technical intelligentsia whose institutes, publishing houses and editorial offices had closed. They were little better than whores for their bosses.

Soon Tanya was sleeping with Nikita. He picked her out from the others, despite the difference in their ages, and took her with him to Turkey on a buying trip. He took her once, a second and a third time, and within two months Tanya, a woman with a commercial streak, had become a shuttle herself, having seen that it really wasn't rocket science.

Then Nikita was murdered, shot by no-one knew whom. One morning they found him at the market with a bullet-hole in his head, and that was that. Nikita's saleswomen migrated across to Tanya and were glad to do so. Tanya proved much more efficient than Nikita, and business began to boom. As a bonus, Tanya was less of a shit than the deceased.

After another six months Tanya stopped travelling to Turkey. Not because she was tired, although life as a shuttle was hard. At that time you had to carry the goods yourself, in enormous bundles which you dragged round airports and railway stations, skimping at every turn, even on luggage trolleys, which had to be paid for. She stopped travelling herself because she had discovered her niche: she was exceptionally good at business.

Tanya flourished and her business soon grew to the extent that she hired at first five and then another five shuttles and became the proprietress of what, in the context of a local market, was a large business. The shuttles travelled, her women traded, and Tanya managed them all. She was already going around, as people put it, "not dressed like a Turk", which meant, like a European. She was a habituée of all the restaurants, where she ate, got drunk, threw her money about and relaxed after work. She had plenty of money left over for herself, her family and her workers. Takings in those years were astronomical. She had lovers befitting her income and years: virtuosos. Tanya got rid of them when she felt like it. Andrey, to be frank, had not been up to much in that department . . .

Another year passed and Tanya decided to refurbish the flat, having first taken over ownership of it. She bought some rather poky flats for Andrey, his brothers and her father-in-law, which made all of them happy. Tanya kept her elderly mother-in-law with her. Pity aside, she needed someone to look after her sons. The elder, Igor, had reached puberty and was causing problems, while the younger boy was sickly.

Tanya did, however, carry through the refurbishment as a kind of retaliation.

"I just really wanted to show them who owned the place!"

She threw everything out, absolutely everything. She sold off all the heirlooms and expunged all traces of her in-laws' dusty gentry past.

Nobody protested. Her mother-in-law went off to the dacha and kept out of the way.

The result was a modern European flat equipped with cutting-edge technology.

After the renovation Tanya decided to move on: she abandoned the shuttle business and went into commerce proper, buying a number of shops in Moscow.

"What? Those shops belong to you?" I couldn't believe my ears. Tanya was the owner of two excellent supermarkets I would drive to after work. "Congratulations! But your prices . . . !"

"I know, but Russia is a rich country!" Tanya parried, laughing.

"Not that rich. You've become an imperialist. A bit hard-nosed."

"Of course. Yeltsin's gone, and with him the easy money and the romance. The people in power now are insatiable pragmatists, and I am one of them. You are against Putin, but I am for him. He almost seems like a brother to me, downtrodden in the past and getting his own back now."

"What do you mean by 'insatiable'?"

"The bribes. The endless bribes you have to give everyone. Just to keep hold of my shops, I pay up. Who don't I give bribes to?! The pen-pushers at the police station, the firemen, the hygiene inspectors, the municipal government. And the gangsters whose patch my shops are on. Actually, I bought them from gangsters."

"Aren't you afraid to do business with them?"

"No. I have a dream: I want to be rich. In today's Russia that means I have to pay them all off. Without that 'tax' I would be shot tomorrow and replaced by someone else."

"You aren't exaggerating?"

"If anything, I am understating things."

"What about the bureaucrats?"

"Some of the bureaucrats I pay myself, and the rest are paid by the gangsters. I give the gangsters money and they keep those other gangsters, our bureaucrats, sweet. Actually, it's quite convenient."

"Where is Andrey now?"

"He died. In the end he couldn't take the fact that I had moved up in the world and he was eating my caviar. He asked me to take him back, but I wanted none of it. I told him to find himself another student. Anyway, I don't want to live with an ugly man. I've decided I like handsome men. I go to male strip shows and choose my partners there."

"You're kidding! Don't you miss family life? Domestic bliss?"

"No. I don't. I've just started living. There is a downside, of course there is. You may think it is all sordid, but what was so pure about the way I used to live?"

"What about the children?"

"Igor, unfortunately, has turned out a weakling, like Andrey. He's on drugs. I've sent him to a clinic. This is the fifth time already ... I am having Stasik educated in London. I'm very pleased with him. Very. He's first in everything there. My mother-in-law looks after him. I rent a small flat for her. Stasik lives in a student hostel during the week, and at the weekends in this flat with my mother-in-law. I paid for her to have a hip replacement. They did it in Switzerland. She's come back to life, running around like a young woman, and she absolutely worships me. I think she really does. It's a great thing, is money."

David swirled into the room bearing a tray. "Time for tea, girls," he crooned. "Just the three of us. All right, Tanechka?"

Tanya nodded and said she'd be right back. She wanted to change for tea. David exuded degeneracy and languor. It was all rather sick-making. A couple of minutes later Tanya returned. She was covered in diamonds, her ears ablaze, her décolletage ashimmer. Even her hair was glittering.

The show was for my benefit. I politely registered appreciation. Tanya was really pleased, as radiant as her diamonds from the pleasure of presenting herself, the new Tanya, to an old friend.

We quickly drank our tea and said our goodbyes.

"Only not for ten years this time!" Tanya proposed as we parted.

"Let's make an effort," I replied, and thought as I went down the stairs that in the Putin era people really did meet up more often. Old friends, I mean. There was a time in Russia, the late Yeltsin period, when everybody was terribly busy just surviving, when people didn't phone each other for years, some embarrassed because they were poor, some because they were rich. It was a time when many emigrated for ever; when many put a bullet in their brains because nobody seemed to need them any more; when people snorted cocaine out of disgust with themselves. Now, however, it was as if everybody who had survived was meeting up again. Society had become noticeably more orderly, and people even had free time.

When the new times had arrived, women were the driving force, going into business, divorcing their husbands. The husbands became gangsters, and many died in shoot-outs in the first years of the Yeltsin period. These things happened because, on the eve of perestroika, many Russian women had felt, like Tanya, that they would never be able to change their lives. Suddenly here was their big chance.

A week later I had to be at a press conference in connection with a by-election to the municipal Duma, I think. And there, quite unexpectedly, I met Tanya again. In our already rather structured and, as under the Soviets, cliquish society, owners of super-markets just don't go to political press conferences.

Tanya manifested herself to the world of journalists with never a hair out of place, in a classic black business suit and without a single diamond to be seen. David was there as well, and he too was top notch, faultlessly performing the role of Tanya's business secretary, modest but not ingratiating. No "girls" on this occasion.

I sat with the journalists. Tanya was on the other side of the barricades. Handed a microphone, she was the last to speak. She was one of the candidates standing for a seat in the municipal Duma. She told the journalists, including me, how she saw the problems of the homeless in Moscow, and promised to fight for their rights if the voters did her the honour of electing her a member of the legislative assembly.

"What on earth do you need this for? You're rich already," I asked Tanya when the press conference was over.

"I told you, I want to be even richer. It's very simple: I don't want to pay bribes to our councillor."

"Is that all?"

"You have no idea of the level of corruption nowadays. Gangsters in Yeltsin's time didn't even dream of this. If I become a councillor that will be one 'tax' less."

"But why have you taken to defending the homeless in particular?" We wandered into a French café nearby. Tanya had chosen it; it was too expensive for me.

"I think that backdrop will make me look good. Anyway, I really can help them pull themselves up by their bootstraps. I've done it myself."

"And why at the press conference, at the end of your speech, did you talk about Putin? About how much you love and respect and trust him. Did your image makers tell you to say that? It's in terrible taste."

"No, it isn't. It's what you have to do nowadays. I know that without any help from 'image makers'." Tanya stumbled over these difficult English words which have immigrated into Russia along with the new life. "If I didn't mention Putin, our local FSB man would be round to see me in the shop tomorrow to complain I wasn't saying what everybody says. That's the kind of life we business people lead now."

"So what if he came round and said that?"

"So nothing. He would just demand a bribe."

"What for?"

"To 'forget' what I hadn't said."

"Listen, aren't you tired of all this?"

"No. If I need to kiss Putin's backside to get another couple of shops I'll do it."

"But what do you mean by 'get'? You just buy them, don't you? Pay for them, and that's it?"

"No, things are different now. To 'get' something you have to earn the right from the bureaucrats to buy the shop with your own money. Russian capitalism, it's called. Personally I like it. When I tire of it I'll buy myself citizenship somewhere and move on."

We parted. Of course Tanya got elected. She's said not to be bad. She puts her heart into battling for the poor of Moscow. She's organised another canteen for the homeless and refugees, she's bought another three supermarkets, and she often speaks on television in praise of our modern times. She rang recently and asked me to write an article about her. I did. The one you are reading right now. She asked to read it before it was published, was horrified and said, "It's all true." She made me promise not to publish it in Russia before her death.

"How about abroad?"

"Go ahead. Let them know what our money smells of."

So now you do.

MISHA AND LENA

Misha was married to Lena, my schoolfriend from early childhood. She had married him when they were at college in the late 1970s. At that time Misha was a very clever, talented boy who translated from German, who dubbed films while still a student at the Institute of Foreign Languages and whose future seemed very bright. When he graduated he was inundated with attractive offers of employment, not something that happened at all often.

Misha landed a job in the Ministry of Foreign Affairs, which was very prestigious, especially towards the end of the Soviet period. It was unusual for a boy without family connections to get into such a closed corporation as our MFA. Misha had none. He had been brought up by his grandmother, a humble cleaning woman. His mother had died suddenly, from a brain tumour, when Misha was only 14. His father had promptly abandoned his orphaned family and run off with another woman.

So there was Misha in the MFA. We were great friends. We would go on picnics together, grill kebabs in the forest over a campfire and enjoy ourselves thoroughly. Lena and I were very close, and Misha was keen to be friends too.

Underpinning our relationship were my two small children. When Misha came visiting he simply couldn't take his eyes off them. He would watch them with delight no matter what nonsense they got up to, talk to them and play with them for hours at a time.

All our friends knew that Misha very much wanted to have children. He was obsessed with it, but Lena was a talented linguist. She was writing her dissertation and kept postponing having a baby until after she had graduated in philological sciences.

Misha was very jumpy as a result. He gradually developed a complex about the fact that they did not have any children. He began to suffer himself and to torment all those around him, most of all Lena. However, Lena was made of stern stuff, and once she had made her mind up nothing was going to change it. She would defend her dissertation and get her degree, and after that she would get pregnant. That was all there was to it.

Misha reacted by taking to the bottle. He put up with his disappointment for as long as he could but then just went off the rails. At first he didn't drink a lot, and people laughed at it and teased him, but then his bouts began to last for several days at a time. He would disappear, and goodness knows where he was spending his nights. Later still he would drink for weeks at a time. Lena thought perhaps she should give in and not finish her dissertation, but how do you make a baby with a man who is permanently inebriated?

Then the new times came: Gorbachev, Yeltsin, and the only reason Misha wasn't fired for his chronic drinking (he would have been sacked instantly under the Communists) was that there was no-one to replace him. MFA staff who knew languages and had experience of working on the other side of the Iron Curtain were suddenly worth their weight in gold. They abandoned the cash-strapped MFA to work for the commercial firms and branches of foreign companies that were springing up. Misha got no offers, even though the Germans were the first to dash into the Russian market and translators from German were the most sought after of all.

Even at the MFA Misha's days were numbered, and he was eventually fired. Late one night at the very end of 1996, in December when there was around 30 degrees of frost, someone rang my doorbell. It was Lena, wearing only her nightdress under a coat. You just don't walk around Moscow dressed like that in winter, and certainly not if you are Lena, who was always immaculately turned out. She was an equable, well brought-up and intelligent young woman. Now, however, one foot was bare as if she were some totally destitute person without a home to go to, while on the other foot the top of a half-laced boot was flapping like a flag. My friend was shivering as if she had fallen through ice and just been pulled out of the freezing water. Something had frightened her half to death, and the shock had made her incoherent.

"Misha, Misha," she repeated over and over again, sobbing loudly, quite unlike her usual self and seemingly unaware of where she was or of the people around her.

The children had woken up by now and came quietly out of their room. They stood by Lena, spellbound by an anguish they could not understand. Lena finally noticed them, pulled herself together, took a tranquilliser with a glass of water and began to explain what had happened.

Misha had been away from home for three nights in a row. Lena wasn't really expecting him back. She had got used to his drinking bouts and his absences, and so she went to bed. She had to go to the institute early in the morning. Shortly after midnight, however, Misha suddenly turned up. This was unusual.

This time he came straight in through the door and, just as he was, in his winter coat and dirty shoes, unwashed and stinking, walked into the bedroom and stood over Lena in menacing silence, staring at her in the semi-darkness. He seemed completely out of his mind. His black eyes were shining unnaturally, and there was a silvery gleam on his cheeks. His once handsome face was contorted in a grimace. Lena pulled the covers up and said nothing. She knew from bitter experience of living with an incipient alcoholic that it was pointless to say anything. Despite appearances, you were talking to someone who could not hear. You just had to wait for him to fall asleep.

Misha, however, moved closer to the bed and said, "That's it . . . It's all your fault . . . that I drink . . . and now I am going to kill you."

Lena heard a note of quiet determination in Misha's voice that left no room for doubt. She jumped up and rushed round the room. At first Misha cornered her on the balcony, and she thought she'd had it, but drunks are clumsy and she was able to slip past him, grab some things by the front door and run out across the snow to the nearest refuge, my block of flats.

After that they got divorced, and although neither was at all maudlin by nature, they would both come to sob in my kitchen and tell me how much they loved each other but how they could never live together again.

I continued to see Misha, although increasingly rarely. He would drop by occasionally, mainly to ask for money, because he was continuing to drink and very hard up. He had only the occasional translation to make ends meet.

On his rare sober visits, he told me he was trying to stop

drinking and start a new life. He had developed an interest in Orthodox Christianity, was reading religious books, had been baptised, had found a confessor whom he trusted, was going to confession and communion and finding solace in that. He was convinced that redemption was possible. Misha's outward appearance was not, however, that of someone on the road to salvation. He was in a bad way, his hair greasy and unkempt. He wore a threadbare and obviously second-hand black coat which was much too short for him, and when I asked where he was living, blurted out some nonsense to the effect that nobody understood him and it was so difficult to live anywhere when nobody understands you.

Under Yeltsin this was not a particularly unusual or surprising sight. A lot of penniless people were wandering the streets, people who had been well-educated, respectable citizens but who had lost their jobs and taken to drink when they could find no place for themselves in the new reality. It was precisely on this fertile ground of general dissatisfaction, unemployment and the redundancy of many who had been members of the professions in the Soviet period that Orthodoxy became fashionable, and all the failures who had lost their work, their spouses or their reasons for being ran to the Church, although not all of them by any means were genuine believers.

Accordingly Misha was seen as one of many people on that path. He came to see me one time, sober and yet joyful, and invited me to congratulate him. He had become a father the day before, he had a son. We hastened to say how pleased we were: at last his dream had come true. For some reason, however, Misha was not in the seventh heaven we expected.

The boy was called Nikita. A long time before, when Misha was still married to Lena, he had often mused that if he had a son he would call him Nikita.

"Who is Nikita's mother?" I asked cautiously.

"A young girl."

"Do you live with her? Are you married ... or going to get married?"

"No. Her parents don't like me."

"Then rent a flat and live with your son. That is so important."

"I haven't got any money."

"Start earning some."

"I don't want to and I can't. I just can't – it's simply not possible."

He cut off any further attempts at conversation.

More than a year passed. Yeltsin abdicated power, nominating Putin as his successor. The Second Chechen War started. Putin was constantly on television. One moment he was flying a military aircraft, the next issuing instructions in Chechnya. The election, a foregone conclusion, was approaching.

Late one night Lena rang. "Do you know what," she said in a barely recognisable voice, completely hoarse, like the voice of a singer after a concert. "I have just had a phone call. Misha has killed the woman he was living with. She has left a 14-year-old son from her first marriage. The boy was in the flat when it happened. Misha got drunk. Apparently the woman was older than him, felt sorry for him and drank with him so he wouldn't feel so lonely. Anyway, they were drinking together yesterday when Misha took a knife and said what he said to me: 'I am going to kill you.'"

Lena burst into tears. "It could have been me," she said. "Do you remember? You were all trying to persuade me not to get divorced. You said he would sort himself out, that he needed treatment. But he would just have killed me."

The court was lenient on Misha, especially after the story of his life was related. He was sentenced to four and a half years. Not much for a murder. The court held that he was not mentally ill or suffering from diminished responsibility, despite his alcoholism.

Misha was sent to a labour camp in Mordovia, in the depths of the forests. Six months later, the commandant of the camp came to see Lena in her Moscow flat, where by now she was living with a new husband and the son she had finally had. The commandant was not the brightest of men but evidently had a kind heart. The decision to visit Lena was his own. He considered it his duty, as he was in the capital on business, to find her, despite the fact that she was divorced from Misha, and tell her that "her Michael" (as the commandant described him, to the horror of her new husband) was the best prisoner he had ever met, the most literate and hardworking person in the camp. The commandant, who evidently had a pedagogical bent, had appointed him to look after the prisoners' library, and Misha had completely reorganised it. He was reading a lot himself and working with the other criminals in the role of psychologist. Misha had single-handedly constructed a wooden church inside the camp's barbed wire and was preparing to become a monk. He was corresponding with a monastery to find guidance on his chosen path. The commandant also informed Lena that he supported Misha's monastic inclinations, since he could see only good coming from them for his contingent of murderers, rapists and old lags. At Misha's request he was going to buy church plate in the shop of the Moscow Patriarchate and take it back to the camp.

The jailer ended by promising he would intercede to have Misha's sentence reduced on the grounds of exemplary conduct.

"Lena, are you not glad?" he asked the divorced wife, noticing that she was practically in tears.

"I am frightened," she replied.

"There's no need for that," Misha's commandant replied. "He has changed a lot, he isn't dangerous. He doesn't drink any more, and he won't kill anyone else. At least, I don't think he will."

The commandant smoothed his hair, drank his tea, rubbed his hands together as if intending to produce fire from his palms, and added, "To tell the truth, I am a bit sorry he will be leaving".

We started readying ourselves for whatever might transpire.

Misha might resurface in Moscow at any moment. In the event it was 2001 before he reappeared. For a few weeks he bobbed around, again with nowhere to stay, his German forgotten, by now completely incapable of adapting to the new life.

I had known he was in Moscow for a long time, but we met by chance on Tverskoy Boulevard. When our paths crossed I barely recognised the features which had once been so familiar. We sat down on a bench and spoke for three hours or so without a break. He didn't ask about my children, and I didn't ask about his son. Misha simply needed someone to talk to, someone to hear him out.

He talked the whole time about choosing the right monastery. I looked closely at the man in front of me. Of the earlier Misha, or what he had been in his youth, almost nothing remained. He looked grey, old and flabby. Of the talent you once could have felt in him, nothing could be seen. There was only a grudge against fate, and a lot of prison slang. In addition, Misha treated me to a lot of banal nonsense about the meaning of life, in the way it is written about in crude brochures for the barely literate. I realised the kind of library they must have in the camp in Mordovia.

"Have you found a job?"

"Where? The pay is low everywhere and they expect a lot."

"Well, we're all in that situation now. We just have to put up with it . . ." I began.

Misha interrupted me. "Well, I don't want to be like everybody else."

He certainly had that in spades.

"How are you getting on with the monastery?"

"They can't take me for the time being. There's a queue and you have to pull strings even for that. You have to know people. Having been in prison doesn't help."

"I suppose it's understandable. You really haven't been out of prison for long."

"Well, I don't understand it." Misha became aggressive.

"What are you planning to do?"

"I shall go into that little church." Misha gestured behind him, and there indeed stood one of the oldest churches in Moscow, solidly rooted in the years. "I'll ask them to take me on as a watchman. They told me you need the right number of points in your CV to get into a monastery."

We both laughed. Only someone born in the USSR and who had spent a fair part of his conscious life there knew how typically Soviet that approach was to getting a good job when you couldn't do it through string-pulling. And here we were, talking about a monastery, faith, religion, the rules of the Church, which couldn't be further removed from the everyday reality of the Soviet way of life. We fell about laughing at the idea.

"It's weird," Misha said, "how in the new Russia the ways of Orthodoxy and of Soviet life have suddenly come together."

From beneath the dropsical eyelids of a man with kidney or heart trouble the old Misha suddenly glanced at me, merry, on the ball, playful, gallant.

"Of course they have. Aren't you afraid the Church you are so keen to sign up to has turned into that local committee of the Young Communist League you once fled from? That everything has just been repainted in new colours, and when you finally get into the monastery you'll be bitterly disappointed and . . ."

I bit my tongue. No glib words came to mind.

"You were going to say I would kill someone again, blaming my problems on them?"

"No, of course not," I stammered, although that was exactly what I had been about to say. Misha and I seemed to be back on the same wavelength.

"That is exactly what you were going to say. I can only reply that I am afraid myself, of course, but I have nowhere else to go. If I stay here I shall certainly end up in prison again. I felt better in prison, in a confined space; the monastery is like a labour camp, only with different guards. I need to live under guard. I can't control myself, seeing the kind of life we have around us."

"And what kind of life is that?"

"Cynical. I can't bear cynicism. That is why I started drinking."

"But why did you kill your woman friend? Was she cynical?"

"No, she was a very good person, and I can't remember why I killed her. I was drunk."

"So, at all events you won't stay in the world."

"Under no circumstances. I couldn't stand it."

I didn't meet Misha again, but I do know that he didn't manage to get into a monastery. The paperwork dragged on. The Orthodox bureaucracy in Russia is much like the State bureaucracy, indifferent to anything that doesn't affect it directly. Misha went along to the Patriarchate, taking them forms, working as a church watchman, actually living in a church. He gradually started to drink again. He turned up at Lena's a couple of times asking for money. The first time she gave him 100 roubles, the second time she refused. She was quite right. She and her husband were not working to enable Misha to get drunk when he felt like it. Of course she was right.

Except that Misha threw himself under a Metro train. We heard about it much later, and only by chance. And we discovered that Misha, one of the most talented Russians I ever met, had been buried as homeless and "unclaimed". More exactly, they buried his ashes, because in such cases the remains are cremated. Nobody knows where his grave is.

RINAT

You can mount a frontal attack or you can make a detour. The compound of the Special Intelligence Regiment of the Ministry of Defence, its most élite subdivision, is not, of course, a place for civilians like me to be strolling around. Sometimes, however, it has to be done. I have been brought here by Rinat, one of the regimental officers. Rinat is a major. Nobody knows who his parents were. He was brought up in an orphanage. His face is oriental, with slanting eyes, and he speaks several Central Asian languages. His speciality was intelligence gathering. Rinat fought clandestinely in the Afghan War for years. He then infiltrated Tadjik armed bands in the mountains and on the Afghan-Tadjik border, catching drug smugglers redhanded. On behalf of the Russian government he also secretly helped some of the current presidents of former Soviet republics to come to power. Naturally, he spent a lot of time in Chechnya during both the first and the second Chechen wars. His chest is covered with medals.

Rinat and I are looking for a hole in the fence. He wants to show me the squalor in which, for all his medals, he lives in the officers' barracks; he wants to show me too the house in the military village which he had hoped to move into but found himself out of luck. Although this regiment is highly trained and very famous, we find the hole we are looking for. An impressive hole it is too, not just big enough for the two of us to squeeze through: you could drive a tank through it.

We walk on for five minutes, and there it is, the village where the spies live. It is morning. Around us we see the unsmiling faces of officers on their day off. The weather is far from cheering. Churned-up clay squelches underfoot. We are not walking but slithering, looking down at the ground in order to maintain our footing.

I look up and, wondrous vision, see before me like a mirage among the other dismal five-storey buildings a fine new grey-green multi-storey block of flats.

"That's how it all started," Rinat says. "Of course, I wanted a flat. I've had enough of wandering the world. My son is growing up, and I am constantly away in wars."

The major falls silent in mid-sentence and suddenly embarks on a manoeuvre that puzzles me. He hides his face and doubles over as if we are being shot at and need to find a trench to shelter in. Rinat whispers quietly that we should pretend not to know each other: he also asks me not to look ahead and not to wave my arms or attract attention.

"But what's wrong?" I ask. "Is it an ambush?"

I'm joking, of course.

"We mustn't make him angry," Rinat says softly, continuing his distracting manoeuvre. Like well-trained spies we quickly, deftly, but without fuss, change direction.

"Whom mustn't we annoy?" I enquire when Rinat raises his head with a sigh of relief, indicating that the danger has passed.

"Petrov, the deputy commanding officer."

Our manoeuvring is explained by the fact that Petrov had been driving towards us. His car had pulled up to the fine new block of flats because that is where Petrov lives. Only after he had disappeared inside did Rinat relax and continue our stroll around the compound. We kept ending up back at the fine building, which Rinat gazed upon with longing and envy.

To tell the truth, I am perplexed. I know a little about Rinat's combat record, his fearlessness, and I am amazed. What is it, I wonder, that he fears most? Death?

"No, I have learned to live with death. I don't mean to boast."

"Being captured?"

"Yes, I am afraid of that of course, because I know I would be tortured. I have seen it happen. But I am not all that afraid of being captured."

"What then?"

"Probably peace, civilian life. It's something I know nothing about. I am not prepared for it."

Rinat is 37. All he has done in his life is take part in wars. His body is covered in wounds. He has peptic and duodenal ulcers, and his nerves are in tatters. He has constant agonising pain in his joints and cerebral spasms after several wounds to the head.

Recently, the major decided it was time to settle down, to come back from the wars to our ordinary world. He found he knew absolutely nothing about it. For example, who would give him a place to live? Surely he deserved a flat for all he had been through defending the interests of the State. Or some money?

As soon as Rinat started asking Petrov about such things, it became apparent that he could expect nothing. Rinat concluded that while he had been carrying out special government missions across mountains, countries and continents, his State had needed him and had rewarded him with medals and orders. As soon, however, as the major's health gave out and he decided to try to settle down, he found there was nothing waiting for him, and the military hierarchy were simply going to turn him out on the street. They were even going to expel him from the squalid nook in the officers' barracks where he and his son were presently sleeping.

Rinat has a son, Edik, whom he is bringing up on his own. The boy's mother died several years ago, and for a long time Edik lived alone in the officers' barracks, waiting for his father to come back from his numerous wars and important combat missions.

"I know how to kill an enemy so he doesn't make a sound," Rinat tells me. "I can climb a mountain swiftly and silently and take out those who are occupying it. I am an excellent rock climber and mountaineer. I can 'read' mountains from twigs and bushes and tell who is there and where they are hiding. I have a feel for mountains, they say it is a natural gift, but I am incapable of getting a flat. I am incapable of getting anything at all in civilian life."

Before me is a helpless professional killer trained by the State. There are many like him now. The State sends people off to yet another war, they live in the midst of war for years, return and do not know what peaceful life is with its law and order. They take to drinking, join gangs, become hit-men, and their new masters pay them big money to take out those they say need to be murdered in the interests of the State.

And the State? It doesn't give a damn. Under Putin it has effectively ceased to interest itself in officers who have returned from the wars. It seems as if the State is actively engaged in ensuring that there are as many highly trained professional killers in criminal gangs as possible.

"Is that what you are thinking of going into, Rinat?"

"No, I don't want to, but if Edik and I find ourselves on the street, I can't rule it out. I can only do what I am trained to do."

Rinat and I finally squelch through the mud and slush to a dismal shack. Called "the three-storey building", it is the officers' barracks. We go up to the second floor, and behind a peeling door is a squalid, spartan room.

In the whole of his life the major has never had a home to call his own. First there was the orphanage in the Urals. Then there was the barracks of the military college he enrolled at from the orphanage. Later still, garrison hostels alternating with tents when he was on active service. He has been 16 years in the Army, a rolling stone under military oath. For the last eleven years Rinat has moved on constantly from one combat mission to the next. It is not a life that has led him to acquire possessions.

"But I was happy," the major says. "I never wanted to stop fighting. I thought it would last for ever."

All that Rinat has acquired is now stored in one parachute bag. The major opens his standard-issue cupboard with an inventory number on its pathetic battered side and shows me the bag.

"Sling it over your shoulder and go off on your next mission," he succinctly summarises his values.

A boy is sitting on the divan and looking at us sorrowfully: this is Edik.

I interrupt the major. "You were married, though, so you must have had a household of some kind."

"No, we had nothing. We didn't have time."

While Rinat was fighting in Tadjikistan, helping the present President, Rakhmonov, to take power, he slipped away and got married in Kirghizia. The newlyweds had met during Rinat's previous combat mission in the city of Osh, where the girl lived and where Rinat had been sent because a bloody conflict had broken out there between ethnic groups.

They got married right there, their passion and love flaring up amid the butchery and the pain. Rinat then presented his young wife to his commanding officer. The commanding officer shrugged and asked him to leave his wife in Osh, because for a spy a sweetheart was an Achilles heel. Rinat left his wife behind and went back to Tadjikistan to join an armed group on the frontier.

One day his commanding officer told him that he had a son and that his wife had called him Edik. Later still, in June 1995, Rinat's young wife, a student at the local conservatory, was killed by people who had discovered who she was married to. She had just turned 21 and that day had been on her way to sit her second-year exams.

At first Edik lived with his grandmother in Kirghizia. The boy was too little to live in officers' hostels, and in any case Rinat rarely spent the night even in the grim, unswept rooms the State provided for him. He was still engaged in secret operations and at large in the mountains of our country. He was severely wounded twice more and spent periods in various hospitals.

"Even so I did not want a different life," Rinat says, "but Edik was growing up."

The time finally came when he decided to collect his son, and after that Edik stayed with his grandmother only when Rinat was away on six-month military missions.

We are sitting in their cold, dismal little room. Edik is a quiet boy with bright eyes which see everything. He is very grown up. He talks only when his father goes out and only when he is asked a question: the son of a spy, in a word. He understands that his father is going through a difficult period now, and that this is why in the next school year he wants to send Edik to the Cadet Officers' College. But the boy does not like this idea.

"I want to live at home," he says calmly and in a very manly way, without any suggestion of whining. Nevertheless he repeats it several times: "I want to live at home, at home."

"And is this your home? Do you feel at home here?"

Edik is an honest boy. He know that when you cannot tell the truth it is better to say nothing, and that is what he does.

Indeed, who could call this pen for combat officers, with the drunken bawling of contract soldiers on the other side of the thin walls, with its inventory of regulation furniture, "home"? Edik knows, however, that they are trying to drive his father out even of here, so let this be home.

Relations between the regiment's commanders and the major began to sour when Rinat asked to be allocated a flat in that fine new building we had been walking around while hiding from the deputy commanding officer. The major supposed he was within his rights, since for many years he had been at the top of the waiting list for accommodation.

"When I asked Petrov he was indignant: 'You haven't done enough for the regiment,'" Rinat relates. "Can you believe it, that is exactly how he put it. I was very surprised and told him, 'I have been fighting the whole time. I rescued pilots from a mountain when nobody else could find them. The State needs me.'"

The major had, indeed, been put forward for the country's highest award of Hero of Russia for his actions when a military fighter aircraft crashed in the mountains of Chechnya near the village of Itum-Kale in June 2001. Several search-and-rescue teams went into the mountains to find the crew but without success. The commanders remembered Rinat with his unique experience of combat, his feel for the mountains and his ability to find men by reading twigs, sticks and leaves.

He found the dead airmen in just 24 hours. One body had been booby-trapped by the Chechen fighters, and Rinat made it safe. So the families have graves to tend.

The active service officers have a saying that commanders who lose their head in combat and in the mountains are best in civilian occupations. Rinat told Petrov, "I know what kind of a hero you were in Chechnya, always skulking in staff headquarters." The deputy commanding officer responded, "Now you're really in the shit, Major. For that little remark I'll make you a down-and-out. I'll discharge you without accommodation. You'll be out on the street with that son of yours."

Petrov set about implementing his threat with a vengeance. First he humiliated the major by setting him to decorate the parade ground and also to manage the regimental club, organising film shows for the soldiers.

Petrov next ordered Rinat to design posters for the parade ground (he is an excellent artist), which was the job of Petrov's wife. She simply ceased to turn up for work, and all the officers knew that Rinat was doing it instead while she took her ease in that fine new block of flats.

Then Edik was taken ill and had to go to hospital. The doctors told Rinat he should stay at his son's bedside. Rinat was constantly asking for time off, and Petrov, ignoring the medical certificate provided by the doctors and backdating the record, took to recording him absent without leave. Petrov convened an officers' court, manipulated the minutes and used them to remove the major from the waiting list for an apartment. He was agitating to have Rinat summarily dismissed from the Army without any privileges. In short, Rinat is in deep trouble.

"What have I done?" Rinat bows his head, aware that he is being outmanoeuvred.

The wars our country takes part in continue afterwards, wherever those who were involved in them find themselves. This means, primarily, within the subdivisions to which they return after completing their missions. The staff officers there are pitted in a fight to the death against the field officers. The latter find themselves discharged for disobedience, their past records ignored, with a barrage of insults hurled after them. Rinat is not the only one. The officers in the Army now divide into two unequal categories. The first are those who have genuinely taken part in combat operations, who have risked their lives, who have crawled their way through the mountains, burrowed into the snow and earth for days at a time. Many have been wounded on numerous occasions. You feel desperately sorry for them. It is difficult for them to find a place for themselves in the civilian life which seems so normal to us. They can't find a common language with the staff officers, who have also been in Chechnya, so they rebel and get drunk and feel terrible. The staff officers, as a rule, outmanoeuvre them at every opportunity: they bear false witness against them, they run to their superiors, they tell tales, they plot. Before you know it, the awkward squad are being lined up for discharge. What have they done? They have been themselves, of course. By the mere fact of their presence in the units, the field officers daily remind the staff officers who is who in this world.

And the staff officers? They rise through the ranks faster than a speeding bullet. They fix themselves up very nicely, get all the flats and dachas.

In the end Rinat gave up. He gave up the Army which he loved so much and went off to who knows where with Edik, a homeless, penniless field officer. I fear for him, because I can guess where he has gone. I fear for all of us.

HOW TO
MISAPPROPRIATE
PROPERTY WITH THE
CONNIVANCE OF
THE GOVERNMENT

Moscow, February 2003. A bolt from the blue: President Putin appoints a new Deputy Minister of Internal Affairs and Head of GUBOP, the Central Agency for Combating Organised Crime. He is Nikolai Ovchinnikov, a modest, low-profile Deputy of the State Duma who never speaks at its sessions, has no known involvement in its legislative work and appears to be politically inert. He isn't even one of Putin's former cronies from St Petersburg, which in terms of current appointments policy is unusual. After the announcement, Ovchinnikov gives an interview saying he will do his best to be worthy of the President's trust, and that he sees his mission as being to reduce corruption "to a minimum" and to ensure that the "healthy sector of society" is no longer at the mercy of the criminal minority. These are splendid sentiments, so why does the new Deputy Minister's pronouncement give rise to such merriment in the Urals?

Let us look at his new job. Where does it rank in Russia's bureaucracy?

The Director of GUBOP occupies no ordinary position in

Russia. This is a key portfolio in the power structure. In the first place, organised crime – the Mafia – rooted in monstrous corruption, permeates everyday life. We say in Russia that where money talks it can't be silenced.

In the second place, the office carries so much clout because of its history. One of our country's top bureaucrats and power-brokers, a man who has stayed afloat under Yeltsin and now under Putin, is Vladimir Rushailo.[8] Formerly Minister of Internal Affairs, today he heads Russia's National Security Council. He began his career as Director of GUBOP. When he was appointed Minister of Internal Affairs, he maintained an interest in his old field and did his utmost to beef the agency up. He inflated its staffing levels relative to other agencies and gave its officers sweeping powers, allowing them to carry out operations involving the use of force without prior sanction, unlike those working in other sections of the police. He also actively advanced his placemen out of the agency and into the highest offices of state, with the result that nowadays "Rushailo men" are a force to be reckoned with in the law-enforcement ministries. Their numbers are comparable only with the "Petersburgers", as those who worked with Putin in St Petersburg and who followed him to various ministry bureaucracies in Moscow are known, and the "Cheka men", products of Putin's old stamping ground, the KGB.

If we look at Nikolai Ovchinnikov the man, everything about his appointment to GUBOP seemed entirely respectable. He deserved the office. According to his official record, before entering the Duma he had been a provincial policeman for 30 years. At the time of his election as a parliamentary Deputy he was chief of police in Yekaterinburg. Yekaterinburg is no sleepy provincial centre nostalgic for past glories. It is the capital of the Urals, the hub of Sverdlovsk Province, which in turn is the Urals' major industrial region. When Yeltsin invited the regions of Russia to "take as much sovereignty as you want", there were entirely serious grand plans to create a Republic of the Urals with Yekaterinburg as its capital. The city's chief of police was a celebrity known to all of Russia. The Urals are a region of great mineral wealth and possess natural and industrial resources sufficient for any country to survive on. Additionally, Yekaterinburg is traditionally the turf of one of the most powerful Mafias, formerly of the Soviet Union and now of Russia. Their official designation is the Uralmash Crime Syndicate. Whether he likes it or not, the top policeman of Yekaterinburg accordingly finds himself combating the Uralmash Mafia.

Needless to say, a good deal of important information is not to be found in Ovchinnikov's official service record. Perhaps, indeed, anything that really matters. What kind of police chief was he? What priorities did he set? Which elements of the Mafia did he prosecute? What were his achievements? And what was the end result: what kind of place was Yekaterinburg under Ovchinnikov, and what kind of place is it today?

It is not my wish to show how a policeman in the Urals rose to giddy heights in Moscow. I am much more interested in that phenomenon of Russian life known as corruption. What is corruption in fact? What constitutes the Russian Mafia – not as it was under Yeltsin but as it is in the Putin era? And why has Putin advanced the career of Ovchinnikov? If we analyse the way in which Ovchinnikov came to be appointed as Russia's principal champion for combating the Mafia, we shall be able to identify the guiding principles behind appointments under Putin and his administration.

The story goes back a long way.

Fedulev

On September 13, 2001 a news story rocked Russia. At the time the Second Chechen War was being waged, and Putin had been appointed Prime Minister because, unlike the other candidates, he was willing to start it. In Yekaterinburg one of Russia's largest engineering enterprises, the Uralkhimmash Corporation, its output used throughout the Russian chemical industry, was seized by the Mafia. Citizens armed with baseball bats, supported by the Yekaterinburg OMON Special Police Unit, burst into the factory's administrative offices, caused major disorder there and attempted to install their own "director" in place of the incumbent, Sergey Glotov.

Urals television duly showed the local Communists shouting, "Hurrah! The people are taking power into their own hands! Down with the capitalists!" The local trade-union leaders repeated the same slogans, declaring the seizure of Uralkhimmash a "workers' revolution" and promising that similar revolutionary renationalisations would spread throughout the country in the very near future.

Nothing was heard from President Yeltsin, but this surprised nobody because he was known to be ill. Newly appointed Prime Minister Putin was also silent, however. In fact, Moscow was silent. Vladimir Rushailo, then Minister of Internal Affairs, had nothing to say in public about policemen under his authority joining in storming an enterprise on behalf of one of the sides in a dispute.

Needless to say, Moscow's failure to comment spoke volumes. This sort of thing doesn't just happen in Russia.

By the evening of September 13 the workers' revolution had quietened down somewhat, the old Uralkhimmash management, unwilling to step down, having barricaded themselves in the Director's office. At this point a veritable armoured column, an armada of dapper black jeeps, swept into the factory grounds. The special police respectfully made way for them.

From one of the jeeps stepped a nondescript, rather short citizen wearing a good suit, expensive spectacles and several gold chains. He was an archetypal New Russian, his face ravaged by a recent drinking spree. On his progress to the Director's office, this citizen enjoyed the protection of a powerful bodyguard provided by the Yekaterinburg police. The special police forcibly cleared the way for them; the workers moved back grudgingly.

"Pashka's spoiling for a fight again. He's here for a show-down," the Uralkhimmash employees muttered.

"Pavel Fedulev, the leading industrialist of our province and Deputy of the Yekaterinburg Legislative Assembly, is attempting to restore justice in accordance with court rulings," Yekaterinburg television broadcast, switching from shots of the concerned expression on the face of the "leading industrialist" to the bloodied faces of the enterprise's defenders. Iron bars were now to be seen among the baseball bats.

The citizen in designer spectacles proceeded inside and presented the beleaguered management of Uralkhimmash with a pile of documents. These were court rulings which showed that he, the bearer, was co-owner of their enterprise and that it was his intention to instal as Director a person of his choosing. Accordingly all unauthorised persons were to vacate the premises.

The citizen sat down uninvited in the Director's chair, his brazen demeanour reflecting his proprietorial status. After a time, during which the displaced management acquainted itself with the documents he had brought, he received a torrent of abuse (which left him unfazed) and a different collection of documents and court rulings which showed that the present Director was in fact the real Director.

In order to make sense of this situation, we need to embark on a further excursion into Yekaterinburg's recent history. How did a society develop in which the seizure of such a large enterprise as Uralkhimmash was possible? And who is Pavel Anatolievich Fedulev? And why, when I asked all sorts of people in Yekaterinburg what on earth was going on, did I receive one and the same reply: "It's all Fedulev's doing"?

How It Started

Ten years ago, when Yeltsin was in power and democracy, as we said then, was on the rampage, Pashka Fedulev was a small-time hoodlum, extortionist and thug. In those days Yekaterinburg was still called by its Soviet name of Sverdlovsk. Major criminal brigades were operating there, carving out their spheres of influence, but Pashka was not associated with any of them. He was a sole trader. Although he had criminal offences trailing behind him like a bridal train, the militia did not go after him because Fedulev was small fry. Such individuals were jailed in those years not because of the crimes they committed, but because it was "time to put them inside", if they failed to reach agreement with other hoodlums, spoke out of turn or in general got above themselves. This was not a problem with Pashka Fedulev. At that time he was very amenable to reason.

In the early 1990s, Pashka became a businessman. This was typical of the majority of his comrades. Pashka, however, was poor. He had no access to the Trough, the criminal underworld's central bank, despite the fact that Yekaterinburg, famous for its criminal underworld, had one of the largest troughs in the country. As a small-time hoodlum Pashka did not qualify for credit and accordingly had to accumulate his own capital. This he duly did.

Fedulev built his capital up quickly with a fiery home-produced vodka called Palenka. The mechanism was simple. In the remoter towns and villages of Sverdlovsk Province there had existed since the Soviet period a number of small liquor factories. In the early Yeltsin years they, like all the other State-owned factories of the era, began to fall apart, and there came a time when anybody could buy, for a nominal cash sum placed directly in the hands of the Director, as much liquor as he could drive away.

Of course, this was flagrant theft from State factories, but at the time it was considered a normal feature of post-Soviet life. People were starving, and, in order to feed themselves, half the country robbed the other half, to nobody's surprise. People were surviving as best they could, and this was what was meant by business, which was what we had been dreaming of.

The point of buying the liquor was that the spirit, which cost virtually nothing, could be diluted with water, poured into bottles and sold instantly as cheap vodka. Excise duty had not yet been thought of and the police, even if they had wished to do anything, were powerless in the battle against Palenka. In the event they did not wish to do anything, since they also preferred survival by any means available, which meant participating in illegal business. The underground vodka purveyors paid the police to protect them from their competitors.

This was when Pashka Fedulev, crook and bootlegger, first made the acquaintance of Nikolai Ovchinnikov, policeman. Ovchinnikov, like everybody else at the time, was eager for money. Policemen's wages were wretched, and frequently not paid at all. Accordingly, Pashka and Ovchinnikov apparently came to an understanding. Ovchinnikov would not notice what Pashka was doing, and Pashka, more successful by the day, would not forget Ovchinnikov. The policeman began to have more than enough for his daily bread and butter.

The moment finally arrived when Pashka's accumulated capital was sufficient for him to start playing a bigger and, importantly, a legal game. This has been a typical feature in Russia: just as every soldier dreams of becoming a general, so every little crook dreams of graduating into legal big business.

It was, and still is, a peculiarity of the Russian economy that there are three conditions for success in big business. The first is that success comes to those who first get a slice of the State pie – that is, a State asset as their own private property. This is why the vast majority of big businessmen in Russia now are former members of the Communist Party *nomenklatura*, the Young Communist League or Party workers.

The second condition is that, once you have been successful in appropriating State assets, you stay close to the authorities – that is, you bribe, or "feed", officials regularly. This should guarantee that your private enterprise will prosper.

The third condition is to make friends with (i.e., bribe) the law-enforcement agencies.

Not being in a position to meet the first condition, Fedulev concentrated on the second and third.

The Forces of Law and Order

In those years there lived in Yekaterinburg a certain Vasily Rudenko. He was Deputy Director of the city's CID and a friend of Ovchinnikov. Everybody knew Rudenko, whose position meant that anyone who wanted to succeed in business needed to keep on the right side of him. Rudenko weeded the personal files of new businessmen (and erstwhile gangsters), in effect freeing them from their criminal pasts.

Fedulev too was drawn to Rudenko. This was not the most straightforward period in Pashka's life. He had already made a reputation in Yekaterinburg as a wealthy liquor baron and was being invited to sponsor local almshouses and orphanages. He was flying to Moscow for the weekend to enjoy the nocturnal entertainments now provided there, taking with him (a special privilege, testifying to his intimacy with the authorities) officials of the provincial administration. This meant it was time to set about cleaning up his image. Pashka no longer needed to have the documentary record of his criminal past preserved in the archives of the Yekaterinburg police.

No sooner decided upon than done.

Fedulev was introduced to Rudenko by a man called Yury

Altshul. All who knew Altshul remember him warmly, even with admiration. Not originally from the Urals, he had been sent there by the Motherland. Altshul was a soldier, a military spy, and he had arrived in the Urals as captain of a Special Operations Company of the GRU (the Central Intelligence Directorate of General Headquarters, Russia). They had been pulled out of Hungary after the Berlin Wall had come down, when the West Army Group had been disbanded.

Altshul retired from the Army and stayed on in Yekaterinburg. The country was not paying its servicemen, and Altshul couldn't wait to set up in business. Like many other members of special units who left the Army at that time, he set up a private security service, as well as a private detective agency and a charity for "Veterans of Special Units".

In Russia there are many such organisations, built on the ruins of the Army. Any large city has its veterans, and their main occupation is protecting its traders. Fedulev accordingly became one of Altshul's clients, and it was this former GRU officer who helped Pashka, through the agency of Rudenko, to delete his picaresque past from the computer database of the Yekaterinburg police. His wish had come true.

Altshul was soon not only Fedulev's bodyguard but his trusted lieutenant. It was he – astute, decisive and educated, unlike Fedulev – who introduced the latter to the Urals stock market. Pashka soon found his feet there and became an adept player. As he was a bit short of money, he allied himself with Andrey Yakushev, famous in the mid-1990s as Director of the Golden Calf, a successful Urals company.

Together with Yakushev, Fedulev was very successful in buying up the shares of a number of enterprises, including the Yekaterinburg Meat Processing Factory, the largest such factory in the Urals. The scale of the "meat deal" brought Pashka to within an inch of the status of a Yekaterinburg oligarch, with corresponding access to the ear of the provincial governor, Eduard Rossel.

At this point it became evident that Fedulev did not like to share success. He was able to form alliances to overcome difficulties but not to share the financial and concomitant social success. As a result, portentously, for the first time in his career he hired a hit-man. This was portentous because people became afraid of Fedulev, recognising that he really had outgrown his earlier limitations. That is how it is in Russia now: you kill someone, you get respect.

At about this time Fedulev borrowed a large sum of money from Yakushev for another deal. He put the deal through and gained a profit many times in excess of the stake. However, he categorically refused to repay the debt. Yakushev wasn't pressing him, but in any case he had no opportunity to do so because on May 9, 1995, in front of his wife and child, in the entrance to his own house, Andrey Yakushev was shot dead.

A criminal case? Well, yes. A case was opened, and it even has a number: 772801. The prime suspect is indicated as being Fedulev.

Then what? Then nothing. A case with this number sits in the archives to this day. It is still open, in the sense that nobody investigated it or is currently investigating it. There were to be plenty more such cases involving Fedulev in the years to come, and every time the same thing happened, or rather, didn't happen. Everybody in Yekaterinburg who had any involvement with Fedulev knew that Pashka had made his most profitable investment of all: he had bought the city police force, and it would henceforth loyally shield him from any little awkwardness.

This is the period when Rudenko and Ovchinnikov became Pashka's constant partners. They helped him to grow into a "new Urals industrialist" and to increase his fortune. Naturally, using the technique that had been tried out on Yakushev.

One day Fedulev offered to cooperate with another Yekaterinburg oligarch, Andrey Sosnin. Fedulev and Sosnin pooled their financial resources and pushed through a speculative campaign on the Urals stock market which to this day remains unparallelled in terms of its size. Sosnin became the owner of a controlling share in the region's prime enterprises, effectively its entire industrial potential. This had been created by several generations of Soviet people, beginning during the Second World War when the largest and most important factories of the European part of the USSR were evacuated to the Urals. Among the enterprises of which Sosnin and Fedulev gained control as a result of their speculative coup were the Nizhny Tagil Metallurgical Complex and the Kachkanar Ore Enrichment Complex (both of international renown), Uralkhimmash, Uraltelekom, the Bogoslovskoe Ore Agency and the three hydrolytic factories in the towns of Tavda, Ivdel, and Lobva.

This was a major success for the businessmen, of course, but what about the State? Neither Sosnin nor Fedulev had development in mind for these enterprises. The provincial officials carried the two of them shoulder high, not asking what they were planning to do with the factories, just anticipating their own share of the proceeds. Corruption was attaining new heights. The two companions left nobody disappointed. They shared out what they had stolen, because these were people they could not afford to disappoint.

And then came the moment to divide the spoils between themselves: which goodies should each of the two receive? The earlier pattern was repeated. Shortly thereafter, Andrey Sosnin died from a gunshot wound. Another criminal case was opened on November 22, 1996, No. 474802 this time, the main suspect was again Fedulev and . . . and nothing.

It's not much good having links if they don't work when you need them. By the time Sosnin was murdered, Fedulev's policemen friends were numbered among the more prosperous of Yekaterinburg's citizens. Everyone could see that the richer they became, the more successful their patron, Fedulev, was in business. Case No. 474802 was closed. It was not even archived, it was simply forgotten.

Liquor Wars

It is of course important to note the Urals factories of which, by the end of the 1990s, Fedulev had seized control, but he achieved something even more important than that. Yekaterinburg is primarily Uralmash, the most important institution in the Urals. Not Uralmash the vast machine-tool factory but Uralmash the organised crime syndicate, the largest Mafia grouping in Russia, a detachment many thousands strong with a strict hierarchy and representatives at every level of the State. It is one thing to bribe officials and bump off your partners but quite a different matter to come to terms with the crime bosses of Uralmash. In 1997 Fedulev pulled that off too. He joined forces with Uralmash to buy up the shares of the Tavda Hydrolytic Factory. This made a lot of sense for Fedulev at that moment. He was leading a life of luxury and once more found himself short of cash for gambling on the stock market. Uralmash had money, they had the Trough. The only real surprise is that they decided to do business with Fedulev, knowing the kind of maverick he was.

The reason why Fedulev and the Uralmash bosses were so interested in hydrolytic factories is that they produce spirit, from which Palenka vodka is made. There is tremendous demand for spirit in Russia, and it costs next to nothing to produce. This is the perfect way to make fantastic profits in return for a minuscule investment, and these are profits in ready cash, not involving credit, not going through the banks and invisible to the Tax Inspectorate.

Fedulev and the Uralmash bosses accordingly bought up 97 per cent of the shares of the Tavda Hydrolytic Factory. They then proceeded to asset-strip in a fairly standard way: both partners set up firms, assets were transferred away from the factory to those firms, the shares were divided, and the firms were then either wound up or took over the manufacturing activity. It became clear that the hydrolytic factory as such no longer existed.

Soon after the deal was completed, Fedulev broke the initial agreement on the proportions due and did not even allow Uralmash representation on the new board of directors, packing it with his own placemen.

Why? He wanted to be the first among the first and needed to shake off any partners, even the highly influential Uralmash. Incredibly enough, he got away with it. The Uralmash bosses did not shoot him, as might reasonably have been expected, but simply slunk off.

The reason for their leniency was simple. When the Tavda factory was taken over, Fedulev enjoyed more than just links with the police. He was to all intents and purposes in charge of the provincial police force. He had excellent personal relations with Governor Rossel. It was Pashka who decided the most senior police appointments, choosing, for example, who would head the provincial agency of UBOP, the top policeman whose job was to combat Fedulev himself and organised crime in general. That person turned out to be Rudenko. And Pashka had Nikolai Ovchinnikov appointed chief of police for Yekaterinburg.

The Uralmash bosses were made from the same mould, however, and they had links of their own to pit against those of Fedulev. The day eventually came for them to lock horns when a Uralmash squad arrived at the Tavda factory and took the property back by force of arms. Fedulev responded in full measure. A special rapid-reaction unit of UBOP was deployed, and the State's police paramilitaries were ready to use force as well.

But against whom? It turned out that it was against other police paramilitaries. Those going head to head in the fight at the Tavda factory were not so much the heavies of the Fedulev and Uralmash gangs but the forces of the people behind them. On Fedulev's side were Rudenko and Ovchinnikov with one unit of armed police. On the other side were Uralmash supported by the head of the entire provincial police force, General Kraev, and the police under his command. In other words those on either side of an armed stand-off over the illegal division of the province's property were the police forces at the disposal of those whose task it was to maintain the rule of law.

How did the Ministry of Internal Affairs in Moscow react? They presented the matter as a conflict within the police force in Yekaterinburg, as a personality clash between Kraev on the one hand and Rudenko and Ovchinnikov on the other. Kraev and Rudenko were moved from their posts. Kraev was publicly accused of having close links with the Uralmash crime syndicate, while Rudenko was declared to have been the victim of an irreconcilable power struggle against the most serious criminal grouping in the Urals. As the wronged party he was transferred to Moscow, where the Minister of Internal Affairs, Vladimir Rushailo, had him appointed Director for Moscow Province of UBOP! Since then, that agency, under Rudenko's direction, has been causing alarm bells to ring in the capital.

Back in Yekaterinburg, meanwhile, there were vacancies to be filled in the wake of Rudenko's departure. The staffing of the Urals UBOP was arranged personally by Fedulev. Rudenko's replacement as Director was Yury Skvortsov, not only Rudenko's right-hand man but someone to whom all of Fedulev's affairs had been confided over many years. As Skvortsov's first deputy Fedulev appointed a certain Andrey Taranov. This individual was believed in the Urals to be the protector (or "roof") within the police force of Oleg Fleganov, the region's leading supplier of wines and spirits. Fleganov was key to the marketing of bootleg vodka since most of it was sold through his retail network. The other deputy Fedulev chose for Skvortsov was Vladimir Putyaikin. His task was to purge the ranks of the police in the whole of the province. He began by forcing out anybody who still had anything to say against the Mafia and anybody who refused to work under the tutelage of Fedulev.

The servile Putyaikin set to work with a will. We shall give just a single example of how he went about it. On one occasion Skvortsov demanded documentary evidence from Putyaikin regarding who in the police was working against Fedulev. Putyaikin had no such documents. That night he took home a young member of the UBOP team, got him drunk and demanded that he should immediately denounce any of his colleagues who were opposed to Fedulev and his stooges in the police. The young officer refused to be an informer, whereupon Putyaikin appears to have bullied him into shooting himself with his service revolver.

"This is unbelievable!" I hear my reader cry.

Believe me, it is true. This is exactly how, during the Yeltsin years, organised crime syndicates were born and grew to maturity in Russia. Now, under Putin, they determine what happens in the State. It is precisely to them – powerful, influential and super-rich – that the President is referring when he says that any redistribution of property is impossible and that everything should stay as it is. Putin may be God and Tsar in Chechnya, punishing and pardoning, but he is afraid of touching these Mafiosi. Money is in play here beyond the dreams of most of us, and the price of a life, or a man's honour, is peanuts when the profits are counted in millions.

The Untouchables

With the coming of the Fedulev group the Urals stopped living "by the rules", to use the criminal jargon which has found such fertile soil in Russia that even the President uses it in his speeches.

I asked people in the streets of Yekaterinburg whom they respected: Governor Rossel? Fedulev? Chernetsky, the city's Mayor? Their answer: "Uralmash." Taken aback, I asked them how they could respect crooks. The answer was a simple one: "They live by their thieves' law, but at least they have laws. The new crooks do not even observe those."

That is what we have come to: the Russian people respect one Mafia in preference to another, because the latter is much worse than the former.

Let us go back to 1997. Fedulev had the Yekaterinburg police in his pocket and had swept the board in the marketing of illegal vodka. He continued to play the stock market and defrauded a certain Moscow firm. This was not just any old firm but belonged to the consortium of a well-known metropolitan oligarch who was sponsoring Yeltsin and his family. To try to defraud him was tantamount to suicide in those times. Twice the firm reported fraud to the Sverdlovsk UBOP, but any information which could embarrass Fedulev was blocked there and the CID refused to open a criminal case. Only after the intervention of the prosecutor general's office was Criminal Case No. 142114 opened: in Moscow, not in Yekaterinburg. Fedulev went on the run. An all-Russia arrest warrant was put out for him.

Remember Yury Altshul, the former spy who became Fedulev's minder? Remember that all who knew him spoke of him as a thoroughly decent person, a man of his word and entirely fearless?

Having set up his own detective agency and security firm, Altshul continued to provide the Russian security services with intelligence. Information passed by him to the prosecutor general's office and the FSB put several big wheels of the Urals underworld behind bars. Altshul did, however, have a particular bee in his bonnet: the struggle against the Uralmash crime syndicate. Although the idea may seem totally bizarre, this was exactly what drew Altshul to Fedulev.

Faced with an all-Russia warrant for his arrest and knowing about Altshul's *idée fixe*, Fedulev summoned him for a talk. Fedulev was afraid that during his enforced absence Uralmash would take control of the two other hydrolytic factories in Sverdlovsk Province on which he had his eye. Fedulev asked Altshul to defend by all the means at his disposal his, Fedulev's, interests against Uralmash. In return he promised Altshul 50 per cent of the profit from the Lobva Hydrolytic Factory, which he was in the process of taking over.

Off Altshul went to Lobva, a town with nothing apart from the hydrolytic factory. There he confronted the dismal picture of the complete and deliberate running down of the factory's manu- facturing capacity. Altshul could not help asking himself why Fedulev was buying up so many shares.

Before Fedulev had become involved, the Lobva factory had been running fairly successfully. Once he began transferring its assets to his own dwarf companies, these started selling or processing spirits illegally. The money from sales naturally came back to the factory through the accounts of these companies, and even then not in full. Month by month, Fedulev sucked the factory dry.

When Altshul arrived at Lobva, the workers had not been paid for seven months. The factory was one step away from bankruptcy. As all the town had grown up around the factory, without it the town would die.

It was at this point that Altshul decided to act on his own initiative rather than on Fedulev's behalf. He gave the workers his word that he would restore order and that as a first step there were two individuals the workers would not see at the factory again because Altshul would not let them in the door. These were Sergey Chupakhin and Sergey Leshukov, Fedulev's hatchet men.

Chupakhin and Leshukov had formerly been officers of the Serious Fraud Office of the province's Directorate of Internal Affairs. They were also personal friends of Vasily Rudenko and "colleagues" of Nikolai Ovchinnikov, and had left the police in order to look after the latter's financial interests in Fedulev's businesses.

Some time passed before Fedulev was finally arrested. In Moscow, naturally. Even from his isolation cell he did everything he could to influence the course of events in Yekaterinburg. Members of the police who were under his control (Rudenko was after all in Moscow by now) arranged for Altshul to come, on Fedulev's summons, to see him in prison. At this meeting Fedulev insisted that Altshul should hand the management of the factory back to Chupakhin and Leshukov. Rudenko was demanding this of Fedulev, not wishing to lose his share in the business.

Altshul, however, refused and flew back to Yekaterinburg with Rudenko following in his wake. Altshul was summoned to the UBOP for a talk, and there Rudenko insisted that he should give up the Lobva factory.

Altshul categorically refused again. A couple of days later, on March 30, 1999, the former army spy was shot in his own car. A criminal case was opened, this time No. 528006. Once again the prime suspect was Fedulev. This was the third criminal case in which he was implicated in contract killings, but can you guess what happened? Nothing. Case No. 528006 was shelved, like the others.

Fedulev's calculation was criminally simple: with Altshul out of the way the factory was his. Altshul, however, had left a friend and deputy in Lobva: Vasily Leon, another former spy and special operations veteran. Leon categorically refused all the demands from Fedulev's people that he should get out.

The Rudenko–Chupakhin–Leshukov trio offered Leon a compromise, or rather a share-out. Leon could stay on as Director, but Chupakhin and Leshukov would return to handle the wholesale side of factory liquor sales, which was what really mattered. They didn't just ask Leon to agree, they did their best to intimidate him. He was openly summoned by Skvortsov himself, "Fedulev's" head of the UBOP, who did his best to cow Leon into submission. Rudenko had in the meantime been further promoted and transferred to the Ministry of Internal Affairs' CID.

The third person pressuring Leon was a certain Leonid Fesko, a friend of Rudenko and another high-ranking police official in Sverdlovsk Province. Fesko was shortly to depart for Moscow to manage the so-called Defence and Aid Fund for Members of the Sverdlovsk Province UBOP. This fund was a familiar institution for legally transferring illegal payments, bribes and bonuses. Such "defence and aid funds" had been devised by gentlemen like Fedulev in the mid-1990s. Large numbers of them exist to this day.

Fesko later became Fedulev's deputy for security and discipline in the enterprises his Mafia controlled. In emergencies, if competitors were turning up the heat, it was Fesko's job to mobilise the special operations police units to crush the resistance. It was Fesko, in fact, who masterminded the seizure of Uralkhimmash in September 2000.

In 1999, however, Vasily Leon defied the lot of them. But then, in December of that year, Yevgeny Antonov, a UBOP agent, a man from Skvortsov's immediate entourage, shot Leon's chief assistant, the very person who supervised the wholesale marketing of liquor at the Lobva factory. According to the official written statements about the events leading up to the shooting of his colleague which Leon made to the FSB in the immediate aftermath of the killing:

In mid-January [2000] I had a conversation with Sergey Vasiliev, departmental head of UBOP. He complained stridently that by my presence at the Lobva factory I had deprived UBOP of financing. He further said, "You have stolen the Trough of the FSB, UBOP and other security agencies of the Province." Vasiliev categorically demanded that I should work with them. I asked what that work would consist of, and Vasiliev replied, "You are to bring money here!"

Every line of Leon's statements testifies to a criminal case which should at least have been opened. Once again, however, things got bogged down. Appeals by Leon to the prosecutor general's office, the Ministry of Internal Affairs and President Putin himself produced not the slightest reaction.

Great concern was, however, shown over the fate of Fedulev. In January 2000 on the personal instructions of Vasily Kolmogorov, Deputy Prosecutor General of Russia, Fedulev was freed from prison. Just like that.

On his return to Yekaterinburg, the authorities welcomed him like a conqueror. Governor Rossel showered favours upon him. On Rossel's initiative Fedulev was declared Urals Entrepreneur of the Year. Following his spell in jail, the shooting of Altshul, the intimidation of Leon and the murder of their colleague, Fedulev had attained the exalted status of "Yekaterinburg's leading industrialist". From this time on the mass media of the Urals invariably used this formula when writing about him. A little later Fedulev was elected a member of the Provincial Legislative Assembly, thereby receiving parliamentary immunity.

If we step back a bit and look at the bigger picture, what do we see? Fedulev is a Urals oligarch, a member of the provincial legislature, a major property owner. What really matters, however, is that he is the founder of what the Russian Criminal Code calls an organised crime syndicate. By the autumn of 2000 when Uralkhimmash was seized, which is where we came in, Fedulev's syndicate had all the attributes of a fully fledged Mafia entity. The only snag was that the Godfather was in prison, and while he was there his factories and industrial complexes started slipping out of his control. The syndicate panicked: "What about our money?" At that point Fedulev was released.

The New Deal

Fedulev's release from prison was a crucial turning point in the modern history of the Urals. Even before he got back to Yekaterinburg, as soon as people knew he had been released, before his countless hugs from Rossel, those in the know realised that matters were not straightforward. There was going to be a new share-out of property, and Fedulev was going to be used as the battering ram. He had been released for good reason, to do something important. Certainly so that he could get back what he had controlled before but also so that those working for him (and perhaps whoever he was working for himself) should again receive their remittances.

Fedulev did not disappoint them. His first priority on being freed was to get his hands on the Lobva Hydrolytic Factory.

Here is how he did it. As Vasily Leon put it in a statement to the FSB: "Fedulev informed me that previously matters had been resolved through the law courts: privatisation, acquisition of shares. Now, however, things were settled by force."

Leon's statement is dated February 2000. At that time he presented the FSB with a written request for help to resist the Mafia. He asked to be protected from blackmail by an organised crime syndicate. Firstly he was being blackmailed by members of the provincial UBOP, who were pressuring him to leave the Lobva factory in favour of Fedulev. Secondly, he was being blackmailed by Fedulev himself, who, on his release from prison, demanded not only that Leon leave but that he should pay Fedulev 300,000 dollars in compensation.

Leon's request went unanswered. The State renounced the rule of law and left the factory to be torn apart by the Mafia.

On February 14, 2000 Fedulev decided to set up a committee of creditors of the Lobva factory. He did so by personal invitation despite having no legal authority. His aim was to push out the factory's current management and replace it with a new one under his control.

Of the five principal creditors Fedulev managed only to bend two to his wishes. A forged proxy then appeared from a third creditor, thereby providing a quorum. This "committee" adopted the resolution Fedulev required: that the meeting of creditors should be held not in Lobva but in Yekaterinburg, at Fedulev's office. Nobody made any bones about why it had to be held there. If some of the real creditors suddenly turned up, they would need to be stopped, and by cordoning off the office this would be a simple matter.

As the day of the meeting approached, Rudenko flew in from Moscow. The main matter he and Fedulev needed to resolve before the meeting was what to do about Leon.

Twenty-four hours before the meeting, on February 17, Fedulev sent a couple of his employees round to the UBOP. These gentlemen, Pilshchikov and Naimushin, were well known there since for many years they had been coming in for questioning as suspected hit-men in the lethargic investigation into the murder of one of Fedulev's partners. On this occasion, however, Pilshchikov and Naimushin wrote a denunciation to the UBOP claiming that Leon had extorted 10,000 dollars from them. In a single hour, with a rapidity unheard of in the Russian legal system, a criminal charge was brought against Leon, naturally without any pre- liminary investigation, recorded interview or checking of facts. At this same time a police car was cruising the streets of Lobva throwing out flysheets to the effect that Director Leon was evading arrest and could no longer be regarded as the factory's Managing Director.

The day of the creditors' meeting in Fedulev's office arrived. Everything began, quite properly, with registration. The entrance, corridors and offices were under the control of men in police uniform armed with assault rifles, the boys from the UBOP. Seemingly nothing could derail Fedulev's strategy.

But then something unforeseen did happen. Galina Ivanova, the representative of the factory's trade union committee, who had a right to be present at the meeting on behalf of the factory's workforce, suddenly took a power of attorney out of her handbag. This was an immensely valuable proxy from the main creditor; Leon, while on the run, had found time to organise it. The proxy represented 34 per cent of the votes, so how Ivanova voted would determine the outcome.

Fedulev gave the order and Ivanova was removed to the UBOP. This was done by plainclothes UBOP officers mingling with the crowd in the hall. She was held at the UBOP for precisely three hours and twenty minutes, until Fedulev rang to say that the registration had been completed.

Alexander Naudzhus was Vasily Leon's deputy. Here, taken from his official statement to the FSB, is how he describes events during the night after the meeting:

> I arrived at the factory at about 22.30. At about 1.30 I went to sleep. At 4.30 I was awakened. The door to the factory management offices had been broken down, also the grilles on the windows. There were a lot of armed people around, and about 30 cars and a bus. We were allowed through to the management offices, where the factory's security officers were standing with their hands up. They were being guarded by people with assault rifles and wearing

police uniform. Oleshkevich, a UBOP lieutenant, was sitting at the table. I went into the office of the Commercial Director. Fedulev was sitting there. I asked, "On what grounds has this occupation taken place?" I was shown the minutes of the creditors' meeting and the contract with the new Director. The contract was inauthentic.

Thus was the joint operation of Fedulev and the provincial UBOP to illegally seize the Lobva Hydrolytic Factory crowned with success. There were manifest glaring violations of the law and *ultra vires* actions by civil servants.

Who has been called to account as we look back from the heights of 2004, the fourth year of the "dictatorship of law" proclaimed by Putin? Nobody. Not so far, at least. Today the Lobva factory ekes out a miserable existence. Fedulev has sucked it dry and moved on. As was to be expected. In 2000, having reconquered Lobva and acquired a cash pile over the following months, there being no-one to stop him, Fedulev was moving in on the minerals market. The first item on his menu was Kachkanar.

Kachkanar

The internationally known Kachkanar Ore Enrichment Complex is one of Russia's national assets. It is one of the very few enterprises in the world that mine ferro-vanadium ore. Its output provides an essential component for blast-furnace smelting. In our country, at least, not a single rail for the railways network would have been produced without it.

In the mid-1990s, like many other nationally important Russian enterprises, the Kachkanar OEC was subjected to a succession of privatisation measures which left it financially crippled. The situation became particularly dire in 1997–8. At this point Fedulev became chairman of the board of directors and proceeded as he always did to emasculate the enterprise, besieging it with his own dwarf marketing companies. By the end of 1998 Fedulev had brought Kachkanar to the point of bankruptcy, and only the arrest of the Urals Entrepreneur of the Year made a revival possible as other shareholders became able to play an active part. They hired a team of knowledgeable managers under the direction of Dzhalol Khaidarov, and large-scale investors appeared on the scene.

In 1999 the enterprise was transformed. Production rose to capacity, the net asset value rose, the workers began to be paid their wages again. Kachkanar's situation was similar to that of Lobva. The town had grown up round the plant, and 10,000 people, almost the entire working population, were employed there.

The results of the recovery were obvious: the plant's shares again became sought after on the stock market.

Almost every Russian provincial governor has the same kind of individual in his entourage as Yeltsin had in Putin: a successor, someone astute and loyal, proclaimed as his patron's heir apparent because someone is needed to cover the principal's back when he retires from the political arena, to ensure his continuing financial well-being and personal security.

For Eduard Rossel, Governor of Yekaterinburg, this person was Andrey Kozitsyn, the Copper King of the Urals, who managed the copper-smelting factories of Sverdlovsk Province. As the next election for governor approached, Yekaterinburg saw "Copper" Kozitsyn expand into the iron industry, under Rossel's patronage, of course. Rossel was not going to be Governor for ever, so with re-election time approaching, he started taking steps to concentrate all the juiciest bits of Urals industry in one set of hands: Kozitsyn's.

As you may recall, one of Fedulev's first visits in Yekaterinburg after his release from prison was to Governor Rossel. What they talked about we do not know exactly, but immediately after the audience Fedulev transferred to a trust managed by Kozitsyn all his shares in two enterprises, the Kachkanar OEC and the Nizhny Tagil Metallurgical Complex. To all appearances this was a straightforward deal between Fedulev and the Governor. Fedulev bought himself the right to do as he pleased in the province, and Kozitsyn moved in on Kachkanar.

It has to be said that at that moment Fedulev owned only 19 per cent of the shares of the Kachkanar complex, and even those were a bit suspect as we shall see. The shares transferred to Kozitsyn thus did not confer control, which meant that it wouldn't be easy to parachute in a Director of their own choosing. In any case, the managers, headed by Khaidarov, opposed the new Fedulev–Kozitsyn invasion and had the owners of 70 per cent of the shares behind them.

What was to be done? Usurpers use force to get their way. On January 29, 2000 the Kachkanar complex was seized by armed men. There was shooting, there were forged documents, and the law-enforcement agencies were actively involved in the mayhem. In fact it was a repetition of the scenario used at the Lobva Hydrolytic Factory. There was also "active non-involvement" on the part of Governor Rossel, just as in Lobva. At dawn on January 29 the complex was vouchsafed a new Director, Andrey Kozitsyn, and Pavel Fedulev strolled proprietorially through the empty offices of the management. *Plus ça change.*

It was clear, however, that the power of the cuckoos would last only until the firstly shareholders' meeting, which could simply throw them out. They concluded that they needed, firstly, not to allow a shareholders' meeting and, secondly, to bankrupt the enterprise as soon as possible in order to deprive the shareholders of their powers. Under Russian legislation, if an enterprise is declared insolvent the shareholders become non-voting owners.

Fedulev and Kozitsyn prevented the meeting by a method successfully practised by our State in Chechnya. They simply blocked off all entry to and exit from the town. The shareholders on their way to the complex, accompanied by the dispossessed managers, were stopped at police checkpoints. How was that possible? Easy! Sukhomlin, the Mayor of Kachkanar, issued Emergency Directive No. 14 banning the entry into Kachkanar of "citizens from other cities". All the shareholders and managers of the complex came from cities other than Kachkanar.

It was ridiculous of course, a farce, but a farce taking place in real life. The shareholders' meeting was not held, and the partners-in-crime set about implementing the second part of their plan: the artificial bankrupting of the Kachkanar OEC.

How was this to be done, given that the complex was functioning successfully?

Kozitsyn took a credit of 15 million dollars from the Moscow Business World Bank, secured on the assets of the complex. He had no trouble getting it, because who would not like to get their hands on the Kachkanar plant? Equipped with this credit he issued promissory notes from the enterprise. The money received was invested not in the complex but in another of his businesses, Svyatogor, which was also located in Sverdlovsk Province, supposedly in order to create a joint enterprise. The next step was for Kozitsyn seemingly to transfer the Kachkanar promissory notes to Svyatogor.

Why supposedly and why seemingly? Well, because actually none of this really happened. All the transfers were "virtual", and the promissory notes from the complex all ended up in the hands of a tiny nominee firm. This firm was registered to the address of a modest Yekaterinburg apartment seemingly belonging to a lady who subsequently, despite everyone's best efforts, could not be traced, and this virtual lady was instantly transformed into the main creditor of the most influential ferro-vanadium producer in the world. How? The ephemeral firm bought the complex's promissory notes for 40 per cent of their nominal value and promptly presented them to the enterprise for payment at 100 per cent. It then declared the enterprise bankrupt because it could not buy back its own promissory notes at 100 per cent of the nominal value. In this way, the phantom nominee lady was found to have 90 per cent of the votes at the creditors' meeting. The fraud was played out brazenly under the eyes of the provincial government.

Brazenly a straw creditor was created.

Brazenly artificial indebtedness was created.

Brazenly was the theft perpetrated of millions of dollars from the real owners of the enterprise, who found themselves without any rights to assets or refund of their investments.

While all this was going on, a round-the-clock guard was mounted in Kachkanar by the provincial UBOP in order to avoid any more annoying intrusions like a new Galina Ivanova, chairman of the trade union committee. The guard were the same lot as in Lobva when the factory there was seized.

When nobody stops a thief, he gets more impudent. Which brings us back to Uralkhimmash. Just as Lobva was followed by Kachkanar, so Kachkanar was followed by Uralkhimmash. In September 2000 that enterprise too was seized by force of arms, following the same scenario. During 2001, there was a quiet stifling of the shareholders by artificially bankrupting the enterprise, again with the total indulgence and connivance of the authorities. The "managed democracy" proclaimed by Putin was on the march.

Or perhaps it was just cowboy capitalism under the management of Mafia syndicates which had the law-enforcement agencies, a corrupt bureaucracy and a corrupt judiciary in their pockets.

The Urals Judiciary Is the Most Corrupt in the World

Let us recall that, on the night following the seizure of Uralkhimmash, both Fedulev and the supporters of the deposed Director were waving a collection of mutually exclusive legal rulings at each other.

The documents were not forgeries. As soon as you start looking into the documents relating to Uralkhimmash, the Kachkanar OEC and the Lobva factory, you see that all these armed invasions were sanctioned by the courts of Sverdlovsk Province. We find certain judges invariably on the side of one party, while other judges are invariably on the side of the other. It is as if no laws existed, as if there were no Constitution. Even as the Mafia syndicates of the Urals were slugging it out to claim their territories, a civil war was going on within the judiciary. The courts were being used, and continue to be used, as a rubber stamp for decisions in favour of one party or another.

Here is an excerpt from a letter to Vyacheslav Lebedev, chairman of the Supreme Court of Russia, from I. Kadnikov, Award of Merit of the Russian Federation, former chairman of the October District Court of Yekaterinburg, and V. Nikitin, former chairman of the Lenin District Court of Yekaterinburg:

It is Ovcharuk [Ivan Ovcharuk, chairman of the Sverdlovsk Provincial Court from Soviet times until the present day] who over a period of years participates directly in the formation and training of the Bench in the Urals, personally chooses and controls the selection of judges for each appointment. Without his personal approval not a single candidate can be appointed to the Bench, and none of us can have his appointment extended. Any judges who fail to find favour with him personally are squeezed out and persecuted. They are compelled to leave their jobs, and individuals are often selected for membership of the Bench who have neither qualifications nor experience of the work but who are in some respect vulnerable and hence manipulable. At the present time a great number of highly qualified judges who have worked for many years and have immense experience, who possess such important qualities as high moral principles, independence and firmness in arriving at verdicts, incorruptibility and courage, have been forced out of judicial work. The sole reason is that if you are not corrupt it is impossible to work normally under the direction of Ovcharuk.

What, in the opinion of Ovcharuk, are the characteristics of a good judge?

Anatoly Krizsky, until recently chairman of the Verkh-Isetsk District Court of Yekaterinburg, was not just "good", he was "the best in the profession". For many years it was Krizsky who loyally looked after the interests of Ivan Ovcharuk. What did that entail?

The Verkh-Isetsk court is the quirkiest in Yekaterinburg. Yekaterinburg prison is located on its territory, which means that, in accordance with the law, it is this court which examines all cases relating to changes in the terms of judicial restraint of those in the prison. Everybody in Yekaterinburg knows that the main factor influencing a verdict altering the terms of judicial restraint is not the nature of the crime, not what a person actually did and hence whether or not he remains a danger to society, but – quite simply – money. A crook from a powerful crime syndicate will usually spend less time in prison than other criminals. His colleagues will simply buy him out.

This results in financial prosperity for certain district courts. Russia's district courts are in general as poor as church mice. They are chronically short of resources, even of paper; plaintiffs have to bring their own. The judges' salaries are barely enough to make ends meet. This, however, is not at all the picture at the Verkh-

Isetsk court. The court building is surrounded by jeeps, Mercedes and Fords costing several thousand dollars. The owners who step out of these cars in the mornings are modest district judges whose salaries are a few thousand roubles. One of the flashiest cars invariably belongs to Anatoly Krizsky.

Krizsky had a close relationship with Pavel Fedulev. For many years it was Krizsky who personally presided over cases in which Fedulev figured in one capacity or another. Krizsky never allowed himself to prevaricate or get tied up in red tape. He always examined the cases in which Fedulev was involved under the "fast-track system", letting nothing hold him back: neither the need to call witnesses nor the question of whether his decisions were in accordance with the law. If, for example, Fedulev asked Krizsky to pronounce that certain shares belonged to him, Krizsky would not bother with the proof necessary in such cases. He would simply state: "These shares belong to Fedulev." With such rulings under his arm Fedulev appeared at Uralkhimmash after the armed invasion.

Another curious detail is that Krizsky's rulings-to-order were sometimes obligingly made in the comfort of the customer's place of business. Krizsky would record his rulings on Fedulev's writs not in the courtroom, as the law specifically requires, but in Fedulev's office. Sometimes it was not even Krizsky who made the ruling but Fedulev's lawyer in his own handwriting, with Krizsky merely adding his signature.

When in the autumn of 1998 Fedulev began to have problems with the prosecutor general's office over his defrauding of a Moscow company, it was Krizsky who, accompanied by Fedulev's lawyer, flew to Moscow to see the then prosecutor general, Yury Skuratov, to argue for the criminal proceedings against Fedulev to be dropped. Skuratov, who had been on friendly terms with Krizsky since they were young, received him personally, and although no-one knows how it happened, the case was closed. On his return to Yekaterinburg, Fedulev's wife met Krizsky. She made no secret of the fact that she thanked him for his trouble, and Krizsky in turn made no secret of how pleased he was: a few days later he bought himself a new Ford Explorer.[9]

It may seem to the Western reader that this is not such a big deal. The chairman of a court is hardly going to be a beggar, so it is not so surprising if he has a car of this kind. In Russia for the chairman of a district court to be able to afford such a car means one of two things: either he has just come into a large (by our standards) inheritance, or he is taking bribes. There simply is no third possible explanation. In Russia a Ford Explorer is something only a successful businessman can afford, and under Russian law the chairman of a court is not permitted to engage in business. A Ford Explorer costs the equivalent of a judge's salary for 20 years.

Nor was this the end of Krizsky's miraculous good fortune. Barely a month passed after the appearance of the Ford Explorer when Fedulev was again in trouble with the prosecutor general's office. Krizsky flew off to talk to Skuratov, not in Moscow this time but at the Black Sea resort of Sochi, where the prosecutor general was on holiday. The storm clouds hanging over Fedulev were again dispersed. Krizsky changed his Ford Explorer, which had already sent shock waves through Yekaterinburg society, for a Mercedes 600, the ultimate status symbol of a New Russian.

Krizsky's birthday parties were the talk of Yekaterinburg, festivals of conspicuous consumption to rival the name-day celebrations of overstuffed pre-Revolutionary merchants. On those occasions the court was suspended, and, by order of the chairman, the doors were locked. Krizsky hired a restaurant in the centre of town, money flew right and left, and vodka flowed in torrents. Every bureaucrat in Yekaterinburg kicked over the traces under the astonished gaze of the almost completely impoverished Yekaterinburg public. What did those drinking and dancing care that a judge had no business conducting himself in such a manner, not only according to unwritten rules of common decency but according to the writ of law? The law on "the Status of Judges in the Russian Federation" categorically requires that judges maintain a modest demeanour outside work, to say nothing of how they behave in working hours. They are to avoid any personal associations which might adversely affect their reputation, and show the greatest circumspection at all times in order to maintain the highest level of respect for the authority of the judiciary.

So what are we to make of the fact that it was Krizsky, with his associations with Fedulev and others like him, who was the favourite of Ivan Ovcharuk, chairman of the provincial court? What was going on? At every assembly Ovcharuk would emphasise that Krizsky was one of the best judges in the Urals.

The simple truth of the matter is that almost all of us living in Russia today were born in the Land of the Soviets and, to a greater or lesser extent, lived by the Soviet code of conduct. Ovcharuk had the old Soviet ways of thinking and behaving baked into him. In other words, he was a typical diehard Soviet legal boss. For the whole of his life he had been trained not, under any circumstances, to argue with his superiors. He was used only to doing as he was told, carrying out his superiors' orders, even trying to guess his superiors' moods, which way their eyebrows were going to move. This is no journalistic exaggeration. This is a description of Soviet servility as it was. Ovcharuk is what we have inherited from this past of ours, a man whose career progressed so well because he never in his life challenged the opinion of his superiors, no matter how lawless or stupid it was.

When the new times came, and democracy and capitalism with them, there was a moment, eyewitnesses tell us, when Ovcharuk panicked. Whom could he serve now?

His perplexity was soon dispelled. A special Soviet flair for sniffing out whom it was most profitable to subordinate himself to, who the new powers were, soon came to his rescue. Ovcharuk chose two new tsars. The first was the nascent business world, those accumulating capital. The second was the civil-service bureaucracy, which, however much people complained about it, remained as monolithic as ever and as solid as a granite cliff. For Ovcharuk it was represented by Governor Rossel. Since these twin tsars had united in Yekaterinburg in tender friendship and a new Mafia had emerged alongside the old Uralmash, Ovcharuk had no further qualms: he began serving Rossel and Fedulev.

Only at the end of 2001 did Yekaterinburg get rid of Krizsky as chairman of the Verkh-Isetsk District Court. It was a messy business, and the outcome was hardly satisfactory.

The provincial directorate of the FSB was well aware that Krizsky had been servicing Fedulev's criminal activities in the Urals for many years, but their agents had been unable to catch him red-handed. In the end, covert (and illegal) round-the-clock surveillance was set up, and the chairman of the Verkh-Isetsk court was caught engaging in . . . paedophilia. The FSB presented its evidence to Krizsky himself, to his patron Ovcharuk and to Rossel. The outcome? Krizsky was honourably retired. There was no public scandal. He was not stripped of his judicial status. He was redeployed to become the Mayor of Yekaterinburg's legal adviser, and that was it.

But what of those judges who did not want to be part of the turning of an independent judiciary into one totally subservient to the criminal underworld?

In Yekaterinburg in recent years a majority of judges have been found to be intractable. Those who chose not to serve the emergent crime syndicates have been dismissed from the Bench in dozens, and have had insult and abuse heaped on them.

Olga Vasilieva worked eleven years as a judge, a fair stint. Outwardly she was a calm, unfussy person, the kind of judge who refused on principle to stamp the judicial directives and rulings which Fedulev needed for the games he played. She simply refused. Vasilieva worked, moreover, in that same Verkh-Isetsk District Court with Krizsky as her immediate superior and was subjected to immense pressure, including occasional threats to her life and her family. She remained unbowed, never once gave in, and turned down not only Fedulev but Krizsky too when he demanded summary directives from her for the release of one or other of his criminal protégés from prison by changing the terms of judicial restraint.

The last straw was when Vasilieva accepted a writ against the chairman of the provincial court, Ivan Ovcharuk. Krizsky insisted she should have rejected it in order not to create a precedent. The plaintiffs were citizens of Yekaterinburg whom Ovcharuk had subjected to unreasonable judicial delay, wilfully failing to examine their application to the court within a reasonable time because it was directed against the interests of high officials in Governor Rossel's administration.

For Yekaterinburg, a city under the heel of the Mafia, where everybody knew that stepping out of line in such matters usually ended not in a quarrel but in a shooting, accepting a writ of that kind was revolutionary. It was unbelievable. Other district courts, in order not to bring major trouble down upon their heads, would refuse even to register such writs, although by law they had no right not to do so.

The system took savage revenge on Olga Vasilieva for acting within the law. She was not only fired, she was endlessly vilified. Complaints were appended to her personal file when it was submitted in order to have her expelled from the Bench. These came from Krizsky's criminal protégés whom she had refused to release from jail. The complaints were written by inmates on official court forms which they could have received only by Krizsky's having brought them to the prison himself.

Vasilieva had to start a pilgrimage round official institutions to prove these were all false accusations, that she was a judge and not a teapot. It took a year for the Supreme Court of Russia to restore her rank, but even then her trials were not over. The Supreme Court sat in Moscow, but she practised in Yekaterinburg, where she was entirely on her own. As soon as she got back she handed the Supreme Court resolution to Krizsky, but he refused to allow her to return to work and wrote an official representation against her to the Provincial Judges' College of Qualifications, an institution of the Russian Bench. He advised them that, despite having been restored to office, Vasilieva "had failed to mend her ways", a formulation traditionally used in reference to prisoners.

Judges in Russia need to have their status reconfirmed periodically, effectively to be reappointed, and hence need a recommendation from the College of Qualifications in their republic or province. This leads to more or less automatic reappointment by directive of the President. Now, however, Ovcharuk added his weight to Krizsky's denunciation, and the College of Qualifications resolved "no longer to recommend" Vasilieva for appointment as a judge.

Needless to say, nobody in this Mickey Mouse College of Qualifications made any attempt to corroborate the facts. These were the very same allegations, based on the statements of convicts, which the Supreme Court had just rejected as unsubstantiated.

Olga Vasilieva is a courageous and principled woman. She naturally applied once again to the Supreme Court, insisting on her right to justice. Years of her life are being wasted on this exhausting, debilitating campaign, however, and in the meantime she is being prevented from working for the good of the State.

Can we expect the majority to tread the path Olga Vasilieva has chosen? Many Yekaterinburg judges commented, begging me under no circumstances to publish their names, "It is easier for us just to rubber-stamp the rulings Ovcharuk demands than to find ourselves in Vasilieva's shoes." They had many harrowing tales about what had happened to colleagues of theirs. The tale of Alexander Dovgii, another Yekaterinburg judge, is one of them.

Dovgii's offence was the same as Vasilieva's. On one occasion he ignored Krizsky's demand to release a protégé from prison. A few days later the judge was savagely beaten with iron bars in the street. The police refused even to look for the attackers, although as a rule they investigate attacks on judges very thoroughly. Dovgii was hospitalised for a long time, came out crippled and, although now back at work, hears only divorce cases. He asks not to be given any other kind of case.

> With things as they stand, professionalism is regarded as the ability not to have one's own judgment. People who cannot dispense with Bolshevik methods are appointed in the name of the State to administer justice. They wag a finger in admonition and see nothing amiss in demanding the passing of a particular verdict. They call judges to account before the present-day equivalent of the Communist Party activists, the College of Qualifications. They see nothing wrong with condemning or pardoning in our name and by our hand . . .

This was written by a promising young judge, who also asked me to forget his name, after he had been pressured by Ovcharuk and Krizsky in much the same manner as Vasilieva. He buckled under the pressure and simply walked away. He wrote these lines in a letter addressed to Krizsky applying for retirement, adding, "I request that the matter be considered in my absence," and left Yekaterinburg for good.

This young judge had had no intention of resigning, it was just that one fine day the expected happened. A case involving the latest criminal machinations of some Mafia groups came his way, and Krizsky demanded that he should close the case immediately. The young judge asked for time to reflect. He received threats from persons unknown, anonymous telephone calls to his home, notes left where he would find them. He was "coincidentally" beaten up in the entry to his house, not too severely, just as a warning, and his assailants were never found.

The young judge wrote requesting permission to resign, and the Mafia case was promptly passed on to another judge. On the eve of the hearing this other judge received a telegram from the provincial court signed by Ovcharuk himself, instructing him to stop proceedings. The following day that case was closed.

Sergey Kazantsev, a judge of the Kirov District Court in Yekaterinburg, ruled that a certain Uporov who was accused of robbery and grievous bodily harm should be imprisoned as a danger to society until his case could be fully considered. Judge Kazantsev then moved on to consider another case. He was in the conference room and writing up the verdict – a time when, under Russian law, nobody is allowed to disturb a judge. To do so virtually guarantees that the verdict will be set aside by a higher court. Nevertheless, Ovcharuk rang Kazantsev to demand that he should alter the restraining order and let Uporov out of prison. Kazantsev refused and was told by Ovcharuk that he would be sacked.

He was sacked.

There are any number of such episodes in Yekaterinburg, and they are as alike as peas in a pod. As a result the judges who are still working there are also as alike as peas in a pod. In the first place, they are completely manipulable, willing to rubber-stamp any judgment just as long as they can avoid unpleasantness from their superiors. Resistance has been crushed. It is the rule of duplicity under the guise of the "dictatorship of law".

This explains how it came to be that when Uralkhimmash was seized, both sides had in their hands contradictory rulings on the same matter. For years any sign of judicial independence was brutally suppressed, and judges were conditioned to servility. Senior judges have long experience of working in the shackled Soviet courts. Where, under these circumstances, are courageous and fair judgments to come from? Anybody prepared to stand up and boldly refuse has long since been dismissed. Those capable of saluting promptly when required to serve the cause of lawlessness are hard at work and progressing up the career ladder.

Behind each of Fedulev's coups stood his special intimacy with the Bench of the Urals. He was friends with judges and they were friends with him. Bags of reciprocity. The most frequently heard names in this connection are those of Judges Ryazantsev and Balashov. Ryazantsev is a humble judge of the Kachkanar Municipal Court, which is subordinate to Ovcharuk. Ryazantsev it was who rubber-stamped the rulings Fedulev needed in the Kachkanar OEC case, validating the deals of the ephemeral firm which purchased promissory notes on the cheap and cashed them at their full face value, thereby sealing the fate of an enterprise of international importance. Our second judge is Balashov, also very humble, who works in the Kirov District Court of the City of Yekaterinburg. He ruled in favour of Fedulev in respect of Uralkhimmash and at several other important moments in Fedulev's business career. Here is how he did it.

It was Judge Balashov who effectively fired the first bullet in the Uralkhimmash affair. On the Friday evening he accepted a writ in support of Fedulev's interests at the factory, and on Monday morning, with a rapidity unheard of in the history of Russian jurisprudence, he issued the ruling Fedulev needed. Balashov managed to do this without calling any witnesses, gathering supplementary information or making enquiries of third persons.

In fairness, it has to be said that Balashov does in fact operate within the framework of the law. He is just very good at exploiting loopholes. The fast-track procedure he resorted to is entirely legitimate. The injunction he issued "in satisfaction of the plaintiff's demands" is appropriate in cases where the defendants have begun to take executive decisions and measures leading to the embezzlement of property. The primary task of such an injunction is to freeze the situation. The court is within its rights in intervening to forbid any managerial actions until the substance of the dispute is resolved.

Accordingly, Balashov's lightning resolution on Uralkhimmash had nothing to do with resolving the ownership dispute. He was merely preventing anyone from managing the plant or making use of its assets. On the surface all was innocence, sweetness and light. The result, however, was asphyxia.

Under Russian law, if a verdict has already been given in a dispute, it is impermissible for another court to hear the dispute again. In granting the injunction required, however, Balashov pretended not to know the crucial detail that an arbitration court had already pronounced on the dispute over Uralkhimmash. He had an entirely respectable explanation for this: there was no unified information system in the province (which was true), and people in the district courts never got to hear about anything as a result . . .

A few hours after his injunction was issued, the ink barely dry on his signature, Fedulev descended upon Uralkhimmash with his armed brigades, waving it before him.

An Important Detail of Modern Russian Court Procedure

If a modern Russian court is clearly biased, openly favouring one side in a dispute, it can do so precisely because the courts in Russia are supposed to be independent. All that matters is whether or not a judge has the support of his superiors. If the top judges who oversee the procedural actions of those below them want the same thing, the lower court can please itself. After the ructions at Uralkhimmash, Valerii Baidukov, chairman of the district court and Balashov's immediate superior, called him in for an explanation. Balashov informed him that his judgment was what the provincial court had wanted, it had all been agreed with Ovcharuk. There were no further questions.

What, however, about the perplexed public? The brazen seizure of Uralkhimmash did get the Yekaterinburg public asking a lot of questions.

Baidukov explained everything very straightforwardly. He assured people that the courts understood that every minute counted when assets could be siphoned off to who knows where. This was why, in the interests of citizens and owners alike, a ruling had been given with such rapidity.

Incidentally, the Baidukov who was doing all this explaining is the chairman of the provincial council of the Bench, the corporate conscience of the judiciary. The case of Olga Vasilieva had naturally passed through his office several times, and each time he had endorsed it as required by Ovcharuk. The council of the Bench is another institution of the community of judges, like the College of Qualifications. Only people agreeable to Ovcharuk become members of either of them, and whatever representations he makes to them produce the desired conclusions. Valerii Baidukov is additionally chairman of the Kirov District Court of Yekaterinburg. One has no sense that he is capable of standing up for anyone. If he ever does have an opinion of his own, it remains purely hypothetical. He can pontificate theoretically about the district court as "the basic link of the Russian judicial system" but falls silent when asked to discuss facts.

Ninety-five per cent of all criminal and civil cases in Russia are heard in the district courts, and to that extent they really are the basic link of the country's judicial system. In reality, however, this is a fiction. The district court is exceptionally dependent and manipulable. The main reason is that the senior judges of the provincial and republican courts have no wish to implement judicial reform and lose the control they enjoy over their inferiors in the district courts. The latter enjoy independence only according to the Constitution, and the fact that the Russian Constitution has legal pre-eminence makes no difference. The district courts have simply not been given procedural independence.

The law gives provincial courts procedural control of district and municipal courts – that is, the responsibility for monitoring their judicial practice. This procedural management means that the verdicts of district and municipal courts are reviewed and evaluated by the provincial courts, which decide whether they are correct or flawed. Procedural dependence develops into organisational and career dependence. A lower judge whose face does not fit is as vulnerable as a baby. A superior judge has the right to criticise and annul his verdicts as he sees fit, but without any accountability. The provincial court can annul the verdict of a district court without explaining what is wrong about it or how it should be improved.

The provincial court does not take responsibility for the final verdict, but it does keep statistics to show how many cases, and from which district judge, have been found to be "erroneous". These statistics are the basis for calculating bonuses for judges, awarding or depriving them of various privileges, holidays in the summer or winter months, advancement in the waiting list for a flat (which is in the gift of the provincial court and matters because judges' salaries are insufficient for them to buy flats for themselves), confirmation of their tenure of office and so on.

This is the mechanism through which the district court judges, who according to the Constitution are "fundamental" to the system, have found themselves more dependent on their superiors than under the Soviet regime. The Constitution seems to preclude such hierarchical relations since it declares that all judges are equal and independent, being individually appointed by directive of the President. The reality is rather different. They may be equal when they are appointed, but they are not equal when they get the sack. If the chairman of a provincial court wishes to get even with district judges, he holds all the aces; but if the chairman of a provincial court is objectionable to district judges, that is just their hard luck. They cannot facilitate his removal.

It is the very laws and rules regulating the Bench as they have developed since the end of the USSR which have allowed Ivan Ovcharuk to become what he is: the official who keeps the Urals legal system safe from judges who might deliver an unpredictable verdict. The legal system has no safeguards to curtail the activities of those at the top of the hierarchy who might go off the rails. The constraints are purely moral. The only way the system could function satisfactorily would be if the person occupying Ovcharuk's office had different moral and ethical attributes. What sort of a system is that?

To come back, however, to District Judge Balashov. Could he have acted differently in the Fedulev case, and, if so, what should he have done? He had only to postpone consideration of the injunction, which he had every right to do.

It the course of preparing their seizure of Uralkhimmash, Fedulev and his accomplices checked out many district courts in Yekaterinburg to see whether or not they would play ball.

The whole lot agreed to act like Balashov with the exception of one, the Chkalov Court. Ivan Ovcharuk invited the chairman of that court, Sergey Kiyaikin, to go and work in Magadan in the extreme north-east of the country. Traditionally, "to be sent to Magadan" has meant to be exiled there, but Kiyaikin, an obstinate judge who had grown up in Yekaterinburg, a man with roots and pride in the city and the Urals region who had himself worked at and graduated in chemical engineering from the prestigious Uralkhimmash, was only too glad to get as far as possible away from his native region. He did not want to be killed or to have his family attacked.

Balashov is a loyal guardian of Fedulev's interests. He has got the production of verdicts to safeguard them down to a fine art. Here, for example, is one of Balashov's rulings, delivered on February 28, 2000.

Fedulev had decided to sell Uralelektromash, not a factory but a company that handled transactions in shares he owned. These happened to include his shares in the Kachkanar OEC and Uralkhimmash.

Fedulev decided to sell in return for a certain sum of money, as he had every right to do. Some time later the new owners of Uralelektromash discovered that, although they had paid the money, they had not received the corporation's documents. Fedulev had *sort of* sold Uralelektromash, only he had kept all the shares himself. The purchasers realised they had been swindled and naturally demanded an explanation. Fedulev told them he had changed his mind. They countered, "Give us our money back, then you can keep everything yourself." Fedulev replied, "I'm not going to give you any money back. You haven't got any documents. You are nobody. Go away." His Uralkhimmash shareholding was in the same situation. Emerging from prison in Moscow and eager to keep hold of what he had already sold for several million dollars, Fedulev said, "I know nothing about it. It wasn't registered in the prescribed manner. The deal is invalid." He went to Judge Balashov, who found in Fedulev's favour.

In order to understand what Fedulev did, you need to appreciate that Russian legislation still has many loopholes. In this instance the flaw was that any company, when it issues shares, is required to register the fact. In the early days nobody in Russia knew how to go about this. There had been no stock market in the

USSR and hence no shares. After the collapse of the USSR the relevant governmental institutions took a very long time to find their bearings. They could neither explain nor decide how shares should be registered. As a result, shares in many companies were unregistered. They were, and still are, traded in. The stock market continued on its way.

What should be done? Naturally, it was assumed that you just needed to be honest with your partners. That, however, is not the basis on which Fedulev operates. Having spotted an opportunity, he first contracted to sell the shares of Uralelektromash and only then applied to have them registered with the appropriate State agency, the Federal Commission for Securities. When the shares were eventually registered, after a fairly long delay because everything got bogged down in a morass of discoordination, Fedulev informed his purchasers that the contract to sell Uralelektromash had been concluded before the shares had been registered. He looked them straight in the eye and said, "The money is mine too. It was your mistake and you have to pay for it." The court once again rubber-stamped in Fedulev's favour.

Is Fedulev so much cleverer than other people that he knows all these details and exploits them? Of course not. He is just so rich that he can afford to hire the savviest lawyers who spot the loopholes. He has managed to create an oligarchic pyramid which ensures that, whatever he undertakes, all those involved are links in a single chain. None can do without the others.

So Judge Balashov ruled in Fedulev's favour in the Uralelektromash case. The judicial process followed the same pattern we observed with Uralkhimmash: a highly complex case, running to many volumes of evidence which could only be made sense of by calling in experts in the subtleties of the Russian stock market, was examined by Balashov in next to no time.

After that, things took off. The exiling of a judge to Magadan was the least of it. The writ regarding the disputed

Uralelektromash shares was the prologue to the bloody events at Uralkhimmash.

Another budding Balashov, the obliging Judge Ryazantsev, works in the Kachkanar Municipal Court. On January 28, 2000, as we have seen, the complex had been brazenly seized by Fedulev's armed heavies. How did the courts react? On February 1, 2000 Judge Ryazantsev found no infringement of the law in the conducting of a meeting of the board of directors under the muzzles of assault rifles. The hearing was conducted à la Balashov, at high speed, without any pre-hearing submission or involvement of those whose rights had been trampled underfoot. And, of course, the writ was presented the day after.

On February 15, just a fortnight later, the Judicial College for Civil Cases of the Sverdlovsk Provincial Court (i.e., Ovcharuk's diocese) confirmed Ryazantsev's ruling, again without a hearing. This represents incredible speed for the Russian appeals machinery, which normally takes six months.

The mocking of Themis did not end there. On the same day, when it was clear that the provincial court was not going to overturn his earlier verdict, Judge Ryazantsev, in order to scotch the possibility of any further mishaps, prohibited the holding of any more general meetings of shareholders of the Kachkanar OEC.

A municipal court has not the slightest right to do anything of the sort. More than that, nowhere in the Code of Civil Procedure is there provision for prohibiting acts of persons not party to a dispute.

But who among the guardians of the law in Sverdlovsk Province cares about that? Was Ryazantsev removed for acting illegally? No way. The courts rolled out their verdicts without even bothering to check whether Fedulev was the legal owner of the complex. In fact, the 19 per cent of Kachkanar shares which Fedulev flourished so effectively did not actually exist. They had long ago been impounded in the course of an examination of

Fedulev's affairs in Moscow by the investigative committee of the Ministry of Internal Affairs. The reason he had been imprisoned on fraud charges was that he had twice sold this same 19 per cent to different companies!

After February 2000 people began to take notice of what was going on. The Supreme Court in Moscow tried to challenge the rampaging of the Sverdlovsk Provincial court on more than one occasion, but nothing really changed. Fedulev retained control of the Kachkanar OEC, those he had duped hid abroad, and the Kachkanar Municipal and Sverdlovsk Provincial Courts enjoyed the benefit of a mass of cases ancillary to the effective recognition of the Kachkanar complex as bankrupt.

The judiciary of Sverdlovsk Province thus facilitated a succession of deals which together deliberately brought about the complex's insolvency. This, incidentally, is a criminal act, but who is going to bother looking into it? As we have seen, when Putin came to power he made it clear that his loyalty lay with the likes of Fedulev and Rossel. On July 14, 2000, shortly after his first election, Putin flew to Yekaterinburg. He participated in the solemn laying of the foundation stone of Mill 5000 at the Nizhny Tagil Metallurgical Complex, the largest enterprise of its kind in the world. The players at that complex are the same people as in Kachkanar. Fedulev has pride of place, and Mill 5000 is a major investment project of Eduard Rossel. The image of the President laying its foundation stone was excellent PR for Fedulev's continuing expansion of his criminal empire. Indeed, new money "followed Putin". In response to this beneficence Fedulev and Rossel are now active supporters of Putin and underwrite the functioning of the Urals section of his United Russia party. They supported Putin in the election campaign for his second term of office in 2004.

It remains to say only that on the surface everything in Russia is going swimmingly and is frightfully democratic. The principle of a completely independent judiciary has been proclaimed, and any obstruction of justice is a criminal offence. The Federal law on "The Status of Judges" is progressive and supposedly safeguards their independence. The reality, however, is that all these constitutional and democratic principles are violated with the utmost cynicism. Lawlessness is demonstrably more powerful than the law. The kind of justice you get depends on what class you belong to, and the upper echelons of society, the VIP level, are reserved for the Mafia and the oligarchs.

What about those who are not at the VIP level? Well, you don't miss what you never had.

Since we are now building capitalism, there is private property. If there is property there will always be someone who wants to get his hands on it and someone else who does not want to part with it. It is just a matter of what methods are used to resolve the issue, the rules by which people play in a state. In our totally corrupt state, for the time being, we live by the rules of Pashka Fedulev.

One final scene before we bring down the curtain. It is March 2003 in Yekaterinburg. Life in the province is sluggish, but for several days in a row, from March 25 to 28, an ongoing protest demonstration has been taking place. The protestors are the civil-rights activists of Sverdlovsk Province: the International Centre for Human Rights, the Social Committee for the Defence of Prisoners' Rights and an umbrella organisation called "Our Union Is the Land of People's Power". They are collecting signatures demanding the immediate retirement of Ivan Ovcharuk. They chant that Ovcharuk, with his long-standing ties of collaboration with the crime bosses of the Urals, is the mainstay of judicial arbitrariness in the Urals and of opposition to the introduction of judicial reform. They tell all who will listen that Ovcharuk is continuing to choke off any signs of democracy and will fight to the death against the introduction of trial by jury, declaring that it "is contrary to the interests of the inhabitants of Sverdlovsk Province". His only real concern is to keep out anything which might cramp the corrupt legal system he has created for the benefit of the criminal underworld of the Urals.

March 2003 again, but Moscow this time. The President has reappointed Ivan Ovcharuk as chairman of the Sverdlovsk Provincial Court.

MORE STORIES FROM
THE PROVINCES

The Old Man from Irkutsk

The winter of Putin's third year in office, 2002–3, was very cold.
We are a northern country, of course: Siberia, bears, furs, all that
sort of thing. So you might expect we would be ready for it.

Unfortunately everything always takes us by surprise, like
snow falling off a roof on to your head. This includes our frosts,
which is why the following terrible events came to pass.

In Irkutsk, in the depths of Siberia, an old man was found
frozen to the floor of his flat. He was past 80, an ordinary
pensioner, one of those the emergency services refuse to turn out
for because they are just too old. Their response to a telephone call
is a straightforward and unreflecting: "Well, what do you expect?
Of course he's feeling ill. It's his age." This elderly citizen lived
alone, a veteran of the Second World War, one of those who freed
the world from Nazism, with medals and a State pension. He was
one of those to whom President Putin sends greetings on May 9,
Victory Day, wishing him happiness and good health. Our old
men, our war veterans unspoiled by too much attention from the
State, weep over these form letters with their facsimile signature.
Anyway, in January 2003, this old man died of hypothermia. He
froze to the floor where he fell. His name was Ivanov, the most

common Russian surname. There are hundreds of thousands of Ivanovs in Russia.

War veteran Ivanov froze to the floor because his flat was unheated. It should have been heated, of course, like all the flats in the block where he lived; like all the blocks of flats in Irkutsk in the third year of Putin's stewardship.

Why did this happen? The explanation is simple. The heating pipes wore out throughout Russia, because they had been in service since Soviet times, and those times have been gone for more than a decade, and thank God for that. For a long time the pipes leaked and leaked, and Communal Services, whose responsibility they are, did nothing about it. Communal Services is a centralised, State-run monopoly. Every month we have to pay them quite a substantial sum for their non-existent technical support, but they virtually ignore us, carry on not doing their job and periodically demand a rate increase. The government gives way, but those employed by Communal Services are so used to doing nothing that that is what they continue to do.

The day finally came when the monopolised pipes which had been leaking for so long, and which had not been repaired for so long, burst. At that moment, in the middle of winter, in severe frosts, it was discovered that there was no way of replacing them. Communal Services had no money to pay for this. Nobody knew what the money we had been paying them had been spent on. All the communal facilities which had been in service since the Soviet period had finally deteriorated. The fact that there was nothing to replace them with was not to be expected because we produce thousands of kilometres of all sorts of pipes every year. "The country has no funds available for this purpose," the agents of Putin's government announced with a shrug, as if it was nothing to do with them. "What do you mean there is no money?" the opposition politicians parried feebly, making their customary show of standing up for the rights of the people. The President publicly ticked off the Prime Minister. And that was the end of it. The politicians agreed to differ. There was no scandal. The government did not resign. Even the appropriate minister did not resign. So what if people had to keep pacing around their flats to keep warm, sleeping and eating in their winter coats and felt boots? The pipes would be repaired come the summer.

The old man who died was hacked with crowbars off the icy floor by the other people living in his communal flat and quietly buried in the frozen Siberian earth. No period of mourning was declared.

The President pretended that this had not happened in his country or to a member of his electorate. He remained totally aloof during the funeral and the country swallowed his silence. In order to consolidate his position, Putin even changed tack. He gave a grim speech to the effect that terrorists were responsible for everything wrong in Russia and that the State's main priority was the destruction of international terrorism in Chechnya. Apart from that, national life was back on the rails. The public could not be allowed to reflect on the imperfection of the world developing before their eyes.

Soon it was spring. Putin began preparing for his re-election in 2004. There could be no place for regret at defeats suffered, only joy at victories. Accordingly, a whole lot of new holidays were announced; in fact, an unheard-of quantity of them. Including the observance of Lent.

The nearer summer came, the less people talked about the complete collapse of Russia's heating infrastructure the previous winter. Citizens were called upon to rejoice in great numbers at the preparations for celebrating the tercentenary of St Petersburg, and to take pride in the sumptuousness of refurbished Tsarist palaces fit to dazzle the world's élite with their splendour. And that is exactly what happened.

Putin invited all the world's leaders to St Petersburg, and the city was subjected to an insensitive repainting of façades. The old man in Irkutsk, and indeed all the old men in St Petersburg, were forgotten by everyone, including Putin.

"Mind you, if he had died in Moscow . . ." the metropolitan pundits would say, suggesting that then there would have been a scandal and a half, and that the authorities would have replaced the pipes before next winter.

Schroeder, Bush, Chirac, Blair and many other VIPs proceeded to our northern capital and effectively crowned Putin as their equal. They were received with pomp and ceremony. They pretended to regard Putin with respect, and old Mr Ivanov and the millions of Russian pensioners who can barely make ends meet weren't given a thought. Putin's reign reached its high point, and almost nobody noticed. He decided to base his power solely on the oligarchs, the billionaires who own Russia's oil and gas reserves. Putin is friends with some oligarchs and at war with others, and this is called statecraft. There is no place for the people in this scheme of things. Moscow is life-giving warmth and light, while the provinces are its pale reflection, and those who inhabit them might as well be living on the moon.

Kamchatka: The Struggle to Survive

Kamchatka is at the furthest reach of Russia. The flight from Moscow takes more than ten hours. The planes on the Petropavlovsk–Kamchatsky route are pretty basic and predispose you to muse on the immensity of our complicated Motherland and about the fact that only a tiny proportion of our people live in Moscow, playing their big political games, setting up their idols and knocking them down, and believing that they control this enormous country.

Kamchatka is a good place to recognise how remote the Russian provinces are from the capital. In fact, distance has nothing to do with it. The provinces live differently, they breathe a different air, and this is where the real Russia is to be found.

There are as many sailors living in Kamchatka as there are fishermen, indeed even more. Despite the massive cutbacks in the armed forces, the power base here remains the same: whoever the Kamchatka Flotilla of the Pacific Fleet votes for wins the elections.

As you might expect in a coastal town, there is a predominance of black and navy-blue everywhere: reefer jackets, sailors' vests, peakless caps. The only thing missing is the fleet's legendary smartness. The jackets you see are worn, the vests much laundered, the caps faded.

Alexey Dikiy is the commander of a nuclear hunter-killer submarine, the *Vilyuchinsk*. He is the élite of our fleet, and so is his vessel, part of the armament of the Kamchatka Flotilla.

Dikiy received an outstanding education in Leningrad – today's St Petersburg – and then made brilliant progress up the career ladder as a highly talented officer. By the time he was 34 he was a uniquely qualified submariner. In terms of the international military labour market, every month of service raised his value by thousands of dollars. Today, however, Alexey Dikiy, Captain First Class, is eking out a wretched existence, there is no other way of putting it. His home is a dreadful officers' hostel with peeling stairwells, half derelict and eery. Everybody who could has left this place for "the mainland", throwing their military careers to the winds. The windows of many now uninhabited flats are dark. This is cold, hungry, inhospitable terrain. People have fled mainly from the poverty. Captain Dikiy tells me that in good weather he and other senior naval officers go fishing in order to put a decent meal on their tables.

On the table in his kitchen he has placed what our Motherland pays in return for irreproachable loyal service. Dikiy has just brought a captain's monthly rations home from his submarine in one of the fleet's bed sheets. The rations consist of two packets of shelled peas, two kilograms of buckwheat and rice in paper bags, two tins of the very cheapest tinned peas, two tins of Pacific herring and a bottle of vegetable oil.

"Is that all?"

"Yes. That's it." Dikiy is not complaining, just confirming a fact. He is a strong and genuine man. More precisely, he is very Russian. He is used to privation. His loyalty is to the Motherland rather than to whoever happens to be her leader at any given time. If he allowed himself to think any other way, he would have been out of here long ago. The captain accepts that anything can happen, including famine, which is precisely what his rations evoke.

These tins and paper bags contain the month's supplies for the three members of Captain Dikiy's family. He has a wife, Larisa, who qualified as a radio-chemist. She has a degree from the prestigious Moscow Institute of Engineering and Physics, whose graduates are headhunted straight from their benches in the lecture room by the computer firms of Silicon Valley in California.

Larisa, however, living with her husband in a closed military township of the Pacific Fleet, is unemployed. This is a detail of no interest to naval headquarters or to the faraway Ministry of Defence. The recruitment policies of staff headquarters mean they stubbornly refuse to see the gold lying at their feet. Larisa cannot even get a teaching job in the school for submariners' children. All the posts are filled, and there is a waiting list. Unemployment among the non-military personnel here runs at 90 per cent.

The third member of Captain Dikiy's family is his daughter, Alisa, a schoolgirl in second grade. Her situation is also unenviable. There is nothing in this military township to bring out the abilities of Alisa or the other children. No sports centre, no dance floors, no computers. All the garrison's children can lay claim to is a dismal, dirty courtyard and a building with a video recorder and a selection of cartoons.

Truly, Kamchatka is at the outer reach of our land and at the extremity of State heartlessness. On the one hand we find here cutting-edge technology for the taking of human life, and on the other a troglodytic existence for those who supervise it. Everything relies entirely on personal enthusiasm and patriotism. There is no money, no glory and no future.

The place where Dikiy lives is called Rybachie. It is an hour's drive from Petropavlovsk-Kamchatsky, the capital of the Kamchatka Peninsula. Rybachie is perhaps the world's most famous closed military township, with a population of 20,000. It is the symbol and the vanguard of the Russian nuclear fleet. The township is packed with the most modern types of weaponry. This is where Russia's east-facing nuclear shield is situated, and where those who keep it intact and in working order live.

Captain Dikiy's submarine is one of the most important constituents of this nuclear shield, from which it follows that Dikiy himself is a vital component. His submarine is a technologically perfect piece of weaponry the like of which is to be found nowhere else in the world. It has the capability to destroy entire surface flotillas and the best submarines of the world's powers, including the US. Under Dikiy's command is a unique weapon armed with nuclear missiles and an impressive array of torpedoes. While we have such a defence capability, Russia is not seriously vulnerable, at least not from the direction of the Pacific Ocean.

Captain Dikiy himself, however, is highly vulnerable, and primarily from the direction of the State he serves. But he rarely thinks along those lines. Like many other officers, he is skilled at surviving without any money at all. His salary is low and paid irregularly, often as much as six months late.

When there is no money, Dikiy declines to eat on board his submarine (though officers are entitled to meals there). He takes home his entitlement in the form of a packed meal and shares it with his family. He has no other way of feeding them. As a result, Dikiy is a pale shadow of a man. He is unconscionably thin. His face has an unhealthy pallor, and it is clear why: the captain of the main constituent of Russia's nuclear shield is undernourished.

Of course, constantly being in a radiation zone also takes its toll. In the past this had its compensations, because submariners were highly eligible as bachelors, but everything has changed. Nowadays the girls look away when naval officers walk past.

"Actually, the poverty is not the real problem," Dikiy says. He is an ascetic, a penniless romantic, an officer to the marrow of his bones, almost a saint in our times when all values are assessed in the cynical language of the dollar. "You can live with poverty as long as you have a clear goal and understandable operational tasks. Our real misfortune is the parlous state of the country's nuclear fleet, the sense of hopelessness. They don't seem to understand in Moscow that these armaments have to be taken seriously. In ten years' time, if the present level of financing is maintained, there will either be nothing here in Rybachie, or NATO will be refuelling at our piers."

In order to escape from the hopelessness of what is occurring in front of his eyes, Dikiy has decided to continue his studies at the General Headquarters Academy. He wants to write a dissertation about the state of Russia's national security at the end of the twentieth and beginning of the twenty-first centuries. He hopes when he has concluded his research to be able to give an academically grounded answer to the question that troubles him: In whose interests was it to undermine Russia's national security?

His interim conclusions are not favourable to Moscow, but the captain is not antagonistic or offended at what has been going on. He thinks it is appalling that Moscow behaves as it does, but there is nothing to be done about it. Except to tough it out, because we are stronger and more intelligent than our superiors.

Dikiy's job means his life is not his own. His cannot do things which everybody else can. In order to be on five-minute standby for his submarine, he can never go off anywhere. He must always be contactable. He can't just go into the countryside berrying, picking mushrooms or walking with friends. He has to live at the post he has accepted and cannot pass it over to anyone else. He has to be with his officers to make sure they do not become demoralised in these difficult times. He has to find time to look in at the barracks to keep a fatherly eye on what the ratings are getting up to. He is a busy man.

Many a military officer, living like a beggar much as Captain Dikiy does, can at least go out to earn a bit on the side after a day's work, feed his family and afford to buy clothes and even his uniform (a majority of officers actually have to do this). Captain Dikiy has neither the time nor the opportunity to do so. In the short hours that remain after work he is literally *required* to relax, to catch up on his sleep, to restore his equanimity. When he boards his submarine he must be relaxed. It is a requirement of the job. The consequences of nervous debility could be catastrophic.

"I have to be as calm and balanced at work," Dikiy explains, "as if I had just come back from holiday, as if everything was sorted and I didn't have to worry about how I am going to feed my wife and daughter tomorrow."

"You say you have to. It seems to me that this is viewing the situation the wrong way round. You are serving the State, and so surely it is up to the State to create the right conditions for you to come to work in a calm frame of mind."

Dikiy smiles a rather patronising smile, and I am not sure who this strange, tough, special man is feeling more condescending towards: me for asking such questions, or the State which spurns those who serve it best. It turns out that it is towards me.

"The State is not able to do that at present," the captain says finally. "It isn't, and there's an end to the matter. What point is there in demanding something that isn't there? I am a realist and not quick to anger. All the sentimentalists and the bad-tempered people left here long ago. They resigned from the Navy."

"I still do not understand, though, why you yourself have not resigned. You are a nuclear specialist with an engineering qualification. I am quite sure you could find yourself a decent job."

"I can't resign because I cannot abandon my ship. I am a commander, not one of the ratings. There is no-one to replace me. If I left, I would feel a traitor."

"A traitor to whom? The State, surely, has betrayed you?"

"In time the State will come to its senses. For now we just have to be patient and preserve our nuclear fleet. That is what I am doing. Even if the Ministry of Defence pursues a policy of betrayal, my duty is to Russia. I am defending the people of Russia, not the State bureaucracy."

There you have the portrait of a Russian submarine officer in our times. He is stuck out there at the furthest reach of our land, and, true to his military oath, he daily covers the embrasure with his own body because there is nothing else to cover it with.

In order to fulfil his obligations in the midst of the profound financial malaise which has befallen the armed forces, complete dedication is demanded of the commander. He leaves home at precisely 7.20 in the morning and returns at 10.40 at night every day. He is on board his submarine for ten hours and more. There is no other way. The Navy is falling apart before our eyes, and with technology which is not being serviced and properly maintained, incidents are possible at any moment, including a major disaster. The only thing that hasn't changed at all is the raising of the flag. This ritual is observed every day at 8 a.m., come hurricane, blizzard, accident or change of government.

Incidentally, Dikiy walks from his home to where the *Vilyuchinsk* is moored. It takes him precisely 40 minutes. He walks not because the exercise is good for him but because, of course, he doesn't have the money for a car of his own, and because no other transport is provided by the Navy. Actually, it is laid up. The Second Flotilla, to which the *Vilyuchinsk* belongs, is in the throes of a fuel crisis, as indeed is the rest of Kamchatka. No cars or buses run to the jetties. The Navy does not have enough petrol. No petrol in a country selling oil to all and sundry! But that is the least of it. What if they run out of bread? The garrison is constantly in debt to the local bread factory, which goes on supplying the ships on tick.

Can you believe it? The service personnel who maintain the nuclear shield of an international superpower are being fed on charity!

I wonder how the President feels when he attends the G8 summit meetings.

Well, okay. All the officers in Rybachie walk to work in the mornings. On the road the officers' corps is usually buzzing like an angry beehive. They are discussing the questions on all their minds: How long can they put up with this situation? What kind of an abyss are we rushing towards?

Their heated political discussions are fuelled by the view in front of them. As you walk towards No. 5 Pier, for example, where the *Vilyuchinsk* is moored, you can contemplate Khlebalkin Island, where there is a derelict ship-repair yard. Two or three years ago, 15 or 16 submarines would be in the Khlebalkin yard for servicing. Today the surface of the water is calm and mirror-like, and not a single ailing vessel is to be seen. The officers were informed that even the servicing of submarines was now subject to a regime of rigorous economy.

"It's an appalling sight," Dikiy says. "We know exactly what it signifies. Our technology must be properly maintained. You can't just go on expecting miracles. Submarines are not like spry old men who never need to see a doctor. Accidents are inevitable."

This disintegration has demoralised some of the Rybachie officers completely. It has turned others to debauchery. They have seen it all in the garrison of late: wholly bizarre behaviour and suicides.

"The present situation makes the officers bitter," Dikiy tells me. "That is why I am so insistent that everybody should be there for the raising of the flag on the dot of 8.oo. The men should see the eyes of their commander, and read in them that everything is in order, everything is being held steady, we are continuing to fulfil our duty no matter what. In spite of everything."

"Officers' bullshit! Fine words for soft heads!" Many reading these lines may dismiss Dikiy's sentiments in that way. To some extent they will be right. These really are lofty sentiments, but the situation of those officers who have not yet resigned from the disintegrating Pacific Fleet is that today they continue to perform their demanding duties solely because those fine words are their anchor. They are men with ideals and principles. That's why they are in the Navy. They volunteered for the submarines because of the prestige and in the expectation of dazzling military careers with high salaries. They have known different times and expect them to continue.

As real life does not have the consistency of a film or a novel, the sublime coexists very happily in Rybachie with the ridiculous and the routine.

"It's impossible to live the way your husband does! Sometimes at least a man needs time to himself!"

Larisa Dikiy is a chortling beauty born in Zhitomir in Ukraine, a woman who has sacrificed her own life to live on the verge of starvation so that her husband can fulfil his duty. She laughs mischievously in reply: "Well, actually I rather like things the way they are. At least I always know where my husband is! He has nowhere to hide from me, so I'm saved all those pangs of jealousy!"

Dikiy is standing beside us. He smiles an awkward smile, like a schoolboy who has just received a declaration of love from the prettiest girl in his class. I discover that the captain is a shy man. He blushes. I could almost weep. I see clearly that the enormous burden of responsibility the commander of a nuclear submarine bears is completely incompatible not just with his standard of living and way of life but also with his age and appearance.

At home, without his uniform, Alexey Dikiy, Captain First Class, looks just like the boy who comes top of the class, thin and melancholy. By Moscow criteria, where young people still mature rather late, that is precisely the situation. Dikiy, remember, is only 34.

"But you have already clocked up 32 years of service in the Navy. It's time you retired!" says Larisa.

"Actually, I could," the captain says, again embarrassed.

"What do you mean? You joined the fleet when you were two? Like the son of a noble family who was registered in a regiment when he was born and by the time he came of age already had a good service record and epaulettes?" I press him for an answer.

The captain smiles. I can see he is looking forward to what he is going to tell me. His father was indeed a naval officer, now, of course, retired. Dikiy grew up in Sevastopol, at the Black Sea naval base. "As regards my 32-year service record at 34 years of age . . ." he begins, but is promptly interrupted by his vivacious wife.

"It means that he has spent his entire service life in the most difficult sector of all, the submarine fleet, in the immediate vicinity of reactors and nuclear weapons. One year's service there is counted as three."

"You don't feel that on those grounds alone the State should long ago have showered you with gold?" I persist. "Are you not insulted that you have to share your dinner between three people as if you were a student?"

"No. I am not insulted," he replies calmly and confidently. "It would be quite senseless for us submariners to come out on strike. In our closed city everybody lives just the same way I do. We survive because we help each other to survive. We are constantly borrowing and reborrowing food and money from each other."

"If somebody's relatives send them a food parcel, that family will immediately organise a feast," Larisa tells me. "We have a visiting circle. We get fattened up. That's how we live."

"Do your parents send you parcels from Ukraine?"

"Yes, of course. And then we feed all our equally hungry friends."

She laughs loudly.

As one of our writers put it, you could make nails out of these people.

It is a curious fact that the years are passing – a great deal of time already separates us from the fall of the Communist Party – yet certain habits from the past remain untouched. Foremost among them is a pathological lack of respect for people, especially those who, in spite of everything, work devotedly and selflessly, who truly love the cause they are serving. The government has never learned how to say thank you to people who are dedicated to serving our country. You are working hard? Well, great, carry right on until you snuff it or we break your heart. The authorities become more brazen by the day, crushing the will of the very best of our citizens.

With the single-mindedness of a maniac, they stake their money on the worst.

There is no doubt that Communism was a dead loss for Russia, but what we have today is even worse.

I continue my discussion of lofty matters with Captain Dikiy at the central control point of the *Vilyuchinsk*. Rybachie is completely closed to outsiders and the inquisitive, and even officers' wives are not allowed access to the classified piers. For me, however, Military Intelligence has unexpectedly made an exception.

The predatory, combative ethos of the *Vilyuchinsk* is evident already from the shore. On the bow, on a black background, is a daunting piece of artwork: a grinning killer whale's head. The naval artist in his desire to make the monster as intimidating as possible has given it a good many more teeth than are likely to be encountered in nature. The whale's depiction there is not random. From the day it was built, the submarine was called *Kasatka*, "Killer Whale", and it was renamed only recently. Quite why is a puzzle to the officers, but they have no problem with it.

My introductory tour provides me with an extremely important insight, which is probably why I was allowed on to the submarine in the first place. I wander past the mouth of a terrifying volcano – God forbid it should ever be stoked up the wrong way. An atomic reactor plus nuclear missiles is an explosive mixture. The submarine is packed with nuclear weapons, the economy is in crisis, and the armed forces are in a state of disarray. What could be more scary than that?

As we continue the tour, Dikiy hammers his views home, and in ideological matters he is really quite pedantic. There can be no compromises in the armed forces, no matter what changes are taking place in society. He categorically rejects the notion of a right to disobey a "criminal order", an idea that has been circulating stubbornly through Army units since 1991. His view is that giving an inch, allowing a subordinate to fail to carry out even a single instruction or order because he considers it foolish or inappropriate, will cause the whole system to fall apart in a domino effect. The Army is a pyramidal structure, and you cannot take that risk.

I see that both Captain Dikiy and the others who join in our conversation, all of them serving officers whose uniforms are decorated with ribbons for heroic submarine campaigns lasting many months, discriminate between two concepts. There is the Motherland, which they serve, and there is Moscow, with which they are in a state of conflict. There are, they say, two separate states: Russia and her capital city.

The officers are frank. Viewed from Kamchatka, nothing of

what goes on in the Department of the Armed Forces makes any sense. Why does the Ministry of Defence obstinately refuse to pay for the maintenance of the nuclear submarine fleet, when it knows full well that it is not only impossible but indeed categorically forbidden for them to undertake such work locally using their own resources? Why do they mercilessly write off ten- to fourteen-year-old vessels which still have many years of life in them? Why, in fact, are they systematically turning their nuclear shield, created by the efforts of the entire nation, into a leaky old sieve? And at a time when a real threat exists, primarily in the form of large numbers of Chinese nuclear submarines constantly lurking adjacent to Russia's territory?

Also present on my exploration of the *Vilyuchinsk* is the most important person in the region, Valerii Dorogin, Vice Admiral of Kamchatka and commander of the North-East Group of Troops and Forces. Shortly afterwards Dorogin is to end his military career to become a Deputy of the State Duma. The officers speak frankly in his presence, in no way inhibited by his seniority. One feels none of the hierarchical pressure or barriers of rank which are usual in a military setting.

In large measure this is because Dorogin is flesh of the flesh of Rybachie. There is nothing the officers and commander are going to conceal from each other. Dorogin has served here, in this closed naval township, for almost 20 years. For a long time he was, like Dikiy, commander of a nuclear submarine. Now his elder son, Denis Dorogin, is serving in Rybachie. Just like everyone else, the commander walks to the pier in the morning. Like everyone else he observes the disintegration. Like everyone else he is here without any means of subsistence, waiting for friends to "fatten him up".

The North-East Group, the agglomeration to which Kamchatka belongs together with Chukotka and Magadan Provinces, has been set up again as a result of the swingeing cutbacks. A similar grouping existed before the 1917 Revolution and under the Bolsheviks in the 1930s.

In any grouping one category of troops inevitably dominates. In Kamchatka, home of the nuclear shield, it is predictably the submarines, and this is why a vice admiral is in command. Accordingly, he has under him infantry and coastal troops, aviation and anti-aircraft defence forces. At first there was a certain amount of contention and dissent, but then everything settled down. To a large extent this was due to Dorogin's influence. He is a legend on Kamchatka.

The vice admiral has spent 33 years in the Navy. His total service record is 48 years because of his time in the submarines. However, the legend of Dorogin is based not on his military past but on the present. He lives in Petropavlovsk-Kamchatsky. Until recently his monthly salary as the military man responsible for an enormous territory and second in rank only to the governors of three major Russian provinces was 3,600 roubles, or just over 100 dollars.

In reality, as we say in Russia, along with his pension, which he paid up long ago, he receives just under 5,000 roubles a month. By way of a comparison, a city bus driver in Petropavlovsk-Kamchatsky earns 6,000 roubles a month.

Dorogin lives in a military apartment on Morskaya Street, in exactly the same conditions as the other officers. There is no hot water, and it is cold, draughty and uncomfortable.

"Why don't you just buy a basic boiler?"

"We don't have the money. If we get some we'll buy one."

The thing Dorogin values most is his reputation. His life is ascetic. The apartment is not bare, but there is no way it befits an admiral. His most precious possessions are concentrated in his study. These are nautical knick-knacks from decommissioned ships which once served in the Russian Far East. His great love is naval history.

"What about your house in the country? You must have a dacha. Every admiral in Russia has one."

"I do, certainly," Dorogin replies. "And what a dacha. Oh, dear! We'll go and take a look at it tomorrow, otherwise you won't believe it."

Tomorrow arrives and I see a patch of land planted with potatoes and cucumbers on the outskirts of Petropavlovsk-Kamchatsky. These vegetables will feed the vice admiral's family over the winter. A decommissioned iron railway carriage stands on bricks in the midst of the vegetable garden: a place to work. If we compare it with Moscow expectations about the living standards of a military commander, it is a complete disgrace.

Kamchatka, as we have seen, is not Moscow. Everything here is more straightforward and more good-hearted. Some fishermen present me with a sack of red fish they have just caught, silversides. I give the fish to Galina, the vice admiral's wife, feeling a bit awkward because I am sure the wife of the Commander-in-Chief of Kamchatka must have tons of such fish brought to her door, but I simply have no way of cooking them myself.

To my great surprise, Galina thanks me effusively and bursts into tears. In her poverty she sees these fish as great good fortune. She cooks dinner and is able to invite guests, even to pickle fish for the future. To crown it all, by luck some of the fish have gold inside them: red caviar.

Galina Dorogina tells me that although the wives of the senior officers have lived all their lives on the peninsula, they have seen very little of exotic Kamchatka. "Our lives have passed in training courses and campaigns, brief reunions and long partings," she says.

For all that, Galina has no regret, not even for what have in effect been wasted years. "The truth of the matter is that nothing has changed much for the officers' wives. If 20 years ago we were cold and hungry and I had to queue all day for a dozen eggs and they wrote my number in the queue on my hand, the only difference now is that we have absolutely no money. There are eggs in the shops, but the officers have no money to buy them with."

Vice Admiral Dorogin's thinking is an ideological mishmash, an amalgam of Communist and capitalist notions. This probably is to be expected from a man who spent almost all his life under the Soviet regime, was a member of the Young Communist League and the Communist Party, and now has to live with the realities of the free market. From my point of view, his ideas are outmoded; they are stale ideology which lost its validity with the demise of the USSR. Against that, the vice admiral fully understands democratic aspirations and why they are needed.

Towards which of these ideological poles is his heart really drawn, and in which of these dimensions does he really feel at home? It is not easy to tell, but I decide to try.

Dorogin is answerable for everything in Kamchatka, from the submarines to the state of the military museum. Here is just one episode from his life.

Among the units of the North-East Group is 22 Chapaev Motorised Division. It bears that name because it is the same division as was formed in the Volga region in 1918 by Vasily Chapaev, a legendary hero of the Civil War. It was here that his girlfriend, Bolshevik Anka, who figures in hundreds of questionable Soviet jokes, was a fighter.

After the Second World War, the Chapaev division was redeployed to the Far East, and today it is famous in Kamchatka for the fact that its first company retains a soldier's bed for Vladimir Ilyich Lenin, leader of the world proletariat. In 1922 Lenin was made an honorary Red Army soldier in the division and the bed was accordingly allocated. Since 1922, wherever the division has been sent, it has been a tradition to transport Lenin's bed along with the other equipment. Even today the bed enjoys a prominent position in the barracks. It is neatly made up, and the walls around comprise a Lenin Corner with drawings on the topic of "Volodya was a good student!" All these items are registered in a logbook kept in a secret location in the division.

The commander of the First Lenin Company, Captain Igor Shapoval, 26, considers that the spirit of Lenin keeps his soldiers up to scratch.

"Are you serious?"

"Yes. They see this neatly made bed and try to emulate it."

I find this laughable, but then I find that Vice Admiral Dorogin believes no less than Captain Shapoval in the lofty ideological role of Lenin's bed.

"New recruits find it a bit odd at first, but they come to respect it," Dorogin says. "When democracy triumphed in Moscow, there were attempts to get rid of Lenin's bed in Kamchatka, but we managed to save it. It's hardly in the same category as your monument to Dzerzhinsky at the Lubyanka."

Dorogin does not believe in change for its own sake. History is what it is, and you didn't need to be all that clever to demolish a monument to the founder of the Bolsheviks' secret police. He also considers that since the Lenin Corner was established in the Chapaev division by a special resolution of the Council of People's Commissars, at the very least it would require a directive from the government of Russia, signed by the Prime Minister, for the bed to be dispatched to the scrap heap.

We talk about which example soldiers in Kamchatka should now be invited to follow. The present commander of the division, Lieutenant-Colonel Valerii Oleynikov, says unambiguously, "The example of those who fought in Chechnya and Afghanistan."

The previous commander of the First Lenin Company had indeed fought in Chechnya. Lieutenant Yury Buchnev received the award of Hero of Russia for fighting in Grozny. We continue this discussion about example, and I suggest that educating soldiers on the example of what is going on in Chechnya can hardly be a good idea. Dorogin keeps out of the discussion, which, as a senior officer, he should. He is serving his country, and as a matter of principle his political views should be of no concern to anyone. But about the future he is entirely willing to speculate. Ideology is one thing, the Army cutbacks are quite another. The officers feel they are sitting on a powder keg.

"We are half expecting that at any moment the State will give a very raw deal to those who have served it loyally," comments Alexander Shevchenko, the division's chief of staff. The other officers, including Dorogin, agree. None of those likely to be retired have civilian qualifications commensurate with their rank and status in the services, and of course they will have nowhere to live. If they have to leave the armed forces, they will lose their homes, because at present all of them are living in military flats. Igor Shapoval is an engineer who maintains military vehicles. He is skilled in the cold working of metals, so when he ceases to be an officer he can look forward to a career repairing tractors, or serving the civilian population in a key-cutting kiosk. Shevchenko already has experience of civilian employment. For two of the three years he studied in Moscow at the Artillery Academy, he earned money on the side as a watchman in a florist's basement, covering the 24 hours jointly with three other student officers.

The view in Kamchatka is that the Ministry of Defence does not agree that in principle an officer should dedicate himself only to his military duties and not fritter away his time by working on the side.

"With things the way they are, it is only too easy to draw a man into illegal activity," says the vice admiral. "I myself have been offered 2,000 dollars in an envelope. This was by someone who was directed to me by a friend. He offered the bribe in a very respectable way: 'You need money for medical treatment for you, wife.' At that moment he was absolutely right. The condition was that I should approve a contract for the sale of scrap brass on terms unfavourable to the Army, not at 700 dollars a ton but at 450. Actually, my signature was the last in a series of signatures of senior military figures. I could simply have thrown the man with the envelope out, but I called in the prosecutor. I thought it might be an example to others."

Of course, Dorogin is in many ways a saintly man. Like many other officers he is serving his country not for money but from a sense of duty. Only here, at the furthest reach of our land, are such spiritually healthy people to be found.

How long the patience of Dikiy, Dorogin and others will hold out nobody knows, not even they themselves. Today's Navy is dependent on the older and middle generations of naval officers. There are almost no young ones. They don't come out here. The few who do are not willing to resign themselves to the idea that they should devote all their strength to the Navy and receive nothing in return. What kind of officers will the Navy have left in a few more years?

"Patriotism?" A young captain second class from Rybachie smiles wryly. He is an officer on the submarine *Omsk*. "Patriotism is something you have to pay for. It is time to put an end to this nonsense, this playing at being paupers. We need to get back on our feet, not limp through life like Dikiy. He is a commander, yet he always has cheap trainers on his feet and drinks cheap brandy. The way the fleet is being treated is out of order, and the only way to respond is by making up your own rules."

"What do you mean by that?"

By "making up your own rules" the young officer means making a living by fair means or foul. He says that all the officers of his age are quietly trading whatever they can get their hands on from under the counter.

"I get fish and caviar brought to my home now," he says proudly. "Two years ago I was bartering spirits I'd stolen from the ship, and people had no respect for me then."

"For the young officers a good standard of living is beginning to be the main reason for being in the Navy," mourns Vice Admiral Dorogin. In his opinion any thought of responding to State neglect by "making up your own rules" is just as fatal for anybody in the service as questioning a commanding officer's orders.

Old Ladies and New Russians

Two old ladies, Maria Savina, a former champion milkmaid, and Zinaida Fenoshina, a former equally champion cowherd, stand in the middle of the forest, angrily shaking upraised sticks in the direction of a bulldozer. It is roaring away at full throttle, and they are shouting as loudly as they can for all to hear: "Be off! Away with you! How much longer must we put up with this sort of thing?"

From behind ancient trees, surly security guards appear and surround them as if to say, "Leave now while you still can, or we shoot."

Nikolai Abramov – a retired vet, the village elder and the organiser of the demonstration – spreads his arms. "They want to drive us off our own land. We shall defend it to the death. What else is left?"

The theatre of operations is on the outskirts of the village of Pervomaiskoe in the Narofomin District of Moscow Province. The epicentre is the grounds of an old estate formerly owned by the Berg family. It dates from 1904 and is today protected by the State as a natural and cultural heritage site.

When they have calmed down a little, the old people shake their heads sadly. "There, in our old age we've joined the Greens. What else can we do? There's only us to defend our park from this scum. Nobody else is going to."

The scum are New Russians who have hired soulless barbarian developers to erect 34 houses right in the middle of the century-old

Berg Park. Maria and Zinaida are members of a special ecological group created by the village assembly of Pervomaiskoe to organise direct action against the despoilers of the environment.

Paying little attention to the Green activists, the trucks continue to drive and the tractors to roar among the precious ancient trees. After an hour's work they have cut a swath through the woodlands. This is to be the central "avenue" of the future cottage settlement. Pipes, reinforcement wire and concrete slabs lie all over the place. The building work is in full swing and really is being carried out as if to maximise damage to the natural environment. Already 130 cubic metres of timber have been taken as rare species were felled. Wherever you look there are notches on cedars and firs, marking them for slaughter. The machinery brazenly wrecks the environment, churning up layers of clay from the depths and pitilessly burying deep beneath it the ecosystem of the forest floor which has formed over the years.

"Have you heard of the Weymouth Pine?" Tatyana Dudenus asks. She is head of the ecological group and a research associate at one of the region's medical institutes. "We had five specimens growing in the grounds of our heritage park. They were the only ones in the whole of Moscow Province. The Bergs made a hobby of propagating rare tree species. Three of these Weymouth Pines have now been sawn down for no better reason than that the developers wanted to run a street for their new estate just where they were growing. Other precious species are under threat: the Siberian Silver Fir and Larch, the White Poplar, a White Cedar, *Thuja occidentalis*, the only specimen in Moscow Province. In just the last three days we have lost more than 60 trees. It wouldn't be so bad if they were destroying the less outstanding or sickly specimens, but they have quite a different approach. They decide where they want to construct a road and cut down anything that's in the way. They decide where they want to put up a cottage and clear the site, taking no account of the rarity of the trees they are destroying. The forest here is legally classified as Grade One, which means it is against the law to touch these trees. In order to obtain permission to fell them you have to demonstrate 'exceptional circumstances' and support your application with a recommendation from the State Ecological Inspectorate. For every such hectare you need the express permission of the Federal government."

When the fate of Berg Park was being decided, none of this was done. The Pervomaiskoe Greens lodged writs with the Narofomin court to bring the brazen nouveaux riches into line. They petitioned Judge Yelena Golubeva, who had been assigned the case, for an injunction to halt the building work until the hearing, since otherwise, after the trees had been felled, a verdict in their favour would be of little use.

However, as we have seen, this is the age of the oligarchs in Russia. Every branch of government understands only the language of their rustling banknotes. Judge Golubeva did not even consider granting an injunction to halt the construction work and, when it was already in progress, deliberately failed to conduct a hearing.

Nearly all those unique trees were felled.

Valerii Kulakovsky emerges from the posse of guards. He is the deputy director of the Promzhilstroy Company, which calls itself a cooperative of home builders. Kulakovsky advises me to stay out of this. He says some extremely influential people in Moscow have an interest in the estate: they are going to live here. This is soon confirmed. I discover that the "cooperative" has managed to acquire property rights over the Berg hectares, which according to the law are the property of the nation. This is totally illegal.

Kulakovsky just shrugs and tries to explain his own position. "We are very tired of these endless demonstrations by the villagers. What do you expect me to do now, when I have put so much money into this, bought the land, started building? Who do you think is going to give it all back to me?"

He also says they have no plans to back down.

They did not back down. Berg Park ceased to exist. The felling of our finest forests in the interests of the oligarchs and their companies is going on throughout the land.

Not long before the Green old ladies of Pervomaiskoe mounted the desperate defence of their ancient park, the Supreme Court of Russia considered the same matter of principle as it applied to Russia as a whole. The case was known as the "Forest Issue".

"Bear in mind the interests of the property owners. They have acquired the land, built the houses, and now you want to turn everything back." The lawyer in the Supreme Court repeated what Kulakovsky had said almost word for word.

The ecologist lawyers Olga Alexeeva and Vera Mishchenko, who were defending the interests of society as a whole against the caprices of New Russians, had a different take on the matter: "Every citizen of this country has the right to life and enjoyment of the national heritage. If we are truly citizens of Russia, then it is our duty to ensure that future generations receive no less a national heritage than today's generations enjoy. In any case, how can we take seriously property rights which have been acquired illegally?"

The essence of the "Forest Issue" was that Russian ecologists, under the leadership of the Moscow Institute of Ecological Legal Issues, Eco-Juris, which brought the case, demanded the repeal of twenty-two orders of the Cabinet of Ministers transferring Grade One forests to the category of non-afforested land. This permitted the felling of more than 34,000 hectares of prime forest in Russia.

Russia's forests are divided into three categories. Grade One relates to those deemed particularly important either for society or for the natural environment. These are forests containing highly valued species, habitats of rare birds and animals, reservations and parks, and urban and suburban Green Belts.

The Forestry Code of the Russian Federation accordingly recognises Grade One forests as part of the national heritage. Berg Park came into this category.

The formal applicant for this change of categories and subsequent right to fell trees was, oddly enough, the Forestry Commission of the Russian Federation, Rosleskhoz. It is the body which has the right to submit documents relating to the legal status of forests for signature by the Prime Minister. The 22 orders disputed by the ecologists had been made without the statutory State ecological inspection, with the result that the national heritage became the prey of short-term interests. Where forests were cut down they were replaced by petrol stations, garages, industrial estates, local wholesale markets, domestic waste dumps and, of course, housing estates.

The ecologists consider this last option to be the least objectionable, but only providing the new house owners behave responsibly towards the magnificent forests surrounding their houses and do not destroy their roots in the course of laying drainage systems.

While the "Forest Issue" was being considered and the judges were taking their time, almost another 950 hectares of top-quality forests were condemned to destruction under new orders signed by the Prime Minister. The greatest damage was done in the Khanty-Mansiisk and Yamalo-Nenetsk autonomous regions, where trees were destroyed for the benefit of oil and gas companies. Moscow Province also suffered: what happened to Berg Park was the result of deliberate judicial procrastination.

While the paperwork was being taken care of and nobody had the courage to dot the legal "i"s or cross the legal "t"s, the struggle for the forest in Pervomaiskoe became violent. When, at the request of the prosecutor's office, the ecological group went to record the barbaric results of the developers' activities with a videocamera, police reinforcements were brought in. A fight broke out, the camera was broken and the ecologists, all of them elderly people, were beaten up.

"Of course, we do not want to wage a war, but we have been left with no option," Nikolai Abramov, the village elder, says by way of explanation. "The estate was the last place in the village where we could go to walk. There were usually old people and mothers with prams there. There is a school for 300 pupils and a kindergarten in the grounds. All the rest has been developed with cottages for the New Russians."

The veteran ecologists are aware that they are at war primarily with the super-rich, people who command amounts of money the like of which they themselves have never seen. They have heard it talk, however. At a village assembly, Alexander Zakharov, chairman of the Pervomaiskoe Rural District Council, openly declared that the sums of money involved were too great for there to be any possibility of reversing the situation. Here is what Igor Kulikov, chairman of the Ecological Union of Moscow Province, wrote to the provincial prosecutor, Mikhail Avdyukov: "The chairman of the council publicly stated to members of the ecological group elected by the assembly that he had given their names and addresses to the Mafia, which would deal with them if they did not stop their protests."

Alexander Zakharov is undoubtedly one of the central characters in this unseemly tale. If he had stood firm, not one dacha would have encroached on the grounds of the Berg Park. At the foot of the documents which ultimately permitted the felling of the Pervomaiskoe trees, in contravention of the law and against the resolution of the village assembly, is Zakharov's signature.

The scenario is a familiar one. First application is made to the upper echelons in Moscow for the "transfer of Grade One forests to the category of non-afforested land". A short time later, an order is drafted for signature by the Prime Minister. The felling of the forest ensues when, implementing the Prime Minister's order, the local forestry officials and the head of the district council give the go-ahead.

There is not much wrong with our laws in Russia. It is just that not many people want to obey them.

NORD-OST: THE LATEST
TALE OF DESTRUCTION

Moscow, February 8, 2003. No. 1 Dubrovskaya Street, now known to the whole world as Dubrovka. In a packed theatre whose image – just three months ago – was flashed to all the world's newspapers, magazines and television stations, there is an exuberant gala atmosphere. Black tie, evening dress, the whole of the political *beau monde* has assembled here. Sighs and gasps, kisses and hugs, members of the government, members of the Duma, leaders of the parliamentary factions and parties, a sumptuous buffet . . .

They are celebrating a conclusive victory over international terrorism in our capital city. The pro-Putin politicians assure us that the revival of the musical *Nord-Ost* on the ruins of terrorism is nothing less than that. Today will see the first performance since October 23, 2002, when the unguarded theatre, its actors and audience were seized during the evening performance and held hostage for 57 hours by several dozen terrorists from Chechnya. They hoped to force President Putin to put an end to the Second Chechen War and withdraw his troops from their republic.

They didn't succeed. Nobody withdrew from anywhere. The war continues as before, with no time for doubts about the legitimacy of its methods. All that changed was that in the early morning of October 26 a gas attack was mounted against all those present in the building, some 800 people, both terrorists and hostages. The secret military gas was chosen by the President personally. The gas attack was followed by a storming of the building by special anti-terrorist units in the course of which every one of the hostage-takers was killed, along with almost 200 hostages. Many people died without medical attention, and the identity of the gas was kept secret even from the doctors charged with the saving of lives. Already on that evening the President was announcing without a qualm that this was a victory for Russia over "the forces of international terrorism".

The victims of this murderous rescue operation were barely remembered at the gala performance on February 8. It was a typical fashionable Moscow get-together at which many seemed to forget what it was they were raising their glasses to. They sang, they danced, they ate, a lot of people got drunk, and everyone talked a lot of nonsense, which seemed all the more cynical because the event was taking place at the scene of a massacre, even if it had been refurbished in record time. The family members of those who had died in the *Nord-Ost* tragedy refused categorically to come to the celebration, considering it a sacrilege. The President was also unable to attend but sent a message of congratulation.

Why did he send congratulations? Because nobody could break us. His message was couched in typically Soviet rhetoric and proceeded from typically Stalinist values: it was a shame about the people who died, of course, but the interests of society must come first. The producers warmly thanked the President for his understanding of their commercial problems and said that audiences would be in for a treat if they came back. The musical had received a "new creative impetus".

But now: the reverse side of the medal, the individuals at the cost of whose lives the President consolidated his membership of the international anti-terrorist coalition. Let us look at those whose lives were not given a creative impetus by the *Nord-Ost* events but crushed by them. Let us look at the victims about whom today's

State machine is trying to forget as quickly as possible, and to induce the rest of us to do the same by every means at its disposal. Let us look at the ethnic purging which followed the act of terrorism, and at the new State ideology Putin has enunciated: "We shall not count the cost. Let nobody doubt that. Even if the cost is very high."

The Fifth One

Yaroslav Fadeev, a boy from Moscow, is now the first named in the official master list of those killed during the *Nord-Ost* assault. The official version of events insists that the four hostages who died from bullet wounds were shot by terrorists and that the special unit of the FSB, Putin's own service, does not make mistakes and hence did not shoot any of the hostages.

There is, however, no escaping the fact that a bullet passed through Yaroslav's head, although his name is not on the list of the "four shot by the terrorists". Yaroslav was the fifth to die from a bullet wound. In the "Cause of Death" column on the official form that was issued to his mother, Irina, for the funeral, there is a dash.

On November 18, 2002 Yaroslav, who was in the tenth grade of a Moscow school, would have been 16. There was to have been a big family celebration, but standing over the coffin of the now eternally 15-year-old boy his grandfather, a Moscow doctor, remarked, "There now, we didn't get to shave together even once."

Four of them had gone to the musical: two sisters, Irina Fadeeva and Victoria Kruglikova, and their children, Yaroslav and Nastya. Irina was Yaroslav's mother, and Victoria was the mother of 19-year-old Nastya. Irina, Victoria and Nastya survived but Yaroslav died in circumstances which have never been legally investigated.

After the assault and the gas attack Irina, Victoria and Nastya were carried out of the theatre unconscious and taken to hospital.

Yaroslav completely disappeared. He was not on any of the interim lists. There was a total absence of precise official information. The telephone hotline announced by the authorities on radio and television was not functioning. Relatives of the hostages were rushing all over Moscow, and among them were friends of this family. They combed the city, dividing its mortuaries and hospitals into sectors to be checked.

Finally, in the Kholzunov Lane Mortuary they found Body No. 5714 which fitted Yaroslav's description, but they could not confirm it really was him. In his pocket they found a passport in the name of his mother, Irina Vladimirovna Fadeeva, but the page for "Children" contained the entry: "Male. Yaroslav Olegovich Fadeev, 18.11.1988". The real Yaroslav, however, had been born in 1986.

As Irina explained later, "I put my passport in my son's trouser pocket. He did not have any identification documents on him. Since he was very tall, looking to be about 18, I was so afraid that if the Chechens suddenly started releasing children and adolescents, Yaroslav might not be included because of his height. So, right there in the hall, I crouched under the seats and wrote Yaroslav's data into my own passport, changing the year of his birth to make him seem younger."

Sergey, Irina's friend, came to see her in hospital on October 27 and told her that Body No. 5714 had been found. He told her about the passport in the trousers and about the resemblance to Yaroslav. In spite of the frost, Irina ran out of the hospital, straight through a gap in the fence, just in what she was wearing.

The hostages who had survived and been taken to hospitals were still being held hostage there. By order of the intelligence services they were forbidden to return home. They were not allowed to telephone or be visited by their families. Sergey had got into the hospital by bribing everyone he encountered: the nurses, the guards, the orderlies, the police. Our total corruption prises open even the most firmly battened-down hatches.

Irina ran from the hospital straight to the mortuary. There she was shown a photograph on a computer monitor and identified Yaroslav. She asked to see his body, felt carefully all over it and discovered two bullet wounds in the head, an entry and an exit hole. Both had been filled up with wax. Sergey, who was with her, was surprised at how calm she seemed. She didn't sob or have hysterics. She was logical and unemotional.

"I really was very glad that I had found him at last," Irina tells me. "Lying in the hospital, I had already thought everything through and considered my options. I had decided how I would behave if my son was dead. In the mortuary when I saw that this really was Yaroslav and that my life was therefore at an end, I simply did what I had decided on earlier. I calmly asked everyone to leave the hall to which his body had been brought from the refrigerator. I said I wanted to be alone with my son. I had decided I would say that. You see, before he died I had made him a promise. When we were stuck there he said to me at the end of the last day, during the night, a few hours before the gas, 'Mum, I probably won't make it. I can't take much more. Mum, if something happens, what will it be like?' I told him, 'Don't be afraid of anything. We have always been together here, and we will always be together there.' He said, 'Mum, how will I know you there?' I told him, 'Your hand is always in mine, so we'll find ourselves there together, holding hands. We won't lose each other. Just don't let go of my hand, hold on tight.' But see how it turned out. I felt I had deceived him. We were never far from one another while he was alive. Never. That is why I was so calm: we were together in life, and over there, in death, we would still be together. Anyway, when I was alone with him in the mortuary, I told him, 'There now, don't worry. I have found you and I'm coming to be with you' . . . I had never deceived him . . . That is why I was so calm. I went through the side door in order not to see the friends who were waiting for me and asked the assistants to let me out through the service entrance. When I got outside I flagged down a passing car, went to the nearest bridge over the Moscow river and jumped off it. I did not drown, though. There were ice floes in the river, and I fell among them. I can't swim, but I didn't sink. I could see I wasn't sinking and thought, 'Well, I may at least get cramp in my leg,' but that didn't happen either. As ill luck would have it, some people pulled me out. They asked, 'Where are you from? What are you doing swimming?' I told them, 'I've just come from the mortuary, but please don't report me.' I gave them a telephone number to ring, and Sergey came to collect me. Of course, I'm doing my best to cope, but I am dead. I don't know how he is getting on there without me."

When she regained consciousness in the hospital on October 26, Irina found she was completely naked under the blanket. The other women hostages around her all had their clothes, but she had only a small icon clutched in her hand. When she could talk she asked the nurses to give her back at least some of her clothing, but they explained that everything she had been wearing when she was brought in from the theatre had been destroyed on orders from officers of the intelligence services because it was soaked in blood.

But why? And whose blood was it? Irina had passed out in the theatre clasping her son in her arms. The person whose blood it was must have been shot in a way that caused it to gush over her. It could only have been Yaroslav's.

"That last night got off to a very tense start," Irina recalls. "The terrorists were nervous, but then 'Mozart', as we called him, Movsar Baraev, the ringleader, announced that we could take it easy until 11 a.m. A ray of hope had appeared. The Chechens began throwing juice out to us. They did not allow us to get out of our seats. If you needed anything you had to put up your hand and then they would throw you some juice or water. When the government assault began and we saw the terrorists running up on to the stage, I said to my sister, 'Cover Nastya with your jacket,' and I put my arms tightly round Yaroslav. I didn't realise they had released gas, I just saw the terrorists becoming agitated. Yaroslav was taller than me, so that really he was shielding me when I held him. Then I passed out. In the mortuary I saw that the entry wound was on the side away from me. I had been shielded by him . . . He saved me, although my one wish in those 57 hours as a hostage had been to keep him safe."

But whose bullet was it? Was a ballistics test conducted? Was a blood sample taken from the clothing to establish whose it was?

Nobody in the family knows the answers to these questions. All information relating to the case is strictly classified, kept secret even from a mother. In the mortuary register the cause of death was given as "bullet wound", but the entry had been made in pencil. This book too was later classified: "They'll have rubbed it out, of course," the family says with certainty.

"At first I thought it had been done by one of the Chechen women," Irina relates. "While we were stuck in there she was nearby all the time. She saw that whenever there was any danger, any noise or shouting, I would grab my son and hold him tight. It was my own fault that I attracted her attention . . . It seemed to me she was watching us all the time. At one point she said, staring at Yaroslav, 'My son is back there' – in Chechnya, that is. Nothing bad happened to us after that, but I felt she was watching us all the time wherever she was. So perhaps she had shot Yaroslav. I still can't sleep. I see her eyes in front of me, the narrow strip of her face."

Irina's friends later explained to her that the size of the entry wound on Yaroslav's body indicated the bullet was not from a pistol, and the Chechen women only had pistols.

So the question remains: Whose bullet was it?

"It must have been our people," Irina says. "Of course, we were sitting in a very unfortunate position, right by the doors. Anyone who came in was right there at row 11. When the terrorists burst into the auditorium we were the first people they saw, so of course when our soldiers came in we would have been directly in front of them too."

Irina can analyse what happened and how as much as she likes. What she thinks or imagines is of no concern to the authorities. The State's line is that four people were shot, and no-one else. Yaroslav, the fifth person, falls outside the official version of events. Indeed, Yaroslav is not even officially included among the victims in Criminal Case No. 229133 being investigated by a team from the Moscow City prosecutor's office.

"It really hurts me that . . . the authorities are pretending there never was any such person," Irina muses.

Worse, however, is that as soon as Irina shared her questions and conclusions with journalists, she was summoned to the prosecutor's office. The investigator was angry. "What are you kicking up all this fuss about? Do you not understand it is impossible that he had a bullet wound?" He went on to do his best to scare the wits out of the unhappy mother, who was already in a parlous state: "Either you immediately write a statement to the effect that you told those journalists nothing and that they thought everything up themselves, whereupon we shall bring criminal charges against them for slandering the intelligence services, or we dig up your son's grave without your consent and carry out a post-mortem examination!"[10]

Irina did not give in to this wretched attempt at blackmail. Instead, she took her leave after a four-hour grilling in the prosecutor's office and went straight to the cemetery to guard her son's grave. It was late November, which in Moscow is the depths of winter. Again she was saved from death by friends who looked all over the city when she did not return home that night.

Yaroslav was considered a quiet, studious boy. He graduated from music school while others of his age were running wild in the streets swilling beer and exercising their swearing muscles. He suffered a great deal because of this. He wanted to be "tough", to be assertive, bold and unflinching.

He kept a diary, as most of us do at his age. Irina read it after the *Nord-Ost* events. He wondered which aspects of his own personality he could say he liked and which he disliked. He wrote: "I hate it that I am such a coward, scared of everything and indecisive." "And what would you like to bring out in yourself?" the diary asked. "I would like to be tough." He had school friends, but these were not boys who were considered tough or whom girls fancied. At home he had a sense of humour, could show what he was made of, and be bold and assertive. It was outside that the problems began.

Irina is terribly saddened by the things she never said to Yaroslav and by the fact she never properly told him how much she admired him.

"People consider me, for example, a strong person," Victoria, Yaroslav's aunt, tells me. "But in there I was completely distraught. There we three women were sitting next to him, the youngest of us, and it was he who encouraged us, like a grown man. My daughter's nerves went completely. She was shaking and sobbing, 'Mama, I want to live. Mama, I don't want to die.' But he was calm and courageous. He reassured Nastya, he supported us, he tried to take everything on himself as a man is supposed to. For instance, one of the Chechen women saw we had put the children between us, trying to protect them . . . Irina and I thought that if there was an attack we would cover them with our bodies. Then the woman came up to us with a grenade in her hand. She touched Nastya's leg. I said, 'Would you mind going away?' but she looked at Nastya and said, 'Don't be afraid. If I am standing right next to you it won't hurt. You will die instantly, while those sitting further away will suffer more.' Then the Chechen woman went away, and Nastya said to me, 'Mum, ask her to stay with us, ask her. She said it wouldn't hurt us.' Nastya was broken. I knew perfectly well that if we had that Chechen woman standing next to us we really would be out of luck, but if she wasn't, there was at least some hope . . .

"Another time the terrorists were frightening us by saying that if nobody came to negotiate they would start shooting us, and that the first to be shot would be anyone in the police or the Army. Naturally, many people quickly threw away their military ID, but the terrorists picked them up and called out the names from the stage. Suddenly we heard, 'Victoria Vladimirovna, born 1960.' That was me. Only the surname was wrong . . . The situation was very bad. Nobody answered. The terrorists started going through people row by row. They came to me. Irina said, 'We'll go together.' The terrorists demanded that members of the law-enforcement agencies go off somewhere with them, and we all thought they were going to be shot. I told Irina that one of us needed to survive or our parents would be left completely alone . . . The terrorists found the Victoria Vladimirovna they were looking for, but while everything was still unclear Yaroslav came and sat beside me. He took my hand and said, 'Auntie Vicky, don't be frightened. If anything happens I'll come with you. Forgive me for everything. Forgive me.' I said to him, 'That's all right, everything is going to be fine.' . . . I don't know where he found so much courage. We thought he was just a child . . .

"It really was very scary. They let us listen to what was being said about us on the radio. That's how we knew the President was saying nothing, and that Zhirinovsky in typical hard-line fashion had said there was no point in the Duma wasting time on this terrorist act. It wasn't worth discussing because it was all just a hoax . . .

"After we had got through the first day we felt we could sit it out there for a week just so long as we could stay alive and the authorities could come up with a solution other than an assault on the theatre. We found it hard. It was difficult to maintain your composure. But Yaroslav took it."

Irina's life has changed completely. She isn't working now. She couldn't bear to go every day to the job she was doing before, when Yaroslav was alive. Her colleagues were a cheery bunch. They knew each other well and would celebrate every exam Yaroslav passed, every top grade he earned. She can't bear even to walk around Moscow, because she walked all the streets with her son and wherever she turns the memories flood back.

"Look, these are tickets for the overnight train to St Petersburg, for October 25–26, just when he died. We were going there to a tennis tournament, just the two of us. I had been wanting to go somewhere with him by train for a long time, because I always had the feeling that we didn't talk enough and in the train there would be just the two of us, and we would be able to have a heart-to-heart. It wasn't to be."

"Why do you say you felt you didn't talk enough?"

"I don't know . . . We did talk a lot, but all the same that is how it seemed. I wanted to talk and talk to him . . ."

Everybody around her is trying to help and support Irina. She is fortunate in having the love of those closest to her, but still it is hard. It was too much even for the priest she sought out in order to unburden her soul. When he had heard her story, he broke down. "Forgive me," he said, "it's just too painful."

"I went to ask the priest what I could do. It was I who had dragged Yaroslav to *Nord-Ost*. It was all my idea. He wasn't all that keen to go," Irina says. In photographs taken before the terrorist ordeal she is a beautiful, self-confident, very young woman, glowing with happiness, perhaps a little plump. Now she is shrunken and haggard, with a look of despair in her lacklustre eyes. She seems far from young in her perpetual black coat, black beret, black shoes and stockings, always shivering, keeping her coat on even inside.

"Yaroslav and I went to the theatre a great deal. That evening we had tickets for a completely different production in a different theatre," Irina continues. "We had already changed to go out.

Victoria and Nastya had come to collect us, and there, standing in the hallway, we realised the tickets were for the day before. Yaroslav was glad. He wanted to stay at home, but I insisted: 'Let's go to *Nord-Ost*, it's on nearby' . . . I dragged him along, and then I failed to protect him . . . The last thing he said to me was, 'Mum, I so much want to remember you, if anything happens . . .'"

"Did you talk a lot like that in there?"

"No. For some reason it happened that this was the last time we talked together. You know, while I still had Yaroslav I would get up in the mornings feeling I was the happiest woman in the world . . . Now I think you probably aren't allowed to be so happy . . . I brought Yaroslav to such a terrible end. The present I gave him for his 16th birthday was a fence for his grave."

"It is not you who did that to him."

"It's the war. There is a war being waged," Victoria says again and again. "And now we have become its victims."

No. 2251: Unidentified

Before I can tell you this story, there is something I need to explain. It is about the way we are living in Russia in the aftermath of the *Nord-Ost* events, and about the state of the Russian judicial system under Putin.

The fact of the matter is that our courts were never as independent as you might have thought from our Constitution. At the present time, however, the judicial system is cheerfully mutating into a condition of total subservience to the executive. It is reaching unprecedented levels of supine *pozvonochnost'*.

This word is used in Russia to refer to the phenomenon of a judge delivering a verdict in accordance with what has been dictated to him in the course of a phone call (*zvonok*) by representatives of the executive branch of the government. *Pozvonochnost'* is an everyday phenomenon in Russia.

"The victims of *Nord-Ost*" is how people now refer in Russia to the families who lost relatives during the assault, and also to hostages who were crippled as a result of the gas attack. These victims have begun to serve writs on the authorities demanding compensation for the moral harm inflicted on them and naming as defendant the municipal government of Moscow. The victims have claimed that the officials of the municipal government, not wishing to argue with Putin and the FSB, failed to organise timely medical assistance for the victims. The plaintiffs consider that the City of Moscow's culpability is the greater since Yury Luzhkov, Moscow's Mayor and Director of the city's executive authority, was one of the people who urged the President to use chemical weapons against Russian citizens.

The initial writs were served at the Tverskoy Intermunicipal Court of Moscow (a district court) in November 2002. By January 17, 2003, when the first three were being examined by Federal Judge Marina Gorbacheva to see whether there was a case to answer, the number had risen to 61. The compensation demanded totalled the rouble equivalent of 60 million dollars, with the plaintiffs stating that this was the price of a State lie. What they primarily wanted to know was the truth about why their relatives had died. This had proved impossible to obtain, because the FSB had classified anything connected with the October terrorist act as secret. Since Putin's own FSB was involved, the build-up to the court hearings took place amid a barrage of propaganda directed against the plaintiffs by the State media, who accused them of brazenly attempting to raid the country's coffers and of trying to profit from the death of their relatives. All the better-known lawyers of Moscow had chickened out of acting for the *Nord-Ost*ers because they feared the wrath of the Kremlin. Igor Trunov, who did agree to act for them, had buckets of ordure emptied over him by the press.

The authorities did their best to bulldoze their way out of the

Nord-Ost claims, using all the considerable PR machinery at their disposal, as if they were not the guilty ones themselves, but rather the aggrieved party.

On January 23, 2003, Judge Gorbacheva, true to form as a "telephone judge" and basing herself on a technicality, rejected the claims of the first three plaintiffs. The Federal law "The Struggle Against Terrorism" could be read in different ways, and there were contradictions between different provisions. One of these could be interpreted as meaning that the State was under no obligation to compensate victims of terrorist acts for any loss they suffered. In fact, the judge did a good deal more than merely reject the claims. She accompanied her rejection with a barrage of abuse as shameless as that of the authorities themselves, who had no doubt asked her to do so. The hearings developed into a succession of unforgivable insults and humiliations directed at the plaintiffs.

Here are some examples from the January 23 session.

"Karpov, sit down. I said, sit down!"

"But there's something I need to say . . ."

Judge Gorbacheva interrupts Sergey Karpov, plaintiff, in mid-sentence. He is the father of Alexander Karpov, a popular Moscow singer, poet and translator who was asphyxiated during the gas attack.

"Sit down, Karpov, or I shall have you removed. You missed your opportunity to make a written submission before the hearing."

"I didn't miss the opportunity. I was never notified."

"Well, I say you did. Sit down, or I shall have you removed."

"I wish to submit . . ."

"I am accepting nothing from you!"

The judge has a hysterical look. Her eyes are vacant, and she sounds like a street trader. While berating the plaintiffs she is cleaning the dirt out from under her fingernails. It is a disgusting sight. She continues her haranguing of Sergey Karpov: "Karpov, do not put your hand up again."

"I request that my rights be explained to me."

"You are going to have nothing explained to you."

The courtroom has not been swept for a long time. It is crammed. All the journalists have been forbidden to use dictaphones. Why, exactly? What State secrets are likely to be divulged? The souls of the victims are in torment. You are reluctant to talk to them because they immediately start crying. Relatives and friends have come to support them in case they are taken ill. The representative of the Russian Bench continues, however, to drown everything in her vulgarity.

"Khramtsova, V. I.; Khramtsova, I. F.; Khramtsov, T. I. Are you present? No?" The judge reels off the names with a total lack of courtesy.

"I am present," a tall, thin young man replies.

"Khramtsov! You may speak!" From the tone of her voice you would think she was saying, "Here is a rouble, my good fellow, and now be off with you!"

Alexander Khramtsov has lost his father, who played the trumpet in the *Nord-Ost* orchestra. He begins to speak but finds it difficult to hold back the tears.

"My father travelled the world with orchestras and to make personal appearances. He represented our country and this city everywhere. His death is an irretrievable loss. Are you completely unaware of that? It is you who let the terrorists in, you, the city administrators of Moscow. They strolled around unhindered. Of course the assault was not your responsibility, but why were 400 people taken to No. 13 Hospital when there were only 50 staff on duty there and they couldn't treat people promptly? People died before they received any attention. That is how my father died."

The lady in the judge's robes, presiding up there on the bench, appears to be miles away. She lazily shifts her papers from one place to another in order to kill time. She is weary and occasionally looks out of the window, adjusts her collar, checks her appearance in the dark glass. One of her earrings seems to be irritating her. She scratches her ear.

The son continues. He turns naturally to address the three defendants at a side table. These are the "representatives of Moscow", officers of the law departments of Moscow's government. Now the judge is checking her manicure.

"Why did you not at least allow medical students into the building if there was a shortage of doctors? Or on to the buses taking the hostages to hospital? They could have looked after our casualties on the way there. People were choking and dying because they were lying on their backs."

"Khramtsov!" Gorbacheva interrupts tetchily, noticing who the plaintiff is addressing. "Who are you looking at? You must address your remarks to me."

"Fine." Alexander turns his eyes back to the judge's bench. "They were choking on the buses. Choking!"

He is crying. Who could remain unmoved?

Sitting immediately behind the witness stand, Valentina Khramtsova, his widowed mother, is also weeping. She is dressed completely in black. Gorbacheva cannot fail to see her. Next to her is Olga Milovidova, her face hidden in a handkerchief, her shoulders like two sharp humps but nevertheless holding back her tears in order not to disturb the court. All the plaintiffs know they must not anger the judge, since then she could simply have the court cleared and they would have to stand outside for several trying hours. Olga is in the seventh month of pregnancy. Her 14-year-old daughter Nina died in the audience at *Nord-Ost*. Olga had bought the ticket for her. "Why do you keep trying to humiliate us?" shouts Tatyana Karpova, the late Alexander Karpov's mother, wife of Sergey. "How have we deserved that?" Danila Chernetsov, a Moscow student asphyxiated by the gas, was 21 years old and earning a little money in the evenings at *Nord-Ost* as an usher. His mother, Zoya Chernetsova, gets up and walks out of the courtroom. Outside the door she can be heard wailing. "I was looking forward to grandchildren," she cries. Her son's young pregnant widow had a miscarriage nine days after his funeral. "And now I have a court case where I'm insulted to my face."

There is such a lack of any decent legal tradition in this land of ours. We all know Judge Gorbacheva's situation. Those who employ her consider that they, rather than we taxpayers, are paying her salary. They could remove her and the privileges of her office, which are real enough and do make life easier for her than for an ordinary citizen on a low income. Let us suppose there really is nothing she can do other than reject every one of the unfortunate victims' demands.

But why does she have to be so rude? What need is there for all this derision, all these insults? Does she just enjoy kicking those who are already down? Who is Judge Gorbacheva anyway, standing so zealously in defence of the interests of Moscow's municipal exchequer?

Do you think anyone wrote in these terms in the State-controlled press or spoke in this way about the *Nord-Ost* hearings on State-controlled television? Some hope! Day after day the media informed citizens that the government supported Judge Gorbacheva in her defence of the interests of the State, which take priority over personal interests.

Such is our new Russian ideology, Putin's ideology. And there is no getting away from the truth that it was first tried out in Chechnya. It was precisely at the time of Putin's ascent of the Kremlin throne, to the din of the bombing at the beginning of the Second Chechen War, that Russian society first made a tragic and wholly immoral error because of its traditional unwillingness to think clearly. Our society ignored what was really going on in Chechnya, the fact that the bombing was not of terrorists' camps but of cities and villages, and that hundreds of innocent people were being killed. It was at that time that a majority of the people living in Chechnya felt, as they still feel, the complete and diabolical hopelessness of their situation. It was when, taking away their children, fathers and brothers to who knows where and for who knows what reason, the military and civilian authorities said baldly (and still say), "Stop whingeing. Just accept that this is what the higher interests of the war on terrorism require."

Russian society kept almost entirely quiet for three years. The vast majority tacitly condoned this behaviour in Chechnya and ignored those who predicted it would come back to haunt them, since a government which has got away with behaving like this in one part of the country would not stop there.

The *Nord-Ost* victims and the families of those who died are being abused in exactly the same way. "Stop whingeing," they are told. "This had to be done. Society's interests come before personal interests."

Well, perhaps the government is behaving a bit better, some 50,000–100,000 roubles better, towards them, since this time it has managed to squeeze enough out of itself to pay for the funerals at least.

What about the reaction of the Russian people? Not much sympathy has been forthcoming, sympathy as a politically significant impulse which the government could not afford to ignore. Quite the opposite, in fact. A depraved society wants comfort for itself and peace and quiet, and doesn't mind if the cost is other people's lives. People run away from the *Nord-Ost* tragedy and would rather believe the State's brainwashing machine than see the reality.

One hour after Alexander Khramtsov's damning speech, Judge Gorbacheva rattled off her verdict, finding in favour of the government of Moscow. The courtroom emptied, leaving behind only the victors: Yuri Bulgakov, a lawyer in the city's Revenue Department, and Andrey Rastorguev and Marat Gafurov, advisers in the legal department of the metropolitan authority.[12]

"Well, are you celebrating?" I couldn't help asking.

"No," all three replied sadly. "We are human after all. We can see what is going on. It is a disgrace that our State is treating these people in this way."

"Well, why don't you stop doing this disgraceful work?"

They were silent. We went out into the dark Moscow evening, some to warm homes filled with the laughter of their families, others to echoing flats left empty for ever on October 23. The last to leave was a stooping, grey-haired man with expressive eyes. Throughout the hearing he had sat with quiet dignity in the corner.

"What is your name?" I called after him.

"Tukai Khaziev."

"Were you a hostage yourself?"

"No. My son died there."

"Can we meet?"

Tukai Khaziev reluctantly gave me his telephone number.

"I don't know what my wife will make of this. You must understand, it is not something she has any wish to talk about. But you may ring in a week's time. I will talk to her."

The Khazievs, a Moscow family, have really been through a specifically Russian hell. They have not only lost their 27-year-old son Timur, a musician in the orchestra of *Nord-Ost*. They have been on the receiving end of that very ideology which is now so widespread and which, without exaggeration, was Timur's real killer.

"Would it have been so difficult for Putin to find at least some sort of a compromise with the Chechens, the terrorists?" Tukai Khaziev keeps repeating. "Who needed that 'indomitability' of his? Not us, that's for sure . . ."

Tukai is the one person in this house on Volgograd Prospekt in Moscow who can talk about the subject without crying. His wife, Roza, Tanya, Timur's young widow, and the 87-year-old grandmother cannot control their grief. Timur's three-year-old daughter, fair-haired Sonechka, ricochets around the grown-ups. Her daddy was not there to celebrate her third birthday because it came after *Nord-Ost*.

They set the table, and Sonechka climbs up on to a chair. She takes the biggest cup. "This is for Daddy. It's Daddy's cup. You mustn't use it!" she warns in tones that brook no contradiction. Grandmother Roza has explained to her that Daddy is in heaven now, just like Roza's own daddy, and that he can't come back any more. But the girl is only small and really cannot see why he can't come back when she, his beloved Sonechka, so much wants him to.

"I believed in the State," Tukai Khaziev says. "Almost to the very end of the siege I believed in it. I thought the intelligence services would think of something, would come to an agreement, make some promises, fudge some issues and everything would work out. What I really did not expect was that they would do as Zhirinovsky suggested a day before the assault. I remember him saying that what we should do was gas everybody. Everybody would sleep for a couple of hours; then they would wake up and just walk away. Only they didn't wake up, and they didn't just walk away."

The whole of Timur Khaziev's life revolved around music and the House of Culture at No. 1 Dubrovskaya Street. From childhood he had attended the Lyre Music Studio there. There he had signed up for the orchestra of *Nord-Ost*, which rented the premises of the House of Culture. And there he had died.

His parents, Tukai and Roza, used to have a room in a communal apartment near the House of Culture, and both their sons, Eldar, the elder, and Timur, learned to play the accordion there. The teachers recommended that Timur should continue. He was a talented boy, and when after tenth grade it was time for him to choose a career, he remarkably completed the examination course for percussion instruments in a single year with help only from his accordion teacher. He entered a wind-instrument college, which he completed in three years instead of four, and then the prestigious Gnesins Academy of Music as he had long dreamed of doing.

His teacher called him Rafinad, "Sugar Lump", after the refined way he held the drumsticks. He was a subtle, intelligent, even suave percussionist.

Timur combined his studies at the Gnesins Academy with playing in wind and symphony orchestras of the Ministry of Defence. He toured Norway with a military orchestra, and a tour of Spain beckoned after October 23.

"There, I had his uniform all ready, and his morning dress for concerts," Roza says firmly in order not to be overcome by emotion as she opens the cupboard. "They just won't come and take it back, the Ministry of Defence."

Sonechka, whizzing past us, promptly grabs the cap with its shiny rosette, plonks it on her head and gallops round the room: "Daddy's hat! Daddy's hat!" Tanya breaks down and leaves the room.

When he graduated from the Gnesins Academy Timur was invited to play in the *Nord-Ost* orchestra. This was a third job, but he took it on. He was married, and had a growing daughter. Tanya, who had graduated from the Academy of Eurhythmic Art and was an actress and producer, was working as a kindergarten teacher, at a correspondingly low salary.

It is unfashionable to believe in mysticism or presentiments, but a month before the siege at the theatre Timur had trouble sleeping. "I would wake up towards morning," Tanya tells me, "and he would be sitting up. I would ask him what he was doing, ask him to come back to bed, but he would say, 'Something is making me feel anxious.'"

His family supposed that Timur was just very tired. His day began early, when he drove Sonechka and Tanya to the kindergarten. From there he immediately went to his parents' flat, where he kept his instruments, to practise. Recently he had been working on improving his left hand and was pleased when he got everything sorted out. In another couple of years, he told Tanya, he would be a really good percussionist. When he had finished practising, he would jump into the car and drive off to rehearsals with the military orchestra. From there he would give his wife and daughter a lift home from the kindergarten and go on to the *Nord-Ost* performance. He would get home close to midnight and the cycle started again early the next morning. He seemed to be in a great hurry to live his life. Why? He was only 27 after all. Nobody has an answer to that question, or knows why, on October 23, Timur was at the performance of *Nord-Ost* at all.

"It was a Wednesday," Tanya tells me. "We had a rule that Wednesday was our free evening for being together as a family. A different percussionist played on Wednesdays, but on this particular day he asked Timur to swap because his girlfriend was insisting that he spend the evening with her. That girl saved her boyfriend's life, but at the cost of the life of my husband. He was never any good at saying no, and because of that he died."

"You don't want the belongings of someone close to you just left lying around, do you?" Roza asks rhetorically. "So we went there [to the theatre]. Of course there was no sign of his mobile phone. Timur had just started having a bit of money and had bought one. No sign of any of his new clothes either."

In the theatre Roza had broken down when she saw his belongings. All that was returned to Timur's parents were his old jacket with an army bootprint on the back and his shirt. That was it.

We seem to have become very basic in the last few years, even rather ignoble. It is more and more noticeable as the war in the Caucasus continues and broken taboos increasingly become familiar facts of life. Killing? Happens every day. Robbery? What of it? Looting? Perfectly legal in a war. It is not only the courts that fail to condemn crimes, but society as well. What was regarded in the past with repugnance is now simply accepted.

In those terrible October days when the hostages were seized the whole country seemed to have come together in a surge of sympathy, wondering how to help, praying, hoping and waiting. But there was nothing we could do. The intelligence services let no one near, assuring us that they had everything under control. How can we reconcile ourselves to the fact that among the very few allowed special access were people who took the opportunity to do a bit of looting? Whatever was nice and new. Whatever fitted. There is no other explanation for the disappearance of the hostages' clothing and possessions. The families of those who died can never be free of what they felt in those days. If the government suddenly decided to give them all a million dollars in compensation, those memories would still remain.

Judging by the shirt that was returned, Timur had been lying outside in the open. Roza couldn't wash our famous Moscow street muck out of it, a mixture of petrol and oil.

When Timur went to work for the last time he had in his pockets some ten different forms of ID with his photographs, testifying to the fact that he was a musician in the *Nord-Ost* orchestra and in the orchestra of the Ministry of Defence. There were his passport, his driver's licence and an address book with the telephone numbers of all his friends and relatives.

Despite that, on October 28 his body was returned to his family with a tag attached to the wrist by a rubber band which read: "No. 2551   Khamiev   Unknown".

"How could that happen?" Roza Abdulovna asks.

"Why 'Khamiev' instead of 'Khaziev'?" [In Russian the word has an insulting ring to it: to call someone a *kham* is to call them a rat.] "And even if they were going to give his name as 'Khamiev', what was the meaning of 'Unknown'? And why did we have to go to such lengths of find him? They had only to open his address book, ring any number in it, and ask the person who answered if they knew Timur Khaziev. They would immediately have been given our telephone number."

Timur's mother is talking about the day after the assault, the long day of October 26 which the Khaziev family will never forget.

"From the morning until 4.00 in the afternoon there was no mention of his name anywhere, not in any of the lists of hostages given out by the authorities," Tukai Khaziev relates. "When we had already done the rounds of all the mortuaries and hospitals, it suddenly appeared. There was a short list, just some 20 people, and Timur was on it. It said there that he was alive and in No. 7 Hospital. I phoned my wife and told her everything was fine. We wept with joy. Our friends congratulated us. Tanya and I went round to the hospital as fast as we could."

At the gate, however, there was a sentry posted who would not let anyone in. He said the prosecutor's office had forbidden it. Tanya began to cry, and the guard, taking pity, whispered to Tukai that it was bad news that "your one" was in there. It meant there was no hope. Tanya heard and started begging to be let inside. The guard opened the gate.

The hospital corridors appeared to be deserted until a policeman came at them with an assault rifle cradled against his fat belly.

"You know, he was just someone without a heart. No word of warning. No 'Brace yourself for bad news'. He just said, straight in my face, 'He's dead. Go away.' Of course I was in hysterics for 20 minutes, and that brought some doctors running. 'Who let you in here?' they demanded."

When Tanya recovered her composure a bit and asked to be allowed to see Timur's body before the autopsy, she was refused. She begged and begged, but the policeman just said, "Go and ask Putin for permission." Three officials from the prosecutor's office turned up. "Why are you in such a rush?" they asked. "You'll have time to nail down his coffin lid." Then they said, "Surname? Khaziev? A Chechen?"

That turned out to have been Timur Khaziev's undoing. The forces of law and order had taken his Tatar surname to be Chechen, and after that everything had followed automatically in accordance with the prevailing ideology.

The family is convinced now that the cause of Timur's death was that, having been taken for a Chechen, he was deliberately denied medical treatment. When the men of the Khaziev family collected his body from the mortuary, he had written on his chest, in large letters, "9.30", the time of his death in No. 7 Hospital. There were no marks on his body from a drip feed, an injection or the use of a ventilator. Instructions had been issued from above to wipe out all the Chechens, and Timur, mistaken for one, was not entitled to resuscitation. For four hours and more after the assault he just lay there dying. Timur was killed by ideology.

"We have no rights in our own country. We are just human trash. That is why all this happened to my Timurka," are Tanya's parting words to me.

While Tanya and Tukai were standing outside the hospital gate on October 26, about 20 people tried to enter the flat where the young Khazievs lived, some in uniform and some in plain clothes. Their neighbour quickly intervened and just managed to head them off. Tanya was told they had been acting on a tip-off from the hospital that a Chechen lived there.

What should the Khaziev family do now? Accept the humiliations and keep their heads down?

"When we spoke as plaintiffs about all this in the Tverskoy Court," Tukai recalls, "Gorbacheva pretended not to understand what we were talking about. She was certain everybody, without exception, had received medical attention."

The Khazievs do, naturally, have a death certificate, but it contains no mention of the cause of death. The space has been left blank. No hint that there had ever been a terrorist act. In addition to the State ideology that killed him, Timur and his family have working against them a system that avoids providing documentary evidence.

"I imagine you asked the officials at the prosecutor's office why the cause of death had been left blank."

"Of course, on October 28. They assured us this was simply a formality so that we could get on with preparations for the funeral. After the results of the post-mortem were known they said they would be sure to make the appropriate entry."

"Did they?"

"No, of course not."

This is an illuminating answer. Nobody expects fair dealing from the government. The authorities are at best a source of trouble, despite all their popularity ratings, which are officially so high. Recently the President's office set up a special department to engineer a "correct" perception of the country and the President abroad. The idea is to reduce the spread of negative information in order to make Russia look better in the eyes of foreigners. It would be even better, of course, if the government set up another special department to improve the image of the country and the President in the eyes of its own citizens.

"Could Putin really not have backed down? Could he not just have said, 'I am bringing this war to an end'? Our loved ones would still be alive today," Tukai keeps repeating. "All I want to know is, who is responsible for our tragedy? No more than that."

Tanya recently bought Kiryusha and Frosya, a tortoise and a cat, so as to have some company to come home to. Sonechka is still too little to understand what happened to her daddy, but she doesn't like coming back after kindergarten to a home without him. The family were recently phoned by the producers of the revived *Nord-Ost* musical and offered free tickets. They declined but were told that any time . . . We really seem to have lost all sense of propriety.

Sirazhdi, Yakha and Their Friends

Only a madman could envy the Chechens who live in Russia now. In years gone by their situation was unenviable, but since the *Nord-Ost* siege the machinery of racially based State retribution has been in overdrive. Racial attacks and purges supervised by the police have become commonplace. In a single moment people's lives are ruined, they lose their accommodation, their jobs, any sort of social support, and for just one reason: they are Chechens. Their lives in Moscow and many other cities are worse than intolerable: drugs are slipped into their pockets, cartridges are pressed into their hands, and they are promptly banged up for several years in prison. They have been made into pariahs quite openly. They find themselves at a dead end from which there is no escape. It is a way of life that leaves nobody unscathed, regardless of age.

"When they started speaking in Chechen and interrupted the second act, I realised that things were serious, and that they were going to get worse. I somehow saw that very clearly straight away." Yakha Neserhaeva is a 43-year-old Muscovite, an economist by profession. She is a Chechen born in Grozny, but she moved to the capital long ago. On October 23 she went to see *Nord-Ost*. Her friend Galya, whom she has known for many years, is from the north Russian town of Ukhta. She bought tickets for the 13th row of the stalls and, although Yakha was not that keen on musicals, Galya begged her to come along.

"Did you tell them you were a Chechen?"

"No. I was frightened. I did not know whether it was better to tell them or not. They might have shot me for being a Chechen at a musical."

Yakha did not see the gas, although many of the hostages noticed white clouds of something in the air. From where she was sitting she just heard people shouting, "They've released gas!" and a few seconds later she blacked out.

She came to in No. 13 Hospital, to which many victims were taken, including Irina Fadeeva, mother of Yaroslav, the boy who was shot. Yakha felt very sick. She didn't have much idea of what was going on. Soon an investigator appeared.

"He asked my name, surname, where I live, where I was born, and what I was doing at *Nord-Ost*. Then two women came, took my fingerprints and took my clothing away for forensic examination. The investigator came back in the evening and said, 'I have bad news for you.' The first thing I thought was that the friend I had gone to the musical with had died, but he said, 'You are being arrested as an accomplice of the terrorists.' It was a shock, but I got up and walked after the investigator in hospital slippers and a dressing gown. I was first taken for two days to No. 20 Hospital [a special-purpose, secure hospital], where nobody asked me anything or gave me any treatment. In fact, I received no treatment at any time. At the end of the second day the investigator came again. I was photographed, and they recorded a sample of my voice. A few minutes later they brought me a coat and a pair of men's half-boots, put me in handcuffs and said, 'You need treatment in a different hospital.' They put me in a police car, took me to the prosecutor's office for ten minutes or so, and then to the Mariino Prison [a women's isolation holding prison in Moscow]. So there I was, with boots three sizes too big for me on my bare feet, in a dirty man's overcoat, unwashed and unkempt for a week. They took me to a cell, and all the woman supervisor said was, 'Well now, you plague virus . . .'"

"Did they question you frequently while you were in solitary confinement?"

"I wasn't questioned at all. I just sat there and asked the wardress for a meeting with the investigator."

Yakha speaks quietly, slowly, without emotion. She seems barely to be present. Her face is that of a dead person, her eyes dilated, her gaze fixed, her muscles immobile. The photograph in her passport seems to show someone else, the face is that of a proud and beautiful woman.

Yakha does sometimes attempt a smile, but it is as if in the two weeks she spent in prison her muscles forgot how to do it. She thought she was done for and that nothing could save her. The situation was as bad as it could be. The policemen who transferred her from No. 20 Hospital, the only people who had had anything to tell her about her future, had informed her that she would "answer for all of them" since all the other terrorists had been exterminated and she was the only one left.

As normally happens in musicals, however, Yakha's story had a happy ending.

Her friends rallied round and swiftly engaged a lawyer who managed by a miracle to break through the seemingly impenetrable wall surrounding Yakha Neserhaeva. After ten days she was released from prison. Surprisingly, in these racist times, the investigators of the prosecutor's office who were working in the team investigating the *Nord-Ost* incident, finding nothing which remotely incriminated Yakha, simply did the decent thing. They did not set about trying to frame her. They did not tailor the charge to the individual, plant evidence, abuse or mock her. They made no attempt to take revenge on a Chechen woman purely because she was Chechen. Nowadays that is quite something.

They went even further. When they advised Yakha that she was free to go, they apologised and had her driven home. For that, she had Senior Investigator and Lawyer First Class V. Prikhozhikh to thank. She also has the officials of Bogorodskoe Department of Internal Affairs to thank. They issued Yakha's elder sister Malika, who had rushed from Grozny to Moscow to help Yakha get back on her feet, a special permit to remain in the capital on the grounds that a relative was in need of constant care. They issued the permit in the knowledge that without it any

Chechen in Moscow today cannot go out of the front door without being arrested immediately.

Aelita Shidaeva is 31. She too is a Chechen. Since the beginning of the present war she has been living with her parents and daughter, Hadizhat, in Moscow. Aelita was arrested where she worked, in a café by the Mariino underground station. She tells me her story in a calm and restrained manner, without tears or hysteria, smiling politely. You might suppose she had experienced nothing out of the ordinary, if you didn't know that when she was finally released from the Mariino Park police station after seven hours of relentless interrogation she promptly collapsed.

"It was all pretty weird. First there was this one policeman having his dinner in our café. Nothing unusual, they often eat with us. The police station is 100 metres from our front door. I've never hidden from them that I am a Chechen who fled Grozny to get away from the war. Anyway, this policeman finished his meal and went out, and suddenly the rest of them came rushing in. About 15 of them, headed by our local policeman, Vasiliev. He knows me very well too. They stood us all up against the wall, searched us and took me in."

"And what questions did they ask you?"

"What were my relations with the terrorists. I said to them, 'You all saw me yourselves. I've been right in front of you for twelve hours every day, from 11.00 in the morning till 11.00 at night!'"

"What did they reply?"

"'Which of the terrorists did you go to a restaurant with?' I have never even been to a restaurant in Moscow. It isn't something I do. They said if I did not confess to links with the terrorists they would plant drugs or weapons on me. They took it in turns to interrogate me. Some dodgy-looking men in uniform were passing by and staring at me. The investigator said that if I did not confess to links with the terrorists he would give me to these guys and they would 'eat me alive'. He said they were just waiting to get at me because they could make anyone talk."

At the police station Aelita was informed that she had been dismissed from her job. The prosecutor said they had ordered the café owner to sack her if he didn't want them to close his business down. They only released Aelita because her mother, Makka, a Russian language teacher, was a born defender of civil rights. Accordingly to the policemen at the Mariino Park station, she "trumpeted the case all over Moscow". Makka rang the Echo of Moscow radio station, mobilised the lawyer Abdullah Hamzaev and many others and, despite the police constantly repeating that Aelita was not at the police station, eventually pressured them into releasing her.

Aelita is no longer in shock. She fully understands the situation and says she just wants to get out of Moscow.

"Back to Chechnya?"

"No, abroad."

Makka is against the idea. She is not against her daughter taking her granddaughter elsewhere: Hadizhat needs to go to school, in spite of what Movsar Baraev and his supporters did at the Dubrovka theatre and in spite of the special interest the Moscow police take in young Chechen girls. Makka herself is reluctant to leave. She cannot imagine living anywhere other than Russia, but equally she cannot imagine what it is that Russia wants from Aelita, from herself and from Hadizhat. One is an adult who spent the greater part of her life in the USSR. Another is a young woman who has never lived a full life, who has only known fleeing from one place to another, from one war to the next. The third is a very young person who is looking and listening attentively to the world around her and saying nothing, for the time being.

Hadizhat's teacher has just phoned Aelita, painfully embarrassed, to say she needs to bring in a form confirming her status as a single mother. Who issues such forms? All her other documents are perfectly in order, but if she doesn't produce this form, then she, the teacher, "just does not know what to do." They want to expel Hadizhat. After October 26, 2002 there is no place in the fifth grade of No. 931 School, Moscow for a Chechen girl brought here by her family to study.

"I can't even work out", Aelita says, "whether my being a single mother is counted in favour of Hadizhat or against her. Who can you trust?"[13]

Abubakar Bakriev once held a modest technical position in a company called First Republican Bank. Now, however, he is free of any such ties. It all happened very simply and undramatically. Abubakar was called in by the company's deputy chairman for security, who said, "Don't take this the wrong way, but we are going to have problems because of you. Write a voluntary letter of resignation."

At first Abubakar could not believe his ears, but then the deputy chairman added that "they" wanted him to backdate the letter, for example to October 16, so that it all looked quite proper and nobody could accuse them of sacking him as part of an anti-Chechen cull after the *Nord-Ost* incident.

So there we have it: the executioners put you to death (and for any Chechen to be sacked today is the end: no way is he or she going to find another job), but they do hope you'll understand their predicament. It is something specific to our present times for a murderer to approach his victim and say straight out, "I am going to kill you, not because I am a bad person but because I am being compelled to do so. I would, however, ask you to make it look as if you haven't been murdered."

On that day, a Dagestani employee was "voluntarily fired" from the same bank, his "personal decision", too, being backdated. He occupied a modest position but was also ethnically cleansed to avoid any further unwelcome questions regarding people of Caucasian origin working at the bank.

"The First Republican Bank has been cleansed," Abubakar says. "The security services can sleep at night. I am 54. I don't know where to go. The police have come to my home three times to see how I live with my three children. You are turning us into enemies. You need to understand that we have no alternative now but to demand independence, because we do need a land, somewhere we can live in peace. Give us any place on earth you choose, and we will go and live there."

Isita Chirgizova and Natasha Umatgarieva are Chechen women who live in a temporary accommodation centre for refugees in the village of Serebryaniki in Tver Province. We met in No. 14 Police Station in Moscow. Isita was wiping off the ink after being fingerprinted. Natasha was crying inconsolably. They had just been released, a miracle in today's climate. The police had taken pity on them.

On the morning of November 13, 2002 the women were subjected to typical treatment. They had come to Moscow on an early train to collect aid from one of the civil-rights organisations. They were arrested at the station, a couple of metres from the organisation's entrance, because Natasha was limping. She has an open sore on her leg from diabetes, which meant she was suspected of being a wounded fighter. Isita is in the seventh month of pregnancy, which means she has a very evident bulge under her jacket, just where suicide bombers wear their grenade belts. This, at least, is how Major Lyubeznov, who was on duty at No. 14 Police Station, explained the reason for their arrest. *Lyubeznyi* means "amiable" in Russian, but the major proved far from amiable. Indeed, to safeguard Russia from the terrorist threat, he felt obliged personally to grope Isita's Chechen bulge in order to ensure that it was caused by pregnancy.

The story of Isita and Natasha ended well. The policemen just gave the women a lot of stick to the effect, "If you kill us, we'll kill you." Major Lyubeznov didn't have time to disgrace himself any further, and in addition it proved possible to do things that are very important in such cases. In the first place I managed to intercept the women in the police station before they were carted off to the isolation and interrogation unit. Secondly, I managed to persuade Vladimir Mashkin, the superintendent of No. 14 Police Station (and he was perfectly open to persuasion) that people do sometimes come to collect humanitarian aid just because they are poor, having no opportunity of getting a job and no home of their own.

Zara worked as a vegetable seller by the River Station underground station. The owner of the little market came to her and said, "Don't come to work here tomorrow, because you are Chechen." Zara provides the only support for a family consisting of three children and her husband, who has tuberculosis. What need is there for the police to involve themselves in a situation like this one?

Aslan Kurbanov spent the First Chechen War in a tented refugee camp in Ingushetia. In the summer he left to enter a college in Saratov, then moved to Moscow to live with his aunt, Zura Movsarova, a postgraduate student at the Moscow Aviation Technical Institute. He found a job and was officially registered as having the right to live in the capital.

On October 28, 2002 CID officers from No. 172 Police District (Brateevo) came to his home. The day before, Zura had been fingerprinted at the request of the local police, so when the CID said they only wanted Aslan to come with them to have his fingerprints taken, nobody suspected anything. Aslan put on his coat and went off in the police car.

Three hours later Zura became anxious. Her nephew still had not returned, so she went to the police station herself. There she was informed that Aslan had been arrested for possession of drugs. What sort of story was that? He had got up, put his coat on, put some drugs in his pocket and gone to give himself up to the police? Aslan managed to shout to Zura that he had been taken to a room, some cannabis had been produced from under the table and he had been told, "This must be yours. We are not going to give Chechens an inch. We're going to bang all of you up like this."

Aslan does not even smoke cigarettes. On October 30 he passed his 22nd birthday in the Matrosskaya Tishina Prison.

On the morning of October 25, 2002 police burst into the flat of the Moscow Chechen Gelagoev family. Alihan, the owner of the flat, was handcuffed and taken away. His wife, Marek, rushed for help to the Rostokino police station but was told that no officers had gone out from there. She rang Radio Liberty, who reported Alihan Gelagoev's abduction, and by evening he had been released. She had pressed the right button.

Alihan told me that in the car the police had put a sack over his head and beaten him for a long time as they were going to Petrovka, the street where the Moscow Central Police Department is located. They shouted, "You hate us and we hate you. You kill us and we will kill you."

When they arrived at Petrovka, however, they stopped beating him and tried for many hours to persuade him to sign a confession saying that he was the ideological mastermind behind the terrorist attack on *Nord-Ost*. This is exactly the sort of thing that used to happen in the Stalin years. The "confession" had even been written in advance, as was the practice in that era. All Alihan had to do was sign at the bottom.

He refused, but to obtain his freedom he had no option but to sign a statement to the effect that he had come voluntarily to the Central Police Department and had no complaints to make against its officers.

Racism? Yes. Appalling behaviour? Of course. This is, however, also a deeply worrying travesty of a war against terrorism. I
do not believe a single statistic produced by the police about the
progress of their anti-terrorist "Operation Whirlwind", telling the
world how many "terrorists' accomplices" they have caught. The
figures are bogus figures. The police are bogus police producing
bogus reports based on bogus investigations.

In the meantime, where are the terrorists? What are they up to?
Who knows? The police have no time to think about that. Putin is
presiding over a return to the methods of Soviet bogus activity in
place of real work.

The police interrogators were very reassuring, 36-year-old Zelimhan
Nasaev tells me. "Don't worry," they said, "you'll get three or four
years and then you'll be out. They may give you a suspended
sentence. Just sign here. Make it easy on yourself."

Zelimhan has been living in Moscow for many years. His
family moved here to escape the Second Chechen War, following
his elder sister Inna.

"Were you beaten at the police station?"

"Of course. They woke me up at 3.00 in the morning and said,
'Time for the pressure.' They beat me through a hard surface
[evidently a technique to leave no external sign of injury] on the
kidneys and liver to make me sign a confession, but I wouldn't. I
said, 'Pressure me, then. Even if you shoot me I'm not going to let
you pin anything on me.' They kept saying, 'What's a Chechen like
you doing here? Your country is Chechnya. Go back there and get
on with your war.' I told them, 'My country is Russia, and I am in
my own capital city.' They got very angry about that. In order to
make me lose control of myself one of the policemen said, 'Well,
I've just come from fucking your mother.'"

If only that agent in the Nizhegorodsky police station had
known whose mother he was claiming to have raped, whom he

was beating up and trying to coerce into admitting to a crime he never committed in order to boost the policeman's rating in the post-*Nord-Ost* campaign to "crack down on Chechen criminals in Moscow"! But perhaps it's as well he didn't know.

Roza Nasaeva is the granddaughter, and Zelimhan accordingly the great-grandson, of the legendary Russian beauty Maria-Mariam of the Romanov family, a relative of Emperor Nicholas II who fell passionately in love with Vakhu, a Chechen officer of the Tsarist Army. She eloped with him to the Caucasus, converted to Islam, took the name Mariam, bore Vakhu five children, was deported with him to Kazakhstan and, after his death there, returned to Chechnya. She died there in the 1960s, regarded almost as a Chechen saint. This beautiful story of Russo-Chechen friendship and love known throughout the Caucasus is of little help at the moment, however, because nothing could save Zelimhan from today's Moscow police. If he had the blood of ten emperors flowing in his veins, they would treat Zelimhan exactly as they treat any other Chechen.

There are parts of Moscow you really do not want to go to. These are grim places at the backs of factories, within industrial zones or beneath high-voltage electricity lines, and they are where you will find the Chechens who are still trying to survive in our capital city. Frezer Road is one such location, a dour strip of asphalt leading from Ryazan Prospekt out past old barely habitable five-storey brick buildings to industrial slums very remote from the life of the metropolis.

Actually, they weren't ever intended for human habitation. Officially, they are still the workshops of a milling factory that ceased to exist long ago, a victim of perestroika. Its workers departed and today the factory bosses make a living by renting out the derelict workshops and other premises. In one such dirty, looted former factory building the first Chechen refugees appeared in 1997. They had fled the criminal anarchy which reigned between the First and Second Chechen Wars and were mainly members of families opposed to the then Chechen leaders Maskhadov and Basaev. The Directors of the milling factory allowed the refugees to refurbish the workshops, convert them into living accommodation and then pay tribute to the bosses.

The Chechens live there to this day, the Nasaevs among them, one of 26 families. The local police know them all perfectly well. Nobody is on the run or in hiding because nobody has any wish to do so, or indeed anywhere to run to.

When the *Nord-Ost* hostage-taking occurred, the police from the Nizhegorodsky station headed straight here, explaining that they had orders to arrest a quota of 15 Chechens "in every precinct". All the men of the 26 families were arrested and taken away in buses for fingerprinting.

It was Zelimhan Nasaev-Romanov's bad luck that he wasn't at home at the time. He had gone to deliver a batch of the pens the family assembles at home and to collect the components for their next assignment.

The police soon came back to the industrial shack where the imperial family's descendant lives. They needed his fingerprints, they said, and Roza let him go without fuss. The family only began to worry several hours later when their son had not returned. Finally his mother and father set off to the police station where they were told, in typically inane fashion, "Your son had a grenade and a fuse in his pocket. We have arrested him."

"I shouted, 'You have no right to do this! You took him away yourselves. He left the house with you and there was nothing in his pockets. There were plenty of witnesses,'" Roza tells me. "The policemen just said, 'Here Chechens don't count as witnesses.' I was so offended. Are we no longer citizens, then?"

When Zelimhan's mother returned to the police station the next morning, they told her, "Your son is also dealing in marijuana. You can't help him."

"We got there and they took me to an office," Zelimhan tells me. "They said, 'You are dealing in heroin.' The more senior officer was holding a small packet in his hand and announced, 'This is yours now.' I was handcuffed. They put the packet in my pocket. I began to protest. Then they said, 'All right, then, we'll add a fuse from a "lemon".' I saw the senior policeman was already wiping a fuse with a rag to remove other people's fingerprints. He shoved it in my hand and made a note. I again shouted, 'You have no right to do this!' And they told me, 'We have our orders. We have every right, and if you aren't a good boy and don't agree to help us by admitting to the crime, your relatives will follow you. We are going back to your house now to search, and we're going to find another part of the same grenade. Sign the confession.'"

Zelimhan refused to sign anything. They beat him and said they would continue to beat him until he couldn't be seen by any lawyer. They only released him because journalists and Aslambek Aslahanov, a Deputy of the Duma, interceded. Now Zelimhan sits at home in his shack in a deep depression. He is afraid of every knock at the door. Depression is the characteristic mood of all the Chechens living among us. There is not a single optimist to be found among the young or the old. At least, I haven't found any. Everybody dreams of emigrating so as to have a chance to merge into the cosmopolitan background somewhere and never have to reveal their nationality.

"There is an orgy of systematic police harassment of Chechens in Russia," claims Svetlana Gannushkina, Director of the Citizens' Assistance Public Committee to Aid Refugees and Displaced Persons. This is the committee to which people turn in their distress: Chechens whose relatives have been arrested, finger-printed and had drugs or cartridges planted on them; Chechens who have been sacked from their jobs or threatened with deportation. (For heaven's sake, where do you deport Russian citizens to from the capital of Russia?) They come to Svetlana Gannushkina because there is nowhere else for them to go.

"The signal for this new wave of frenzied State racism, officially called Anti-terrorist Operation Whirlwind," Svetlana continues, "was given immediately after the storming of the Dubrovka theatre complex. Chechens are being expelled everywhere. The main problem is when they are sacked from their jobs or driven out of their flats. This is a settling of scores with a whole people in retaliation for the acts of particular individuals. The main method used to discredit them as a nation is the false creation of criminal cases by planting drugs or cartridges. The policemen think they look cool when they mockingly ask their victims, 'Which would you like: drugs or a cartridge?' The only ones who get rescued are those with mothers like Makka Shidaeva. But what about all the others?"

And what sort of a nation are we, the Russian people?

One Chechen family has three daughters. One has passed the entrance exam and got into music school while the other two haven't. The parents have asked their successful daughter's teacher to give private piano lessons to her sisters. The teacher has refused to teach them. The head of the music school, where of course everyone knows everybody else's business, has refused to let her continue, saying she has received orders to that effect from the Department of Culture. If the teacher continues to teach the Chechens, the security services will start taking an interest in her.

This is something we are actively involved in, we, the Russian people. The majority of us go along with the State's xenophobia and feel no need to protest. Why not? Official propaganda is very effective, and the majority share Putin's belief that a whole people must shoulder collective responsibility for the crimes committed by a few.

The upshot, nevertheless, is that nobody yet knows, despite a war that has been going on for years, despite acts of terrorism, catastrophes and torrents of refugees, what the authorities actually want from the Chechens. Do they want them to live within the Russian Federation or not?

In conclusion, a straightforward story of ordinary people living in Russia and suffering from State-induced hysteria.

"Do you often get told off at school?"

"Yes." Sirazhdi sighs.

"And is there a good reason?"

"Yes." He sighs again.

"What do you do that is naughty?"

"I'm running down the corridor and somebody bashes into me and I always give them something back so they don't think they can hurt me, and then the teachers ask me, 'Did you hit them?' and I always tell the truth and say 'Yes', but the others don't and I get told off."

"Perhaps you shouldn't tell the truth either? You might not get into trouble."

"I can't." He sighs very heavily. "I'm not a girl. If I did it, I say, 'I did it.'"

"You know, he tries to trip our children up so the little ones will hit their heads. And die . . ."

Great heavens above! This is not Sirazhdi talking about himself now, this is grown-ups talking about him. Not about a special operations agent trained to destroy terrorists but about a seven-year-old Chechen boy called Sirazhdi Digaev. This is the publicly expressed view of a certain woman member of the parents' committee of Class 2b of No. 155 School, Moscow, which Sirazhdi attends.

"Well, do you know, my child complains, 'Sirazhdi never has anything, and I have and I have to lend it to him.'" This from another mother on the same committee.

Why is this child complaining? Surely if the person next to you hasn't got something and you have, you should bloody well lend it to them!

"He's a nuisance to everyone. You have to understand that. My son told me he didn't write down his homework in the class because Sirazhdi was making so much noise that he couldn't hear the teacher. Sirazhdi is uncontrollable. Like all Chechens. You have to understand that!" opines another mother.

The conversation continues as we sit in an empty classroom. The children of Grade Two have gone home, and now the parents' committee is discussing how to purge the school of a small Chechen so that "our children don't learn bad things from a possible future terrorist".

You think I must be making this up. Sadly not.

"Don't get us wrong. Even though he is a Chechen, we don't discriminate between nationalities. No. We just want to protect our children . . ."

From what? In November the parents' committee of Class 2b convened a meeting in order to warn Sirazhdi's mother and father that, if they did not take him in hand by the New Year, and unless "in spite of being a Chechen" he had started behaving himself in accordance with the parents' committee's understanding of good behaviour, they would demand that the head of No. 155 School should expel him.

"Well, just tell me, why are they all piling into Moscow?" The real reasoning emerges when, one or two weeks later, a member of the parents' committee tries to explain why they adopted that resolution.

Well, why should "they" not come to Moscow? Are the inhabitants of this city so special that being brought into proximity with other citizens of Russia might have a negative effect on their sensibilities?

"Why is it you say they are having a hard time?" another parent almost shrieks. "Who asks if we are having a hard time? What makes you think our children are having it any easier than him?"

Why? Well, Sirazhdi was born in Chechnya in 1995. When his

mother, Zulai, was pregnant there was shelling and bombing all around her. She fled because she had no option when the First Chechen War started. Today Zulai has complicated feelings when she sees that, even though they moved to Moscow in 1996 and her youngest son has been a Muscovite for almost the whole of his life, he is still terrified by firework displays and thunderstorms. He hides and cries but doesn't know why.

"Oh, so it's because they don't feel at home here yet," floats up the ratty voice of one more member of the parents' committee. "So they think they should bring their rulebook to our monastery? No, thank you very much!"

The irritation is caused by the fact that Alvi, Sirazhdi's father, came to the meeting, listening to everything they had to say to him, and then took the floor himself and dared to try to explain his problems, that in front of his children he had been sworn at by a policeman who came marching into their room in his jackboots, and that he, a father, had been unable to do anything about it. The children had seen it all.

Alvi also told them that the main reason his family were in Moscow and not in Chechnya, in spite of how uncomfortable things were for them here, was to enable their children to go to school without a war going on around them. Zulai was a maths teacher, but she had to work as a market trader in Moscow, not something she was good at. They spent their evenings rolling chicken cutlets to sell in the morning. Everything he and Zulai did was for the sake of their children.

"Well, how about that! They're worming their way right into the centre of Moscow! And they expect to be given a 500-dollar flat!" This was the reaction of the parents' committee to Alvi's appeal.

"I do not want my son/daughter being taught in the same class as someone like that." That was the verdict Alvi and Zulai were given at that meeting.

"Who says we're wrong?" the members of the parents' committee demand.

Well, nobody of course.

It is worth remembering something that began in a similar way in the last century but that had a different ending. When the Fascists entered Denmark, all Jews were ordered to sew yellow stars on their clothing so they could be easily recognised. All the Danes promptly sewed on yellow stars, both to save the Jews and to save themselves from turning into Fascists. Their King was right in there with them.

In Moscow today the situation is quite the opposite. When the authorities struck at the Chechens who are our neighbours, we did not sew on yellow stars in solidarity with them. Alas, we did the opposite. We are making sure Sirazhdi never loses the sense of being a pariah.

At my request, he shows me his exercise book for Russian language. His marks range from poor "2"s to average "3"s. Sirazhdi's handwriting is untidy, as Yelena Dmitrievna reminds him on almost every page. She is his class mistress and writes out her words of admonition in a trained calligraphic hand. She has been a teacher for 35 years, all of them in a primary school.

Yelena Dmitrievna did not support the parents' committee in their campaign to get rid of the Chechen boy, but neither did she sew on a yellow star. She did not categorically refuse to be part of it although she could have done, thereby halting in its tracks the Digaev family's persecution by notorious Russian "public opinion".

Sirazhdi is spinning like a top. He really has no wish to show me his Russian exercise book. He does his guileful best to divert my attention to his maths book, where the situation is much happier. Sirazhdi is an ordinary boy who can't sit still. The main thing is that he very much wants to look good. Why should he be any different, a modest little boy keeping his head down as the parents' committee would like him to, to make him less of a Chechen?

Even his maths book soon bores him. Promising to draw a "sword and a man", he goes off in a great rush. He does everything in a great rush. Soon he returns bearing a pad with the outline of a strongman with powerful muscles from *Lord of the Rings*, and a light sabre represented by a smudge of yellow crayon.

"You know, we only wanted what was best for him," the parents of Class 2b now say, realising that the story of their campaign against a small Chechen boy in the wake of the *Nord-Ost* hysteria has been taken up by journalists. "Only what was best . . ."

Is Sirazhdi going to believe in what they think is best for him? He really does fight at playtime. In art lessons he throws paint at the wall. He trips up his classmates too, and the more often he does these things, the more they make it clear to him that he is the odd one out in Class 2b.

This is life in Russia after *Nord-Ost*. The months have passed, and it has gradually become more evident that this appalling tragedy really does have its uses. In fact, it has come in positively handy for lots of people and for a lot of different reasons.

First in line has been the President with his innate folksy cynicism. He has taken to openly clipping useful international dividends from this horror and its deadly outcome. Neither has he baulked at using other people's blood for his own PR purposes inside Russia.

Lying at the bottom of the heap are the petty squabbles in a small school and the rank-and-file police officers who were only too glad to beef up their "anti-terrorist" scores before the New Year in order to qualify for bonuses. The frantic anti-Chechen chauvinism and race attacks of the days immediately following *Nord-Ost* have mellowed to a pragmatic, steady racism.

"Do we take up arms, then?" some of the Chechen men ask.

You can hear them grinding their teeth in impotence. "I can't take this any more," groan others. It is a sign of weakness, of course, which does not suit them at all, especially since their children are watching. What should they do?

AKAKY AKAKIEVICH
PUTIN II

I have wondered a great deal about why I have so got it in for Putin. What is it that makes me dislike him so much as to feel moved to write a book about him? I am not one of his political opponents or rivals, just a woman living in Russia. Quite simply, I am a 45-year-old Muscovite who observed the Soviet Union at its most disgraceful in the 1970s and '80s. I really don't want to find myself back there again.

I am making a point of finishing the writing of this book on May 6, 2004. There has been no miraculous challenging of the results of the March 14 presidential election. The opposition has acquiesced. Accordingly, tomorrow sees the start of Putin II, the President re-elected by an unbelievable majority of more than 70 per cent. Even if we knock off 20 per cent as "window-dressing" (i.e. ballot-rigging), he still received enough votes to secure the presidency.

In a few hours Putin, a typical lieutenant-colonel of the Soviet KGB, a look-alike of Akaky Akakievich, downtrodden hero of Gogol's story "The Greatcoat", will ascend the throne of Russia once again. His outlook is the narrow, provincial one his rank would suggest; he has the unprepossessing personality of a lieutenant-colonel who never made it to colonel, the manner of a Soviet secret policeman who habitually snoops on his own colleagues. And he is vindictive: not a single political opponent has been invited to the inauguration ceremony, not a single political party that is in any way out of step.

Brezhnev was a distasteful figure, Andropov bloody, although he had at least a democratic veneer. Chernenko was dumb and Russians disliked Gorbachev. At times Yeltsin had us crossing ourselves at the thought of where his doings might be leading us.

Here is their apotheosis. Tomorrow their bodyguard from Echelon 25 – the man in the security cordon when VIP motorcades drive by – Akaky Akakievich Putin will strut down the red carpet of the Kremlin throne room as if he really were the boss there. Around him the polished Tsarist gold will gleam, the servants will smile submissively, his comrades-in-arms, a choice selection from the lower ranks of the KGB who could have risen to important posts only under Putin, will swell with self-importance.

One can imagine Lenin strutting around like a nabob when he arrived in the vanquished Kremlin in 1918 after the Revolution. The official Communist histories – we have no others – assure us that in fact his strutting was very modest, but his modesty, you can just bet, was insolent. Look at humble little me! You thought I was a nobody, but now I've made it. I've broken Russia just as I intended to. I've forced her to vow allegiance to me.

Tomorrow a KGB snoop, who even in that capacity did not make much of an impression, will strut through the Kremlin just as Lenin did. He will have had his revenge.

Let us, however, run the reel backwards a little.

Putin's victory had been widely predicted both in Russia and throughout the world, especially after the humiliation of such democratic and liberal opposition parties as the country possessed in the parliamentary elections of December 7, 2003. Accordingly, the March 14 result surprised few. We had international observers in but everything was low key. Voting day itself was a contemporary remake of the authoritarian, bureaucratic, Soviet-style pantomime of "the people expressing its will", which many still remember only too well, myself included. In those days the procedure was that you went to the polling station and dropped your voting slip in the ballot box without bothering whose names were on it because the result was a foregone conclusion.

How did people react this time? Did the Soviet parallel rouse anybody from inertia on March 14, 2004? No. They went obediently to the polling stations, dropped their voting papers in the ballot boxes and shrugged: "What can we do about it?" Everyone is convinced that the Soviet Union has returned, and that it no longer matters what we think.

On March 14 I stood outside the polling station on my own Dolgoruky Street in Moscow. With the advent of Yeltsin its name had been changed from Kalyaev Street. Kalyaev, a terrorist in Tsarist times, was later regarded as a revolutionary. It became Dolgoruky Street in honour of the prince who had his estate there in Kalyaev's time, before the Bolsheviks came.

I talked to people going in to vote and coming quickly out again after participating in the charade. They were apathetic, completely indifferent to the process of electing Putin for a second term. "It's what 'they' want us to do? Well, then. Big deal." That was the majority sentiment. A minority joked, "Perhaps now they'll name it Kalyaev Street again."

The return of the Soviet system with the consolidation of Putin's power is obvious.

It has to be said that this has not only been made possible by our own negligence, apathy and weariness after too much revolutionary change. It has happened to choruses of encouragement from the West, primarily from Silvio Berlusconi, who appears to have fallen in love with Putin. He is Putin's main European champion, but Putin also enjoys the support of Blair, Schroeder and Chirac, and receives no discouragement from the transatlantic junior Bush.

So nothing stood in the way of our KGB man's return to the Kremlin, neither the West nor any serious opposition within Russia. Throughout the so-called election campaign, from December 7, 2003 until March 14, 2004, Putin openly derided the electorate.

The main token of his contempt was his refusal to debate anything with anyone. He declined to expand on a single point of his own policies in the last four years. His contempt extended not only to representatives of the opposition parties but to the very concept of an opposition. He made no promises about future policy and disdained campaigning of any kind. Instead, as under the Soviet regime, he was shown on television every day, receiving top-ranking officials in his Kremlin office and dispensing his highly competent advice on how to conduct whichever ministry or department they came from.

There was, of course, a certain amount of tittering among members of the public: he was behaving just like Stalin. Putin too was simultaneously "the friend of all children" and "the nation's first pig-farmer", "the best miner", the "comrade of all athletes" and the "leading film-maker".

None of it went further than tittering, however. Any real emotion drained away into the sand. There was no serious protest over the rejection of debates.

Meeting no resistance, Putin naturally became bolder. It is a bad mistake to suppose he takes no notice of anything, never reacts and only, as we're encouraged to believe, forges ahead in pursuit of power.

He pays a lot of attention and takes account of what he sees. He keeps a close eye on us, this nation he controls.

In this he is behaving exactly like a member of Lenin's Cheka secret police. The approach is entirely that of a KGB officer. First there is the kite-flying of information released through a narrow circle of individuals. In today's Russia, that is the political élite of the capital. The aim is to probe likely reaction to policies. If there is none, or if it has the dynamism of a jellyfish, all is well. Putin can push his policy forward, spread his ideas or act as he sees fit without having to look over his shoulder.

A brief digression is in order here, less about Putin than about us, the Russian public. Putin has backers and helpers, people with a vested interest in his second ascent of the throne, people now concentrated in the President's office. This is the institution which today really rules the country, not the government which implements the President's decision, not the parliament which rubber-stamps whichever laws he wants passed. His people follow the reactions of society very attentively. It is completely wrong to imagine they aren't bothered. It is we who are responsible for Putin's policies, we first and foremost, not Putin. The fact that our reaction to him and his cynical manipulation of Russia has been confined to gossiping in the kitchen has enabled him to do all the things he has done in the past four years. Society has shown limitless apathy, and this is what has given Putin the indulgence he requires. We have reacted to his actions and speeches not just lethargically but fearfully. As the Chekists have become entrenched in power, we have let them see our fear, and thereby have only intensified their urge to treat us like cattle. The KGB respects only the strong. The weak it devours. We of all people ought to know that.

Let us now go back to late February 2004. At some moment the Kremlin techniques for sounding out public opinion warned that the public was beginning to tire of Putin's insolent refusal either to debate or to campaign and of the absence of any recognisable pre-election campaign.

In order to reinvigorate the languishing electorate, the Kremlin announced that Putin had decided to take "firm measures". These proved to be a Cabinet reshuffle three weeks before election day.

At first everyone really was taken aback. This appeared to be an act of complete lunacy. In accordance with the Constitution, the entire Cabinet does in any case resign after an election. The newly elected President announces his choice of Prime Minister, who in turn proposes ministers for the President to confirm. What sense could it possibly make to appoint everybody now, only to have to reappoint them after the inauguration? What was the point of all this crazy activity which could only further paralyse the functioning of a government riddled with corruption, which already spent a good proportion of its working week taking care of its personal commercial interests?

However, although replacing the Cabinet a month before the Constitution required was entirely daft, it did indeed serve to reinvigorate the election process. The political élite was stirred, the guessing game about whom Putin would appoint took over the television channels, the political pundits were given something to discuss and the press finally got something it could write about the election campaign.

But this reinvigoration of politics lasted one week at best. Putin's spin doctors daily intoned over the television that the President had done this purely because he wanted to be "absolutely honest with you", he did not want to "enter the election with a pig in a poke" (by which was evidently meant following the constitutional procedure for replacing the Cabinet). He wanted to present his future course before March 14.

It has to be said, alas, that people believed him: probably just over half the electorate. The half which fell for and hailed this dishonest, absurd line of argument have an important distinguishing feature. These are people who love and trust Putin without reservation, irrationally, uncritically, fanatically. They believe in Putin. End of story.

In the week preceding the appointment of a new Prime Minister the media images were all of this now familiar "love" for Putin. Those with faith in the genuineness of his proclaimed reasons for changing the Cabinet ignored the obvious non sequiturs.

You really do have to believe unreservedly, as if you have fallen in love for the first time, if you are not immediately to be struck by the obvious question: Why didn't Putin choose a less dramatic way of presenting his future course than sacking the entire government? He had plenty of other ways to do so. He could, for example, have taken part in televised debates. But no. The week after the dismissal of the Cabinet saw hitherto unprecedented levels of cynicism. The people of Russia watching their televisions were told that actually it didn't matter what happened on March 14. Everything had been decided. Putin would be Tsar. The spin doctors got to the point of saying, "He wants to show you his course in advance because it's the only choice you've got."

The day when the name of the new Prime Minister was to be announced was arranged with all the ceremony traditionally preceding the emergence of the hero of an opera to sing his first aria. The President will tell us tomorrow morning. In two hours' time. In one hour's time. Ten minutes to go. Moreover, the one whose name would be revealed might, we were assured over the television, possibly be the President's successor in 2008.

In Russia it is very important not to look ridiculous. It can end badly. People make up jokes and you turn into a Brezhnev. When Putin announced his new government, even his most diehard supporters fell about laughing. No-one could fail to see that the Kremlin had been staging a very bad farce. It was no more than a petty settling of scores, although subjected, of course, to endless spin and veiled behind all manner of claptrap and rhetorical garnishing which invoked the greatness of Russia.

But the mountains truly had brought forth a mouse. Virtually all the old ministers stayed where they had been. Only the Prime Minister, Mikhail Kasianov, was sacked. He had been getting up Putin's nose for many months in a big way, and in many small ways too. He was a legacy of the Yeltsin era. When raising the second President to the throne, the first President of Russia had asked Putin not to remove Kasianov.

Prime Minister Kasianov, alone among the main actors in Russian politics, categorically opposed the arrest of the liberal oligarch Mikhail Khodorkovsky and the gradual destruction of his Yukos oil company. Yukos was the most transparent company in our corrupt country, the first to function in accordance with internationally accepted financial practice. It operated "in the white", as people say in Russia, and what is more it donated over 5 per cent of its gross annual profit to financing a large university, children's homes and an extensive programme of charitable work.

But Kasianov was speaking out in defence of a man whom Putin had for some time counted among his personal enemies, on the grounds that Khodorkovsky was making major financial contributions to the country's democratic opposition, primarily to the Yabloko Party and the Union of Right Forces.

In Putin's understanding of political life this was a grave personal insult. He has publicly shown on many occasions that he is quite incapable of understanding the concept of discussion, especially in politics. There should be no answering back from someone Putin considers his inferior, and if an inferior does allow himself to answer back he is an enemy. Putin does not choose to behave this way. It is not because he is a born tyrant and despot; he has just been brought up to think in the categories inculcated in him by the KGB, an organisation he considers an ideal model, as he has publicly stated more than once. This is why, as soon as anyone disagrees with him, Putin categorically demands that they should "cut out the hysterics". This is the reason behind his refusal to take part in pre-election debates. Debate is not his element. He doesn't know how to conduct a dialogue. His genre is the military-style monologue. While you are a subordinate you keep your mouth shut. When you become the chief you talk in monologues, and it is the duty of your inferiors to pretend they agree. This is a political version of the misrule of officers in the Army which occasionally, as with Khodorkovsky, leads to all-out war.

But to return to the government reshuffle. Kasianov was out. The ministers returned to their original portfolios and Putin ceremoniously parachuted in Mikhail Fradkov as the new Prime Minister. In recent times Fradkov had been quietly enjoying a place in our bureaucratic hierarchy as the Russian Federation's representative to the European institutions in Brussels. He is a nondescript, amiable, forgettable gentleman with narrow shoulders and a big bum. Most Russians learned that our country had a Federal minister called Fradkov only when his appointment as Prime Minister was announced, which, in accordance with Russian lore, tells us that Fradkov is a low-profile representative of that same service to which Putin has dedicated the greater part of his working life.

The country laughed out loud when it heard of Fradkov's elevation, but Putin insisted, and even started explaining his "principled" choice to the effect that he wanted to be open with the electorate and to enter the election with people knowing in advance whom he would be working with in his fight against Russia's main evils of corruption and poverty.

The Russian people, both the half which supports Putin and the half which doesn't, didn't stop laughing. The Kremlin farce continued. If the country as a whole did not know Fradkov, the business community remembered him only too well. He is a typical Soviet *nomenklatura* bureaucrat who, throughout his career, from the Communist period onwards, has been shifted hither and thither to miscellaneous bureaucratic posts quite independently of his professional background and knowledge. He is a typical boss for whom it is not too important what he is driving, just as long as he is in the driver's seat. While he was Director of the Federal Tax Police Service it had a reputation as the most corrupt ministry in the Russian civil service. Its bureaucrats took bribes for literally everything, for every form they issued and every consultation. The service was consequently shut down, and Fradkov, in line with the undying traditions of the Soviet *nomenklatura*, was "looked after". He was transferred once again, this time to Brussels.

Prime Minister Fradkov hastily flew back to Moscow from Brussels, only to provoke further merriment. In his first interview in his new capacity at the airport, he confessed he didn't actually know how to be a Prime Minister. No, he had no plans, it had all come like a bolt from the blue. He was waiting to see what arrangements had been made and what his instructions would be.

Russia is a country where much goes on behind the scenes and most people have short memories. Despite his ignorance of arrangements and the lack of instructions from Putin, which never have been made public, the Duma confirmed Fradkov's appointment by a convincing majority, making reference to its duty to "fulfil the will of our electors who trust President Putin in all matters". This Duma, its composition the result of the elections of December 7, 2003, contains practically no opposition to Putin and is firmly under the control of the Kremlin.

March 14 arrived. Everything passed off in accordance with the Kremlin's scenario. Life went on as before. The bureaucrats returned to their tireless thieving. Mass murder continued in Chechnya, having quietened down briefly during the elections to give hope to those who for five years had been hoping for peace. The Second Chechen War had begun in mid-1999, in the run-up to Putin's first presidential election. In accordance with Asiatic traditions, just before his second presidential election two Chechen field commanders laid down their weapons at the feet of the great ruler. Their relatives had been seized and were held in captivity until the commanders stated that they now supported Putin and had given up all thought of independence. Oligarch

Khodorkovsky took to writing penitential letters to Put[...] prison. Yukos was rapidly becoming poorer. Berlusconi came t[...] visit us, and his first question to his pal Vladimir was how he too could get 70 per cent of the vote in an election. Putin gave no clear advice, and indeed his friend Silvio would not have understood if he had. Berlusconi is after all a European.

They went off on a trip to provincial Lipetsk, opened a production line for washing machines and watched a military airshow. Putin continued to give a dressing-down to high-level bureaucrats on television. That is usually how we see him, either receiving reports from officials in his Kremlin office or tearing one of them apart in monologues. The filming is methodically thought through in PR terms. There is no ad libbing, nothing is left to chance.

Putin was even revealed to the people at Easter instead of the risen Christ. A service was held at the Church of Christ the Redeemer, Moscow's cathedral re-erected in concrete on the site of an open-air Soviet-era swimming pool. Almost a month had passed since his second election. At the beginning of the Great Matins service there stood, shoulder-to-shoulder with Putin as if at a military parade, Prime Minister Fradkov and Dmitry Medvedev, the Kremlin's new *éminence grise*, head of the President's office, a man of diminutive stature with a large head. The three men clumsily and clownishly crossed themselves, Medvedev making his crosses by touching his hands to his forehead and then to his genitals. It was risible. Medvedev followed Putin in shaking the Patriarch's hand as if he were one of their comrades, rather than kissing it as prescribed by church ritual. The Patriarch overlooked the error. The spin doctors in the Kremlin are effective but, of course, pretty illiterate in these matters and had not told the politicians what to do. Alongside Putin there stood the Mayor of Moscow, Yury Luzhkov, who had been behind the rebuilding of the cathedral and who alone knew how to invoke the protection of

...cent manner. The Patriarch addressed Putin
...igh Excellency", which made even those not
...ed wince. Given the numerous ex-KGB officers
...op government positions, the Easter Vigil has now
...er from the May Day Parade as the major obligatory
...ial ritual.

The beginning of the Great Matins service was even more comical than the handshakes with the Patriarch. Both State television channels did a live broadcast of the procession round the cathedral that precedes the service. The Patriarch participated in this, despite being ill. The television commentator, who was a believer and theologically knowledgeable, explained to viewers that in the Orthodox tradition the doors of the church should be shut before midnight because they symbolise the entrance to the cave where Christ's body was placed. After midnight the Orthodox faithful taking part in the procession await the opening of the church doors. The Patriarch stands on the steps at their head and is the first to enter the empty temple where the Resurrection of Christ has already occurred.

When the Patriarch had recited the first prayer after midnight at the doors of the temple, they were thrown open to reveal: Putin, our modest President, shoulder to shoulder with Fradkov, Medvedev and Luzhkov.

You didn't know whether to laugh or cry. An evening of comic entertainment on Holy Night. Really, what is there to like about this individual? He profanes everything he touches.

At about this time, on April 8, two nine-month-old twin baby girls were declared *shaheeds* – martyrs for the their faith – in Chechnya. They came from the tiny Chechen farmstead of Rigakh and were killed before they had learned to walk. It was the usual story. After the March 14 election relentless military operations were resumed in Chechnya. The Army, in the form of the Regional Operational Staff Headquarters for Coordinating the Counter-terrorist Operation, announced that it was attempting to catch Basaev: "A large-scale military operation is under way to destroy the participants of armed formations." They failed to catch Basaev, but on April 8 at around 2.00 in the afternoon, as part of the "military operation", the Rigakh farmstead was subjected to a missile bombardment. It killed everyone there: a mother and her five children. The scene which confronted Imar-Ali Damaev, the father of the family, would have turned the most hard-headed militant into a pacifist for life, or into a suicide bomber. His 29-year-old wife, Maidat, lay dead, holding close their four-year-old Djanati, three-year-old Jaradat, two-year-old Umar-Haji and the tiny nine-month-old Zara. Their mother's embrace saved none of them. To one side lay the little body of Zura, Zara's twin sister. Maidat had had no room and evidently no time to think of a way of covering her fifth child with her own body, and baby Zura herself had had no time to crawl the two metres. Imar-Ali gathered up the anti-personnel fragments and established the number of the killer missile: 350 F 8-90. It was not difficult, the number was easy to read. They started burying the bodies, and the *mullah*, a Moslem scholar from the neighbouring village, declared all those who had been slain to be martyrs. They were buried the same evening, their bodies unwashed, without graveclothes, in what they were wearing when death claimed them.

Why do I so dislike Putin? Because the years are passing. This summer it will be five since the Second Chechen War was instigated. It shows no sign of ending. At that time the babies who were to be declared *shaheeds* were yet unborn, but all the murders of children since 1999 in bombardments and purges remain unsolved, uninvestigated by the institutions of law and order. The infanticides have never had to stand where they belong, in the dock; Putin, that great "friend of all children", has never demanded that they should. The Army continues to rampage in

Chechnya as it was allowed to at the beginning of the war, as if its operations were being conducted on a training ground empty of people.

This massacre of the innocents did not raise a storm in Russia. Not one television station broadcast images of the five little Chechens who had been slaughtered. The Minister of Defence did not resign. He is a personal friend of Putin and is even seen as a possible successor in 2008. The head of the Air Force was not sacked. The Commander-in-Chief himself made no speech of condolence. Around us, indeed, it was business as usual in the rest of the world. Hostages were killed in Iraq. Nations and peoples demanded that their governments and international organisations withdraw troops in order to save the lives of people carrying out their duties. But in Russia all was quiet.

Why do I so dislike Putin? This is precisely why. I dislike him for a matter-of-factness worse than felony, for his cynicism, for his racism, for his lies, for the gas he used in the *Nord-Ost* siege, for the massacre of the innocents which went on throughout his first term as President.

This is how I see it. Others have different views. The killing of children has not put people off trying to have Putin's period in office extended to ten years. This is being done by creating new pro-Putin youth movements on instructions from the Kremlin. The deputy head of Putin's office is a certain Vladislav Surkov, the acknowledged doyen of PR in Russia. He spins webs consisting of pure deceit, lies in place of reality, words instead of deeds. There is a great fashion at the present for bogus political movements created by directive from the Kremlin. We don't want the West suspecting that we have a one-party system, that we lack pluralism and are relapsing into authoritarianism. There suddenly appear groups called "Marching Together", or "Singing Together" or "For Stability" or some other latter-day version of the Soviet Union's Pioneer movement. A distinctive feature of these pro-Putin quasi-political movements is the amazing speed with which, without any of the usual bureaucratic prevarication, they are legally registered by the Ministry of Justice, which is usually very chary of attempts to create anything remotely political. As its first public act the new movement usually announces that it will attempt to ensure the extension of the period of office of our beloved President. Putin was given just such a present for his inauguration on May 7. At the end of April the members of "For Stability" set in motion procedures for prolonging his term of office. Their underlying concept is that Putin is the guarantor of stability. At the same time the members of this pocket-sized movement demanded an inquiry into the results of privatisation. This showed them to be against Khodorkovsky, hence friends of Putin. The Moscow City Electoral Commission hastened to accept the application of the young members of "For Stability" to initiate procedures for a national referendum to extend the President's term of office.

Such was the state of play on inauguration day, May 7, 2004. Putin has, by chance, got his hands on enormous power and has used it to catastrophic effect. I dislike him because he does not like people. He despises us. He sees us as a means to his own ends, a means for the achievement and retention of personal power, no more than that. Accordingly, he believes he can do anything he likes with us, play with us as he sees fit, destroy us as he sees fit. We are nobody, while he whom chance has enabled to clamber to the top of the pile is today Tsar and God.

In Russia we have had leaders with this outlook before. It led to tragedy, to bloodshed on a huge scale, to civil wars. I want no more of that. That is why I so dislike this typical Soviet Chekist as he struts down the red carpet in the Kremlin on his way to the throne of Russia.

POSTSCRIPT

July 10 is just another day in the calendar of Russia. It happens to be the cut-off date for making changes to this book.

Late yesterday evening, Paul Khlebnikov, editor-in-chief of the Russian edition of *Forbes Magazine*, was murdered in Moscow. He was mown down as he left the magazine's office. Khlebnikov was famous for writing about our oligarchs, the structure of Russian "gangster capitalism" and the huge sums of easy money certain of our citizens have managed to get their hands on. Also last evening, Victor Cherepkov was blown up by a grenade in Vladivostok. He was a member of our parliament, the State Duma, and famous for championing the weakest and poorest of this land. Cherepkov was standing for mayor of his native Vladivostok, the most important city in the Far East of Russia. He had successfully got through to the second round and looked to have a real chance of being elected. As he left his campaign headquarters, he was blown up by an anti-personnel mine activated by a trip-wire.

Yes, stability has come to Russia. It is a monstrous stability under which nobody seeks justice in lawcourts which flaunt their subservience and partisanship. Nobody in his or her right mind seeks protection from the institutions entrusted with maintaining law and order, because they are totally corrupt. Lynch law is the order of the day, both in people's minds and in their actions. An eye for an eye, a tooth for a tooth. The President himself has set an example by wrecking our major oil company, Yukos, after having jailed its chief executive, Mikhail Khodorkovsky. Putin considered Khodorkovsky to have slighted him personally, so he retaliated. He not only retaliated against Khodorkovsky himself but went on to seek the total destruction of the goose that laid golden eggs for the coffers of the Russian State. Khodorkovsky and his partners have offered to surrender their shares in Yukos to the government, begging it not to destroy the company. The government has said, "No. We want our pound of flesh." On July 9 Putin strong-armed his loyal supporter Muhammed Tsikanov into the post of Vice-President of Yukos-Moscow, the parent company of Yukos. Nobody has any doubts that the former deputy minister for economic development has been parachuted in for one reason only: to co-ordinate the delivering of Yukos into the hands of those whom Putin favours. The market is in turmoil, investors are running for cover, and all the remotely successful businessmen I know spent May and June this year looking for ways of moving their capital to the West.

They were very wise. On July 8, 9 and 10, queues a mile long formed at ATMs. The authorities had only to hint that a crackdown might close some of the banks, for people to whip out of Alpha Bank, one of the most stable, funds to the tune of two hundred million dollars in seventy-two hours.

All that was needed was a hint. Because everyone expects the State to play dirty. The withdrawal of those two hundred million dollars in seventy-two hours tells us all we need to know about Russia's current "stability".

If we go by the official surveys of public opinion, conducted by polling firms which have no wish to lose their contracts with the President's office, Putin's popularity rating couldn't be better. He has the support of an overwhelming majority of the Russian public. Everybody trusts him. Everybody approves of what he is doing.

AFTER BESLAN

On September 1, 2004 an unprecedentedly horrible act of terrorism was perpetrated in Russia, and from now on the name of the little North Ossetian town of Beslan will be associated with a waking nightmare beyond the imaginings of Hollywood.

On the morning of September 1 a multi-national gang of thugs seized control of No. 1 School in Beslan, demanding an immediate end to the Second Chechen War. The hostage-takers struck during the annual *lineyka*, a celebration of the beginning of the school year which is observed throughout Russia. By tradition this is an occasion to which whole families come: grandmothers and grandfathers, aunts and uncles, and especially the families of the youngest children coming to school for the first time.

This is why almost 1,500 people were taken hostage: schoolchildren, their mothers and fathers, their brothers and sisters, their teachers and their teachers' children.

Everything that happened during the period of 1–3 September, and in Russia subsequently, has been a wholly predictable consequence of the Putin regime's systematic imposition of the power of a single individual to the detriment of common sense and personal initiative.

On September 1 the intelligence services, and after them the authorities, announced that actually there were not all that many people in the school: just 354 in all. The infuriated terrorists told the hostages, "When we have finished with you there really will be only 354". The relatives who had gathered round the school said the authorities were lying: there were more than a thousand people trapped inside.

Nobody heard what the relatives were saying, because nobody was listening. They tried to get their message through to the authorities by way of the reporters who had converged on Beslan, but the journalists merely went on echoing the official tally. At this point some of the relatives started beating up some of the journalists.

The authorities spent September 1 and the first half of September 2 in an unforgivable state of shock and disarray. No attempts were made to negotiate since this had not been sanctioned by the Kremlin. Anybody attempting to lay the groundwork for negotiations was subjected to intimidation, while those whom the bandits called upon to come forward and negotiate – President Zyazikov of Ingushetia, President Dzasokhov of North Ossetia, Putin's adviser on Chechnya, Aslanbek Aslakhanov, and Dr Leonid Roshal (who had mediated in previous sieges) – kept their heads down or fled the country, displaying cowardice at the very moment when courage was essential. Each of them subsequently had his excuses ready, but the obstinate fact remains that none of them entered the building.

Against this background of official cowardice, the hostages' relatives' great fear was that there would be a repetition of the government's tactic for ending the *Nord-Ost* siege at a Moscow theatre in 2002, when they mounted an assault which resulted in an enormous number of innocent victims.

On September 2 Ruslan Aushev, the former President of Ingushetia, entered the beleaguered school. Reviled by the Kremlin for constantly calling for peace talks and a political settlement of the Chechen crisis, Aushev had been forced to "voluntarily" resign in favour of the Kremlin's favoured candidate, FSB General Zyazikov.

Arriving in Beslan, Aushev had found a deplorable situation, as he later recounted. He discovered that, one and a half days after the school had been seized, none of those in the headquarters of the "Operation to Free the Hostages" was at liberty to decide who should take part in negotiations. They were waiting for instructions from the Kremlin and paralysed by the fear of losing favour with Putin, whose displeasure would signal the end of their political careers. Evidently this consideration took priority over concern for the predicament of the hundreds of hostages. The deaths of hostages could always be blamed on the terrorists, whereas falling foul of Putin would be political suicide.

Let us state unambiguously that all the Russian government representatives in Beslan at that time were more concerned to work out what Putin wanted than to work out a way of resolving the monstrous situation in the school. When Putin did speak, no-one dared to contradict. Dzasokhov, for example, told Aushev that Putin had personally telephoned him and forbidden him to enter the school if he didn't want to face immediate criminal charges.

Dzasokhov stayed put. Dr Roshal fared no better. Although himself a paediatrician, he failed on this occasion to save anyone other than himself, having been warned by an unnamed intelligence source that the terrorists were only calling for him as a negotiator in order to kill him. He too stayed put.

The officials in the operational nerve centre all succeeded in saving their careers, but failed to save the children. Even before the showdown on September 3 it was obvious that Putin's "vertical" system of authority, founded on fear of and total subservience to one individual, himself, was not working. It was incapable of saving lives when that was what was needed.

Faced with this situation, Aushev printed off the Internet a declaration by Aslan Maskhadov, the leader of the Chechen resistance in whose name the thugs claimed to be acting. Maskhadov stated categorically that he was against the taking of children as hostages. Aushev took this declaration and went in to talk to the terrorists. He was to be the only person to conduct negotiations of any sort in the course of the Beslan catastrophe.

For his pains he was roundly abused by the Kremlin and accused of collaborating with the terrorists.

"They refused to talk to me in Vainakh," Aushev related afterwards, "although they were Chechens and Ingushetians. They would speak only in Russian. They asked at least to have a minister sent to negotiate, for example Fursenko, the Minister for Education, but nobody was willing to go in without the sanction of the Kremlin."

Aushev was in the school for about an hour and himself carried three babies out in his arms. A further 26 small children were allowed to leave with him. At 2.00 p.m. on September 3 an assault was launched, and fighting continued in the town until late into the night. Many of the terrorists were killed, but many others broke through all the cordons and escaped. Officialdom began counting how many hostages had died, and is still counting today. A field was ploughed up on the outskirts of Beslan and turned into an enormous cemetery with hundreds of new graves. At the time of writing, more than one hundred hostages have simply vanished: they are classified as having disappeared without trace. Some people believe they were abducted by the terrorists who escaped, others, that they were incinerated by the thermobaric warheads of the Bumblebee rocket flamethrowers with which the Special Operations Units were equipped.

In the immediate aftermath of Beslan there was a further tightening of the political screws. Putin announced that the tragedy had been an act of international terrorism, denying the Chechen connection and blaming everything on al-Qaeda. Aushev's courageous intervention was denigrated and the mass media, on instructions from the Kremlin, set about portraying him as the terrorists' principal accomplice rather than as the only hero of the hour. That role was reserved for Dr Roshal, since the masses do need heroes to admire.

In political terms, Beslan did not prompt the Kremlin to any effort to analyse and correct its own mistakes. On the contrary, the Kremlin went on a political rampage.

Putin's favourite slogan after Beslan was that "War is war". His top-down authoritarianism must be strengthened. He knew better than anyone else who was behind what, and only if he held the reins would Russia be safe from terrorist acts in the future. The Kremlin introduced a bill in the Duma abolishing direct election of provincial governors which, in Putin's opinion, only led to their acting irresponsibly.

Not a word was heard about the fact that throughout the Beslan hostage-taking it was precisely Presidents Zyazikov and Dzasokhov, effectively Putin's nominees, who behaved like cowards and liars. They provided about as much leadership as one can expect milk from a billy goat.

The proposed reform of the system for selecting governors was accompanied by a campaign of ideological brainwashing which asserted that the authorities had performed irreproachably throughout the Beslan catastrophe. Nothing could have been done differently, nothing could have been more effective. As a smokescreen, a commission of enquiry of the Russian Federal Council (the upper chamber of the Russian parliament) was set up to monitor the investigation into the hostage-taking. The chairman of the commission, Alexander Torshin, was received in the Kremlin by Putin and sent off with some presidential advice: The commission has not been stepping out of line.

The people of Beslan began to get the distinct feeling that they were being disregarded. Television coverage concentrated on the good news: the help the hostages were receiving, the mountains of sweets and toys sent to them. The question of what had happened to all those who had disappeared without trace was not looked into.

The traditional 40-day period of mourning passed and official memorial services were held. No air time was given to the heartbroken grieving of families.

Then it was October 26, the second anniversary of the *Nord-Ost* hostage-taking in Moscow, when a band of terrorists seized the audience and actors of a musical in the middle of a performance. Two and a half days into the ensuing siege, the security services mounted an assault using an unknown chemical gas which resulted in the deaths of 130 hostages.

After *Nord-Ost* the only action undertaken by the authorities was to whitewash their actions, award themselves medals and preen. Not only were no attempts made to find a settlement to the Second Chechen War, but the noose was drawn tighter. A campaign was launched to destroy or neutralise anybody who might be capable of bringing a peace settlement nearer, or of preventing the Chechen crisis from again spawning terrorism in the region. This was a predictable response to the state terrorism of Russia's "anti-terrorist operation" directed against the peoples of Chechnya and Ingushetia. "Anti-terrorist terror" was the defining characteristic of life in Russia in the period between *Nord-Ost* and the Beslan atrocity. We are ground to dust between the millstones of terror and anti-terror. The number of terrorist outrages has increased exponentially, and the path leading inexorably from *Nord-Ost* to Beslan is plain to see.

On October 26, 2004 at 11.00 in the morning there was a gathering on the steps of the theatre on Dubrovka of all those whose loved ones had died or whose lives had been blighted by the *Nord-Ost* events: the hostages themselves, the relatives and friends of those who died. Earlier that morning they had been visiting the graves of those dear to them, as is the tradition in Russia, and the service of remembrance at the theatre had accordingly been scheduled for 11.00. The *Nord-Ost* Aid Association of those affected by the tragedy publicised the event through the usual channels. The arrangements for the service were broadcast over local radio. Invitations were sent to the office of the Mayor of Moscow and to the President's Office, and assurances were received that representatives would attend.

But now the priest was waiting as the clock ticked past 11.20, 11.30, 11.50. It really was time to start. People began murmuring among themselves: "Surely they can't just not show up?"

Then it was noon. The crowd were getting edgy. Many people had children with them, orphans of those who had died. "We want to talk to the authorities, we came to ask them questions face to face." Finally, more angrily, "We need help urgently, we are being ignored, our children are no longer receiving free hospital treatment."

Still no sign of officialdom. There was no point in waiting any longer: nobody turns up that late. Were they afraid of looking their victims in the eye? The investigation of the *Nord-Ost* incident had led nowhere. The truth about the disaster and about the gas the authorities used remained deeply classified information. Or was something else going on here?

The square around the theatre had been sealed off by police, ordinary young lads who had been sent to ensure that any passions were kept under control. They could hear what people were saying, and they were not looking happy. Eventually, it was the policemen who explained to the *Nord-Ost* victims that the authorities had already been and had already left. They had come for their own cosy, official memorial service while the families were out at the cemeteries, in order not to confront the victims of their actions. At 10.00 representatives of the Mayor of Moscow and the President's Office had come to Dubrovka to act out their own memorial service for the cameras of all the main television channels. Official wreaths had been laid, a guard of honour had performed like clockwork, appropriate speeches, pre-planned and approved by higher authority, had been delivered. It had all been very respectable: no tears, no excessive displays of grief, and the whole sanitised charade was shown repeatedly on all the television channels on the evening of October 26. Russia could rest assured that the authorities were properly mindful of this tragic happening, and that everybody agreed they were doing the right thing. The official nationalisation of Russia's memory of the events slotted neatly into just a few minutes.

Of course, nothing stopped the thousand-strong crowd of friends and relatives, former hostages and numerous foreign journalists from paying respect to the dead. Candles were lit on the steps of the theatre where those gassed had lain barely alive, and where many of them died before medical help arrived. One hundred and thirty portraits of the dead were illuminated by the flickering flame of lovingly placed candles. It was raining, just as it had been two years before, and the rain mingled with our tears, just as it had then.

The rain could not, however, wash away the bad feeling left by this ideological cynicism. It was a sorry reaction by the state to the immense grief of those who had suffered from its incompetence, at the very place where its victims had lost their lives. The authorities' apparent contempt for their own citizens stems from their fear of us. They cannot face our grief, they cannot admit their own shortcomings or acknowledge their responsibility for the many victims of so many terrorist acts, which they have no effective strategy for dealing with.

This, alas, is precisely the future which awaits those who have suffered at Beslan. There will be an official version of the tragedy very different from the unofficial one. Grief will be permitted, within bounds, but the truth will not be told. Nobody will want to hear what those who were there have to say. Higher authority will decide what is to come out. Spontaneous emotion is not wanted, any more than it was under the Soviets. The ideological stance adopted by the authorities since the tragedy of September 1 is that nothing must be allowed to show that the authorities are incompetent (which they certainly were). Tears are permissible, but only in moderation, since everything is, after all, satisfactorily under control. While the tragedy should not be forgotten, there is no call for excessive displays of emotion which might be suggestive of despair. There can be no place for that in the land of the Soviets, because Putin is watching over us and knows better than we how matters should be arranged. There is light at the end of the tunnel, we are all fighting a war on international terrorism, and are, moreover, "united as never before".

On October 29 the Duma voted by an overwhelming majority to pass Putin's new law under which he would nominate candidates for the post of governor and the regional parliaments could rubber-stamp the single name being put to them. If a region's MPs should be so impertinent as to reject Putin's nominations twice, the recalcitrant parliament would be "deemed to have passed a motion of no confidence" and would be dissolved by a directive of, yes, Putin again.

This, of course, makes a mockery of the Constitution and demonstrates complete contempt for the Russian people, but the Russian people took it only too calmly. Certainly the opposition held a few meetings, but these were quiet, local affairs and nobody paid any attention to them. Putin got his way. This is post-Beslan Soviet Russia in action.

So what is the situation after Beslan? "The Party and the People Are One", the old Soviet slogan ran. In reality the rift grows wider by the day, while the images on television convey quite the opposite impression. Soviet-style bureaucracy is growing back and growing stronger, and bringing with it an old-style political freeze. No evidence of global warming here. Russia swallowed the lies about how the *Nord-Ost* siege was ended, and now makes no demand for justice or an objective investigation of the Beslan atrocity. For two years after *Nord-Ost*, most of the population snored peacefully in their beds, or went out dancing at discos, occasionally rousing themselves for long enough to turn out and vote for Putin. It is arguably we ourselves who allowed Beslan to happen as it did. Our apathy after the *Nord-Ost* events, our lack of concern for the ordeal of its victims, was a defining moment. The authorities saw they had us back under their thumb and relapsed into the complacency which brought about Beslan.

We cannot just sit back and watch a political winter close in on Russia for another several decades. We want to go on living in freedom. We so much want our children to be free and our grandchildren to be born free. This is why we long so much for a thaw in the immediate future, but we alone can change Russia's political climate. To wait for another thaw to come our way from the Kremlin, as happened under Gorbachev, is now foolish and unrealistic, and neither is the West going to help. It barely reacts to Putin's "anti-terrorist" policies, and finds much about today's Russia entirely to its taste: the vodka, the caviar, the gas, the oil, the dancing bears, the practitioners of a particular profession. The exotic Russian market is performing as the West has come to expect, and Europe and the rest of the globe are perfectly satisfied with the way things are going on our sixth of the world's land mass.

All we hear from the outside world is "Al-Qaeda, al-Qaeda", a wretched mantra for shuffling off responsibility for all the bloody tragedies yet to come, a primitive chant with which to lull a society which wants nothing more than to be lulled back to sleep.

NOTES

1. The story of the 54 soldiers received extensive publicity with the result that an official enquiry was held under the auspices of the chief military prosecutor's office. The enquiry found that while in their "training" of the soldiers their officers had exceeded their authority, the soldiers' misconduct on the training ground had provoked the officers into losing their tempers. The case did not come to court, and none of the officers received a criminal sentence. The soldiers were dispersed to different units to prevent them causing further trouble. This judgment of Solomon was produced by a justice system specifically for those in the armed forces. Such cases are investigated by military prosecutors and passed on by them to military courts. These prosecutors and the military judges are themselves members of the armed forces who have sworn the oath of loyalty and are subordinate to their own superiors, and so on right up to the Minister of Defence. Accordingly, at every level, prosecutors and judges cannot be independent in their judgments.

2. This incident was handled in much the same way as the case of the 54 soldiers. An enquiry was held by the garrison prosecutor's office, whose employees were effectively subordinate to the commanding officer of the military unit in which the incident occurred. Again the prosecutor's office acquitted the officers. The illegal "sale" and "renting out" of

soldiers as inexpensive labourers, usually by their own junior officers and in order to carry out particular agricultural or building tasks, is common practice in Russia. Payment usually goes to the officers for their role in the deal. It is extremely rare for the soldiers to be paid other than in food, cigarettes and overnight accommodation. Occasionally no payment is involved. If the officer and employer are decent people, the soldiers may be moved out of their units for a time simply because they can be more adequately fed away from the Army.

3. Aslan Maskhadov is the leader of the Chechen resistance forces in the current Chechen War. In 1997 he was elected President of the Chechen Republic of Ichkeria, his legitimacy recognised both by the Kremlin and by the Organisation for Security and Co-operation in Europe, which sent observers to the elections. In 1999, however, Putin declared Maskhadov to be *de facto* deposed. Maskhadov responded by heading up the resistance to the occupation of Chechnya by Federal troops. Since then he has been on Russia's most-wanted list.

Islam Hasuhanov is married to Maskhadov's niece. He was renowned in Russia as a submarine officer, serving on one of the Navy's élite missile cruisers. On completing his service contract, he was honourably discharged and worked for the Ministry of Defence of Chechnya during a period when Maskhadov was internationally recognised as the legitimate President. This did not save Hasuhanov from being sentenced to twelve years in prison, in effect for working for Maskhadov during this period. As the Supreme Court of the Republic of North Ossetia-Alaniya acknowledged, testimony against Maskhadov was extorted from Hasuhanov during the preliminary investigation by means of barbaric torture. The record of these court sessions, containing the admission that torture had been used, was subsequently passed to Amnesty International, which continues to work on the case.

4. The Russian code of criminal procedure provides that the accused should have access to a lawyer irrespective of ability to pay. During the Second Chechen War, however, the law-enforcement agencies began misusing the system to foist defence lawyers on accused persons who, more often than not, were the agencies' own former employees. Such people are known as "insider lawyers". There are also lawyers who work constantly with the FSB and so have a better understanding of its requirements than of the individuals they are supposed to be defending. The function of such lawyers is to be present on occasions when the law requires the presence of a lawyer. FSB officers also appoint insider lawyers to represent suspects the FSB has abducted. The relatives know only that their family member has disappeared. The FSB deliberately hides him, informing them neither of his whereabouts nor of the charges against him. Often no formal accusation is ever made. The detention of the disappeared person is illegal, but the family are prevented from appointing a defence lawyer for him. Such victims can "disappear" for weeks or months; in Hasuhanov's case the period was about six months. Testimony is meanwhile beaten out of them, as happened in Hasuhanov's case. His family had no idea what had happened to him or where he was. All the law-enforcement and security agencies of the republic denied they were detaining anybody by that name, while in fact he was being tortured by the FSB despite the appointment of a lawyer.

5. The Red Cross is often unable to carry out its functions because the Russian authorities withhold permission for prison visits.

6. Abdullah Hamzaev died in Moscow in June 2004 after a serious illness. During the Budanov trial he was subjected to unheard-of pressure for speaking out against the accused and all he stood for. Hamzaev was threatened with retribution, and

members of his family were intimidated both by Russian nationalists from extremist paramilitary groups and by officers who were colleagues of Budanov. He had several heart attacks in the course of the trial and was taken to hospital. Once he suffered infarction and clinically "died", but later on he returned to the trial. Hamzaev succeeded in ensuring that Budanov was sentenced to a long term of imprisonment, something few people believed possible in the spring of 2000.

7. It is important to understand what changed the direction the judicial proceedings were taking, towards justice in accordance with the law. Psychological and psychiatric reports were crucial in the Budanov case. When it became apparent that Budanov might be released from detention right there in the courtroom, the Memorial Civil-rights Centre and the Director of the Independent Psychiatric Association of Russia, Professor Yury Savenko, sent a request to colleagues of his in Germany to produce a report for the trial based on the documentary evidence. Simultaneously, lawyers stated in court that they had no confidence in the politically motivated Russian psychiatric experts and demanded that internationally respected foreign psychiatrists be officially invited to contribute to the trial. Despite the fact that the judge refused this demand, the German psychiatrists soon presented their conclusions, which were passed to members of the Bundestag. This resulted in the spotlight being turned onto the politically biased reports of the Russian psychiatrists, which were contrasted with the German specialists' conclusions. Then Gerhard Schroeder brought up the case in conversation with Putin, who, while not that bothered about public opinion in his own country, is highly sensitive to criticism from abroad. Shortly afterwards, the trial in Rostov-on-Don completely changed direction, which only goes to show once again the dependence of the courts on Russia's

leaders. The state prosecutor who had spoken solely in favour of Budanov was replaced by one who was unbiased. Lawyers were allowed to call witnesses. The judge agreed to attach to the case file the long report by Dr Stuart Turner, a Fellow of the Royal College of Psychiatrists in London. For Dr Turner, Yury Budanov was not the politically sensitive figure he was for us; he was just another patient. Thus it was Western intervention that changed the direction of the Budanov trial.

8. Rushailo was removed from this post in May 2004.

9. The prosecutor general's office subsequently held an inquiry into the allegation that Fedulev's wife had given a bribe of 20,0000 dollars to Judge Krizsky, and into the closing of the case for which he had interceded. The enquiry found the allegation of "thanking" proven, but no criminal investigation followed. In accordance with Russian tradition, Krizsky was allowed to "resign at his own request" in order not to cause a scandal. And resign he did, into "honourable retirement". Soon afterwards Prosecutor General Skuratov left office, having provoked a public scandal in which corruption figured prominently.

10. This was moral blackmail calculated to crush a woman in a state of extreme stress. Under Russian legislation, as the investigator must have known, exhumation can only be authorised after a court hearing. Where exhumation is authorised, it may only take place in the presence of the mother, father or other close relatives whom the court recognises as having suffered as a result of the death of the individual concerned. The investigator who attempted to blackmail Irina was moved to other work as a result of his misconduct. Later still he was quietly sacked.

11. "Telephone law" is the term that has stuck since Soviet times for an informal system of governance based on personal acquaintance. Officials telephone judges directly, and the latter

produce the verdicts required. "Telephone law" operates in every other sphere of our life as well, as can be seen from the saying "What can't be done, can be done over the telephone."

12. This was observed by the bereaved families who came to the court, and also by the journalists who covered the hearing.

13. An enquiry into the arrest of Aelita Shidaeva was conducted by the Moscow prosecutor's office after she lodged a complaint. None of the policemen involved were disciplined.

14. A wave of racism (not only anti-Chechen but directed at people of non-Slavonic appearance) washed over Russia after the *Nord-Ost* events. Many complaints were investigated by Russian civil-rights organisations, primarily the Moscow Helsinki Group, the Memorial Civil-rights Centre and the Citizen's Aid Committee for Assistance to Refugees. Numerous petitions and appeals were sent to the President by Amnesty International and Human Rights Watch. They were fruitless. Nobody was punished. These international interventions did not halt the wave of racism largely because the Russian leadership took no action. Racist harassment and murders continue and show no sign of abating.